*Di Guoyong
on
Xingyiquan*

Volume I

Foundations

Available from **tgl books**

Jiang Rongqiao's Baguazhang

Li Tianji's The Skill of Xingyiquan

Yan Dehua's Bagua Applications

Di Guoyong on Xingyiquan: Volume I, Foundations

Di Guoyong on Xingyiquan: Volume II, Forms and Ideas

Di Guoyong on Xingyiquan: Volume III, Weapons

A Shadow on Fallen Blossoms

Falk's Dictionary of Chinese Martial Arts

Beijing Bittersweet

Shadowboxing in Shanghai

 www.thewushucentre.ca

Di Guoyong on Xingyiquan

Volume I

Foundations

Third Edition of Five Element Foundation

The 2020 Set Edition

邸国勇
形意拳械精解
2020年修订版

translated and edited

by Andrea Mary Falk

霍安娣翻译，主板

Translation copyright © 2005 by Andrea Mary Falk
Third edition copyright © 2021 The 2020 Set Edition

All Rights Reserved

ISBN 978-1-989468-07-4

Library and Archives Canada Cataloguing in Publication of first editions

Di, Guoyong, 1948- . Di Guoyong on Xingyiquan / translated and edited by Andrea Falk. Includes some text in Chinese. Translation of Xingyiquanxie Jingjie originally published by The People's Publishing House of Sports.

Complete contents: v.1 Five element foundation - - v.2. Form and Theory - - v.3. Weapon and partner play. ISBN 978-0-9687517-6-3 (v.1) ISBN 978-0-9687517-7-0 (v.2) ISBN 978-0-9687517-8-7 (v.3).

1. Hand-to-hand fighting, Oriental. I. Falk, Andrea, 1954- II. Title. III. Title: On xingyiquan.

GV1112.D5213   2005 796.815'5   C2005-910938-8

Volume I of a three volume set. Volume I Foundations. Volume II Forms and Ideas. Volume III Weapons.

Translated and edited by Andrea Falk 2005 in Beijing, China, and Morin-Heights, QC, Canada.

With thanks for the assistance of Di Guoyong, Beijing, China.

Second edition by Andrea Falk, June 2009, Quebec, QC, Canada.

Third edition by Andrea Falk, 2021, Morin-Heights, QC, Canada.

The techniques described in this book are performed by experienced martial artists. The author, translator, and publishers are not responsible for any injury that may occur while trying out these techniques. Please do not apply these techniques on anyone without their consent and cooperation.

TABLE OF CONTENTS

About the Author ix
Author's Preface to the English edition x
Author's Preface to the Chinese original xii
Translator's Preface to the Book Set xiii
Translator's Preface to the Second Edition xiv
Editor's Preface to the 2020 Set Edition xiv

CHAPTER ONE: BACKGROUND
 Historical origins of Xingyiquan 1
 Introduction to the five element fists 3

CHAPTER TWO: POST STANDING
 Introduction to post standing 5
 Training progression for post standing 6
 Primordial post standing 7
 Santishi post standing 9
 Descend the dragon post standing 17
 Subdue the tiger post standing 20
 Pounding post standing 22

CHAPTER THREE: SPLIT (CHOPPING FIST)
 Introduction to split 27
 Standard split 27
 Fixed stance split 31
 Reverse stance split 32
 Old style split 34
 Dodging split 34
 Retreating split 35
 Further discussion of split 36

CHAPTER FOUR: DRILL (DRILLING FIST)
 Introduction to drill 43
 Standard drill 44
 Reverse stance drill 47
 Dodging drill 50
 Retreating drill 52

    Coiling drill 53
    Further discussion of drill 55

CHAPTER FIVE: DRIVE (CRUSHING FIST, THRUSTING PUNCH)
    Introduction to drive 59
    Standard drive (rear foot timed) 60
    Lead foot timed drive 66
    Reverse stance drive 67
    Further discussion of drive 69

CHAPTER SIX: CANNON (POUNDING FIST)
    Introduction to cannon 75
    Standard cannon 76
    Aligned stance cannon 81
    Dodging cannon 84
    Reverse stance cannon 85
    Further discussion of cannon 86

CHAPTER SEVEN: CROSSCUT (CROSSING FIST)
    Introduction to crosscut 91
    Standard crosscut 92
    Aligned stance crosscut 96
    Retreating crosscut 98
    Inward crosscut 99
    Further discussion of crosscut 101

CHAPTER EIGHT: SOLO FORM
    Introduction to Five Elements Connected 105
        Names of the movements 105
        Descriptions of the movements 106
        Rhythm and power generation 118

CHAPTER NINE: PARTNER FORMS
    Introduction to Entangling hands 121
        Names of the movements 121
        Descriptions of the movements 121
    Introduction to Five Phases Contend 127
        Names of the movements 127
        Descriptions of the movements 127

CHAPTER TEN: THE TWELVE ANIMAL MODELS

- Dragon 135
  - Description of the movements 136
  - Further discussion of dragon 143
- Tiger
  - Description of the movements 146
  - Further discussion of tiger 161
- Monkey
  - Description of the movements 167
  - Further discussion of monkey 175
- Horse
  - Description of the movements 181
  - Further discussion of horse 192
- Alligator
  - Description of the movements 196
  - Further discussion of alligator 200
- Chicken
  - Description of the movements 203
  - Further discussion of chicken 213
- Swallow
  - Description of the movements 219
  - Further discussion of swallow 225
- Sparrow Hawk
  - Description of the movements 230
  - Further discussion of sparrow-hawk 236
- Snake
  - Description of the movements 241
  - Further discussion of snake 246
- Wedge-tailed Hawk
  - Description of the movements 251
  - Further discussion of wedge-tailed hawk 254
- Eagle
  - Description of the movements 257
  - Further discussion of eagle 262

    Bear
        Description of the movements 265
        Further discussion of bear 269
    Eagle and Bear
        Description of the movements 272
        Further discussion of eagle and bear 274

Pronunciation of pinyin 275

About the translator 278

ABOUT THE AUTHOR

Di Guoyong was born in Hebei province in 1948 and moved to Beijing in 1960. He began his wushu life in 1963 with the well-known Zhao Zhong, apprenticing in Shaolinquan and Xingyiquan to improve his poor health. Later he also apprenticed to Wu Binlou to learn Chuojiao Fanzi, and Li Ziming to learn Liang style Baguazhang. His home in Beijing has given him access to the best martial artists throughout his life, until he has become one of those men that he emulated as a youth. He glows with the health and energy that training in the internal martial arts can bring.

Di Guoyong's main emphasis has for years been Xingyiquan. The work that he does for Xingyiquan sounds like the work of many: founding member, first secretary general, and long-term president of the Beijing Xingyi Quan Research Association; national level one wushu judge; member of the official Xingyi forms development committee; organizer of national and international Xingyi and traditional wushu competitions; Xingyi teacher at Beijing University and other colleges; coach of fighting and forms champions; teacher also of students every morning in the park and of many foreign visitors; author of numerous published articles; presenter of a popular instructional video series; and presenter of an instructional Xingyi series shown on Chinese television. His love for and skill in martial arts, and particularly in Xingyiquan, stands out as a player, teacher, presenter, judge, organizer, researcher, and writer.

Di Guoyong never backs down from any question until he has reached "three levels of why " and this book reflects that attitude. He has combined his open and inquisitive mind with his years of experience to present the reader with a complete resource for training and teaching Xingyi.

Di Guoyong loves the written word and he loves to research every aspect of Xingyi through every means possible, whether modern or traditional. He never ceases to explore any avenue to learn more about martial arts theory and practice. This book represents the result of over forty years of his love, hard work, experience, and examination. It explains the whole of Xingyiquan – the shape and the meaning, the unarmed and the weapons, the practical and the theory, the training and the teaching, with his particular emphasis always on whole body power. He has tried to present the whole picture to the reader, to combine the form – *xing* – and the intent – *yi* – of Xingyiquan.

Andrea Falk

霍安娣

Morin Heights, QC, Canada

June 2005

AUTHOR'S PREFACE TO THE ENGLISH EDITION

I have just received Andrea's email that the English translation of my book is almost done, and that she would like a new preface for this edition. The Five Element Foundation is the first volume of a three-volume translation of my original two-volume book "Analysis of Xingyi fist and weapons ". Due to the size of the original book, Andrea suggested that the English version come out in three volumes, separating the five element foundation techniques, the empty hand forms, and the weapons, to allow the English books to come out more quickly and reasonably priced, which I agreed was a good idea.

Andrea has trained with me since around the year 2000. From that time she has visited Beijing every year to study Xingyi with me and I have come to know her well. She was a bike racer as a youth, and came to the martial arts as a young adult in the 1970s. She was the first foreigner accepted by the Chinese National Wushu Association in the advanced degree program at the Beijing Institute of Sport. During a six-year relationship with the Institute she studied many wushu styles and weapons. She also was the first foreign woman to train sparring here. Andrea had studied Chinese before coming to China, and her language skills developed considerably during her years in Beijing studying wushu. After her return to Canada she continued to teach, research, and translate to spread Chinese wushu. She not only works continuously to popularize wushu, but she herself continues to train and examine what she has learned.

During the time that she has trained Xingyi with me I have found that, with her solidly built foundation in wushu, she learns quickly and knows how to train hard. She has an intuitive and intelligent grasp of any material. Her high level of Chinese ensures that we have no communication problems. Indeed, I have learned many things from her so that, as they say "teacher and student improve together'.

Andrea is a most appropriate person to translate Chinese wushu into English. Firstly, her mother tongue is English. Secondly, she has studied, trained, taught, and researched wushu for many years, and understands the approaches of both student and teacher. Thirdly, her Chinese is excellent, especially the specialized vocabulary of wushu. My foreign students tell me that with these three strengths her translations are the best!

Every specialty has its own vocabulary. People outside the wushu circle cannot fully understand its vocabulary. People without training in wushu, without firsthand experience in performance, cannot properly understand and express this knowledge in words. People who do not understand Chinese culture cannot properly translate the theoretical aspects of wushu. To translate wushu writings, you need to understand the movements, the power, the applications, the theories, and the terminology, and be able to transfer this knowledge to English speakers. It is not an easy matter to do, but I believe that Andrea is able to do it, and furthermore, that she does it very well.

As this volume on the five element techniques goes to print, I would like to thank Andrea again for the work that she does on the translations. If readers come to understand and enjoy Xingyi more from reading this volume, and if it encourages them to delve deeper into Xingyi, then this is great for Xingyi, and great for Chinese wushu. I invite readers with questions from the book to simply contact me. I'll do my best to answer your questions. My email is guoyong1948@hotmail.com.

Xingyi is a simple, powerful, and functional style. It completely combines the mind and the body. First you need to learn the movements. Once you are comfortable with them you need to change the emphasis to the intention behind the action. "The quality of your intent determines the quality of your power " is something that I emphasize throughout the book. Every individual has his or her own background, social history, educational level, habits and hobbies that make up their mental environment. You must find your own concepts that suit your national characteristics, customs and languages, to better accept, enjoy, and train the intent behind Xingyi.

The five element techniques are the "mother fists of Xingyi". They are the foundation of the foundation. But you must first "set the posts" for the foundation with *santishi* post standing. This is the first step in training. The quality of your post standing will directly determine the quality of your five element techniques. Xingyi emphasizes the post standing to an extraordinary degree – the classics say, "If you want to learn Xingyi you must stand for three years. " In former times you were not allowed to learn the five elements before you had done three to five years of post standing. Times have changed and this is no longer a requirement, but you should remember the importance of its lesson. Every time you train, you must absolutely start each session with post standing.

Xingyi is particularly suited to Westerners. Westerners tend to be big, strong, relatively heavy, and tend to like straightforward movements. Xingyi is a simple, practical style with no wasted movement. It moves like a tank in a practical, straightforward, fearless way. Heavier players look like heavy tanks, while lighter players look like light tanks. I think if Westerners are introduced to Xingyi that they will love it, and that they will take to it and reach a high level of skill.

"The more something is of the people the more it is international." Chinese wushu is like a flowing stream, its source is in China but it belongs to the world. I hope that wushu can bring health to the people of the world, and I hope that Xingyi can help to unite the many peoples of the world.

Di Guoyong

邸国勇

Beijing, China

June 28, 2005

AUTHOR'S PREFACE TO THE CHINESE ORIGINAL

I have tried to present in this book the whole contents of Xingyiquan: history, post standing, the five foundation techniques, the twelve animals, many traditional techniques and forms, and weapons. In my presentation of the traditional forms I have held completely to traditional practices. I have, however, added my own understanding of power and meaning gained over years of training and teaching. I have also included some writings based on my experience and research. I have tried to present more than just how to do the movements, and have described the origins and meanings of the techniques and explained the rhythm, breathing, and whole body power within them. Xingyiquan is characterized by whole body power, and I have tried to describe how to achieve this for each technique through detailed analysis and explanation.

Xingyiquan is not an imitative style, but combines the shape and structure of the images available to us in the world with the power available within the human body and mind. Nowadays in martial arts there is great emphasis on the 'form ' and less on the 'meaning'. What type of meaning should we bring to practice, what type of meaning should we use to direct our training? We cannot leave out the meaning in Xingyiquan, because the definition of the style itself is form [xing] and meaning [yi] together. The ideas that we bring to our practice dictate the power [jin] that we will develop. The meaningful concepts that we bring to practice dictate the deep skill [gongfu] that we will attain.

The process of writing this book has been one of learning and improving for me, and has helped to deepen my understanding of Xingyiquan. Although the book has now been published I do not feel a lightening of my burden. The development of wushu gives us a great responsibility. The theoretical examination of Xingyi in particular falls far behind our need for knowledge if we wish it to develop further. I heartily wish that fellow martial artists, masters, and readers raise questions and opinions to help me improve and to help Xingyi develop.

There are many people involved in the writing of this book that I would like to thank. The editor of the Chinese edition, Zhao Xinhua, for his painstaking help. Liu Mingliang and Yang Shudong, for the many, many photographs that they took. My martial friend Kang Gewu, and former president of the national wushu association Xu Cai, for their prefaces to the original edition, which they took time out of their busy schedules to write.

Di Guoyong

邸国勇

Beijing, China

2003

TRANSLATOR'S PREFACE TO THE BOOK SET

I wanted to translate this series of books because it fills in many gaps left by current books on Xingyi available in English. I have, since 2000, come to know Di Guoyong and his Xingyi well enough that I felt well qualified to translate his work with full understanding. The time between the original publication and the translation publication of the first volume was less than two years, and I hope to bring out the following two volumes a year at a time.

Translating this book was a new experience for me, marking the first time that the author was available to help me solve problems. This has been an exciting and fun collaborative writer-translator teacher-student team effort. The first time we met we were finishing each other's sentences, and have continued this way ever since. I have occasionally added things that the author said in class but did not write in the book, without using the device of translator's notes. These additions are what I have seen or heard Di Guoyong do or say while I trained with him or acted as interpreter in his classes.

This English edition is actually an improvement over the original, with all the mistakes taken out and a few things added. I have reorganized and edited some of the original text in a way that is (I hope) more useful to the reader. Most especially I made the introduction from comments made throughout the original, created the chapter on teaching to reduce repetition of comments made throughout the original, and considerably reworked the Appendix on the internal organs and added diagrams to it. I also made the glossary as is usual in my translations.

I would like to thank:

The author, Di Guoyong, for his knowledge of and enthusiasm for wushu, for his patient teaching, and for his help with the translation and easy agreement to my editing.

His daughter, Di Hua, for all her efforts with emailing.

My parents, William Andre and Mary Elliott Falk, for their painstaking proofreading. My students, Haim Behar and James Saper, for their knowledgeable help with Appendix I.

And, always, Xia Bohua and Men Huifeng, for teaching me Xingyiquan way back when.

Please forgive the odd placement of some of the Chinese characters; this is a quirk of the whacked-out computer program I work with. Any other mistakes in the book are mine alone.

Andrea Falk 霍安娣

Victoria, B.C., Canada

July 2005

TRANSLATOR'S PREFACE TO THE SECOND EDITION

With the publication of the third and final book in the series, I decided to reduce the font size in new print runs of volumes one and two to make the set a bit slimmer. This will use less paper while not reducing the contents of the books at all.

I made quite a few changes while I was in there tightening up the text. They were mostly formatting changes, catching mistakes, and some changes in terminology. The only actual content I changed was to add the extra words from Volume II to the glossary. I feel that the second edition is a great improvement but if you have the first edition there is no need to update it.

Andrea Falk

霍安娣

Quebec QC, Canada

June 2009

EDITOR'S PREFACE TO THE 2020 SET EDITION

All three books needed to be redone to enable print-to-order sales, but the original files of the books were lost. As I set up the books again, I went through them to standardise the formatting to make them a more cohesive set. The main changes I made were to move things around. This was in order to even out the sizes of the books as much as possible, because the printer had problems making books of widely different thickness come out with the same look. I tried to do the readjustment in accordance with learning and teaching progressions. I moved the twelve animals to Volume I, to include them as basic techniques to Xingyiquan. I put all the theoretical and teaching discussions, the Protect the Body partner form, and the glossaries to Volume II, making it the next level – learning empty hand forms, more applications, and more thinking about things. Volume III is now specific to the weapons.

I corrected some typographical errors, adjusted some translation, and made some editorial changes while I was doing this work. I had to work on the photos yet again, and one yet again impressed with Di Guoyong's perfection and ease in all the movements and postures. If you already have the books, the original translation was solid, you do not need to buy the new set. This is the final edition of the set, and I really hope there are no remaining errors.

Andrea Falk

霍安娣

Morin-Heights, QC, Canada

January 2021

CHAPTER ONE

BACKGROUND

HISTORICAL ORIGINS OF XINGYIQUAN

Tradition has it that Xingyiquan originated with General Yue Fei (1103 - 1142) of the Song Dynasty. Recent research has questioned the truth of this tradition. General Yue Fei is a national hero because of his spirit, character, and nationalism, so it is possible that practitioners of Xingyiquan borrowed his name to gain more recognition for the style.

In recent years scholars have published much research into the origins of Xingyiquan. There are some differences of opinion, but the general consensus is that the Xingyiquan system grew out of Xinyi Liuhequan. That is, that Xingyiquan originated with Li Luoneng (c. 1808-1890) of Hebei province, on the foundation of Xinyi Liuhequan that originated with Ji Longfeng (1602-1680, also known as Ji Jike). Ji Longfeng taught Cao Jiwu (1662-1722), who taught Dai Longbang (c. 1713-1802), who taught Li Luoneng. This has been confirmed by the research of many scholars, most notably Huang Xin'ge, who spent many years on the topic and methodologically examined a huge number of historical documents. It seems quite certain that Ji Longfeng created Xinyi Liuhequan and Li Luoneng in turn created Xingyiquan.

The three main branches of Xingyiquan – 'three streams from the same source' – are commonly categorized by region: Shanxi, Hebei, and Henan provinces. The 'source of the streams' is Xinyi Liuhequan. At present, Henan province still refers to the style as Xinyi Liuhequan, and has essentially kept the original characteristics of Xinyi Liuhequan, most notably the chicken step and ten animals. Shanxi and Hebei provinces refer to the style as Xingyiquan and really represent one branch with only regional and stylistic differences, both coming from Li Luoneng.

By the Qianlong reign period of the Qing dynasty [1736-1796], Xinyi Liuhequan was already an established style with its own techniques and theory in Shanxi and Henan provinces. Li Luoneng studied Xinyi Liuhequan with Dai Longbang for ten years. Li Luoneng had trained in other styles and had a strong foundation in martial arts before studying with Dai, so after ten years of diligent analysis and practical experience he achieved a high level of skill in Xinyi Liuhequan. Li accumulated a great depth of theoretical and practical knowledge over several decades of training, and this gave him a level of mastery that allowed him to refine the style and germinate the idea of creating a new style from Xinyi Liuhequan – that is, to create Xingyiquan. By 1856 his style was spreading by this new name.

2　HISTORY

- In classical Chinese there is only a small distinction between the meaning of the characters *xin* [心 heart, the emotional mind] and *yi* [意 will, the intentional mind]. So the name *xin-yi* was repetitive – heart also partially means will, and will contains heart in its meaning. Li Luoneng changed only one character *xin* [心 heart] to *xing* [形 form, shape, structure] to make the name *xing-yi* [form and intent] more meaningful.

Although there is a difference of only one character in the names *xin-yi* and *xing-yi*, this was a milestone of reform in martial arts history, and a beautiful new 'martial flower' was created in the 'martial arts garden'. Li Luoneng bravely undertook a systematic reorganization of Xinyi Liuhequan. He established a systematic training method with the *santishi* post standing as the basic training, the five element fists as the foundation, and the twelve animals as the advanced techniques. He based his system on a combination of the ancient Chinese traditional theories of *yinyang* and five elements [metal, water, wood, fire, and earth]; the Daoist life enhancing, training, and refining methods and theories; and martial arts internal refinement training. In this way he developed a three-level martial training (obvious, hidden, and transformed; to 'train essence to transform energy,' 'train energy to transform spirit,' and 'train spirit to transform to emptiness'). These aspects were new, and Xingyiquan towered in the martial world with its systematic approach to training and scientific (for its time) theory. Although the theoretical kernel did not depart from Xinyi Liuhequan, it made a qualitative leap to a higher level. Similarly, the later development of Yiquan on the foundation of Xingyiquan created a new style with its own training methods that emphasized will and spirit.

Of course, the establishment and spread of any style, the improvement of theory and enrichment of the technical system take several generations of work. The Xingyiquan now popular throughout China has evolved in theory and technique as the result of the continued innovation of the 2nd, 3rd, 4th, 5th and 6th generations. With further social advances and developments in scientific understanding, future generations will continue to make Xingyiquan's theory and techniques even more systematic and modern and enrich all of mankind.

The author's lineage in Xingyiquan:

Li Luoneng (c. 1808-1890) 李洛能

Liu Qilan (dates unknown) 刘奇兰

Li Cunyi (1847-1921) 李存义

Shang Yunxiang (1863-1937) 尚云祥

Liu Huafu (dates unknown) 刘华甫

Zhao Zhong (1912-1978) 赵忠

Di Guoyong (1948-) 邸国勇

CHAPTER ONE: BACKGROUND

INTRODUCTION TO THE FIVE ELEMENT FISTS

The five element fists – split, drill, drive [or crush], cannon [or pound], and crosscut – are the basic techniques of Xingyiquan. Because they give rise to all other techniques the classic texts called them Xingyi's 'mother fists.'

The five element fists take their name from the Chinese five element theory – a key component of ancient Chinese philosophy. According to this theory, all phenomena of the world are composed of five basic interacting energies/substances – metal, wood, water, fire, and earth. This ancient scientific method explained the myriad phenomena by correlating them to the relationships between the five elements – how they formed and complemented each other, interconnected, and interacted.

[Metal creates water, water creates wood, wood creates fire, fire creates earth, and earth creates metal. Metal controls wood, wood controls earth, earth controls water, water controls fire, and fire controls metal.

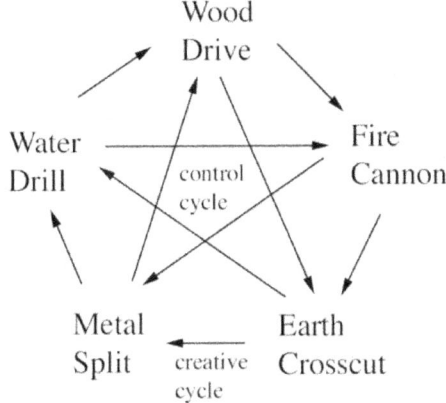

][1]

This theory permeated and enormously influenced every aspect of society, so it was natural that the martial artists who developed Xingyiquan should combine the theory of the five elements with martial techniques. Once they simplified their martial techniques and discarded non-functional moves they pared down to five techniques. They then integrated the resulting techniques with their knowledge of body mechanics and Chinese medical theory to explain martial theory and combat methods. They named the resulting techniques the 'five element fists.'

---

[1] Editor's note: There is no explanation or diagram of the cycles in the original book, so I have added this information briefly here. This knowledge is probably assumed. The author does not emphasize the cycles because in actual application different techniques could combine and function equally well. He emphasizes rather the nature of the elements and the techniques, as you will see throughout the book.

FIVE ELEMENT FISTS

The five element fists are not just five different techniques, five types of applications, and five post standing methods but more importantly, are five methods of generating power and five ways to train the power generation of Xingyi.

- Split (chopping fist) hits mainly forward and down, a vertical downward moving power. [To complete split, the body compresses then lengthens to assist the downward force.]

- Drill (drilling fist) hits mainly forward and up, a vertical upward moving power. [To complete drill, the body settles to assist the upward force.]

- Drive (crushing fist, thrusting punch) hits straight forward, a straight and level power. [To complete drive, the body expands on the straight line.]

- Cannon (pounding fist) drills one hand up to deflect as the other hand punches straight forward, a diagonal power that is effective in all directions. [To complete cannon, the body compresses and expands in a diagonal form.]

- Crosscut (crossing fist) pulls one hand back as the other hand knocks across and forward, a horizontal power that covers all directions from the centre, and it is the key power. [To complete crosscut, the body compresses and expands in a diamond form.]

Each technique hits with whole body power, each shows a complete integrated force. Launched power almost always flows forward, outward, and from the root to the tip of the body. The five techniques form one integrated system, and each one isolates an important power so that you may master it. With mastery you can use the techniques freely and naturally.[2]

---

[2] Editor's note: Note that the author emphasizes action and power flow, which is under-emphasized by some due to Xingyi's tradition of post standing training. For each technique the body needs to generate and balance a distinct power. The body compresses and expands in specific directions to create and launch the power and to counterbalance the forces issued for each technique. This pre-loading is a subtle and functional action – there is no extraneous movement in Xingyi. Compression is often done for the 'defensive' initiation of the action, and release from the compression launches the 'offensive' landing of the action. The author explains this in more detail throughout the book.

CHAPTER TWO

POST STANDING

桩功

INTRODUCTION TO POST STANDING, ZHUANG GONG

Post standing is the foundation of martial arts. Martial arts classics say: "If you desire to learn martial arts you must start with post standing." Xingyiquan is no exception, to the extent that some masters say that to properly learn Xingyi you must stand post for three years.[3] Post standing serves to build a foundation for the skills needed in Xingyiquan and to strengthen the body for its demands.

The first goal is to learn and master the basic body positions for Xingyiquan, such as holding the head up, keeping the chest contained, dropping the shoulders, sinking the elbows, and so on. Once one gains this kinesthetic awareness one gradually develops deep understanding with unremitting practice.

The second goal is to increase leg strength and the strength of the tendons and ligaments surrounding the knees.

The third goal is to master the requirements of all the distinct shapes and body positions. Standing for a long time sets the body into the correct position. The beginner learns to self-correct and gradually builds correct and unchanging positions. This creates a solid foundation for future learning of movements and skills, and the body will naturally hit the correct positions when moving into the stances.

The fourth goal is to regulate the central nervous system and the whole body. Post standing trains the ability to focus and empty the mind of random thoughts, to focus completely on the task at hand. Concentration is on relaxing every part of the body and on regulating the breath. This type of training benefits the circulatory system, improves the metabolism, regulates the qi[4] and blood, and

---

[3] Editor's note: Xingyi is a fast style that hits or throws hard. *Xing* is structure and action – the way the body stands and moves. Standing is done to improve internal power, but also the lines of power, speed and accuracy of the actions, as explained below. Sometimes people underestimate the speed and agility of Xingyi because of its characteristic static training method.

[4] Translator's note: I, along with many translators, have chosen not to translate *qi* into English. *Qi* is the energy, life force, or power that circulates throughout the body and keeps us alive. *Qi* is both energy and the substance that contains this energy, and includes

improves the immune system, thus aiding one to gain a long healthy life. At the same time, it improves the ability to fight by training a focused combative spirit.

Post standing in Xingyiquan includes primordial post standing, meridian post standing (or *santishi*), descend the dragon post standing, subdue the tiger post standing, and pounding post standing. Each standing method serves a particular goal through different positions and focus. Xingyiquan masters created these post-standing methods through practical training experience over long periods. They are all effective training methods that gradually develop and nourish the deep skills required in Xingyiquan. Each emphasizes a different aspect, but they centre on *santishi*, the kernel of all post training.

The martial arts classics say: "If you train martial arts without training deep skill[5] you will arrive at old age with nothing. " Training deep skill means working hard to enhance health and develop fitness in addition to training the basic martial skills. If you train martial arts without making your body strong inside and out, then your body cannot withstand the training. No matter how good your technical abilities they will eventually let you down. This is the integral connection between training and nourishing your body.

TRAINING PROGRESSION FOR POST STANDING

- The first step is to form a correct structure and relaxed body. Each part of the body should be adjusted to the correct position and correct shape. A correct structure is the first requirement, since if the positions are wrong then the *qi* cannot flow. A relaxed body means that every part of the body has released excess tension so it is comfortable and harmonious.

- The second step is to focus the mind. That is to say, discard random thoughts and concentrate until all thoughts blend into one.

- The third step is to breath mindfully. Focus on controlling your breath, so that your breathing pattern becomes slow, even and deep. Mindful breathing permeates to the whole training session. From the opening movement to the closing, at all times the breathing is controlled by the mind. This is one of the most evident characteristics of Xingyiquan.

---

both the life force that you are born with and the life force that you develop through *gong* training. Balanced, flowing, and strong *qi* causes and shows health, while unbalanced, blocked and/or depleted *qi* causes and shows less than full health.

[5] Translator's note: I have translated *gong* as 'deep skill'. *Gong* includes, but it is more than, martial skill, incorporating training to develop basics, fighting, mental and physical health, and strong unimpeded *qi*. Including both internal and external development, *gong* is the result of gradual and continuous training, and its definition implies both the work process and the result of the work.

CHAPTER TWO: POST STANDING

PRIMORDIAL POST STANDING   húnyuán zhuāng   浑元桩

Introduction to Primordial Post Standing

Primordial refers to the time just before heaven and earth began. [Also translated as mixed essence, 浑元 húnyuán can also be written 混元 hùnyuán.] "The mixed essence means the chaos before things were separated, it is the beginning of the original *qi*." When martial artists brought the term 'primordial' into martial arts terminology they used it in the sense of 'amalgamation of heaven and earth into one', or 'endless transformations'. Primordial post standing is used to build the foundation for beginners in almost every martial arts style. It serves to enhance the health, strengthen the body, and develop internal power.

The goals during the beginning stage are to collect the spirit and mind, discard random thoughts, regulate breathing, and release excess tension throughout the muscles, tendons, ligaments and interstitial tissues surrounding the joints. The main purpose of primordial post standing at the beginning stage is to clear random thoughts and focus on training. "Cork up your horse's mind, lock up your monkey's heart." The 'horse's mind' means thoughts that shift about like a horse, which never stands still, even when sleeping. The 'monkey's heart' means thoughts that dart around like a monkey, which constantly looks around and grabs at things. Post standing serves to regulate the body and mind to allow the whole body to release its tension. Once the whole body has achieved a relaxed state the *qi* and blood can flow unimpeded and bring health to your body and mind.

The goal during the middle stage is to use the will to lead the energy and clear all channels in the body so that the *qi* flows throughout the entire body. The goal during the higher stage is to nurture your body and your nature, and join together heaven and man. You feel your own body's internal *qi* intermingle with nature's external *qi*.

Description of Primordial Post Standing

ACTION 1: Stand upright and breathe deeply three times. (image 2.1)

ACTION 2: Step the left foot out to the left to shoulder width, with the feet parallel. Place the weight between the feet. Move slowly and synchronize breathing with stepping by inhaling as you lift the foot and exhaling as you place it. (image 2.2)

8 PRIMORDIAL POST STANDING

ACTION 3: Slowly lift the hands forward and up with the palms facing each other, fingers open, and arms naturally bent. When the hands arrive at shoulder height turn them to form a circle in front of the chest with the palms facing the chest, the elbows bent and set down, the shoulders relaxed, the chest contained, and the head slightly pressing up. Imagine you are holding a big ball of air in front of the chest. The elbows must be set down below shoulder height. At this time bend the knees slightly, release the tension around the hip joints and flatten the lower back to lower the body slightly. Look straight ahead. Hold this position, discard all random thoughts and focus on breathing. Breathe through the nose slowly, deeply, and evenly. The length of standing time is set by your endurance and fitness. (images 2.3 and 2.3 side)

2.3   2.3 SIDE

ACTION 4: Close the position by doing the opposite to the opening. First give your mind a signal, tell yourself that you are about to stop, you are about to complete the standing session. Then shift onto the right leg and bring the left foot in beside the right and stand up. As you start to stand up, lower the hands naturally down by the sides of the body, fingers pointing down. Press the head up and look forward. Once you have completed this action breath deeply three times and stand quietly for two or three minutes.

Pointers

- The three main requirements for primordial post standing are to release excess tension from the body, clear the mind, and regulate the breath. This applies to all post standing, not just primordial post standing. The foundation of post standing is the same as that of most *qigong* training – regulate the body, regulate the mind, and regulate the breath. Relax the body to release the tension from every part of the body so that not a single part of the body holds any stiffness. The key to relaxing is to release the joints, to allow all the joints to hold their natural physiological position. Relaxing the body enables the flow of *qi* and blood throughout the body. Calm the mind to withdraw into yourself and focus on your training, to bring all the activities of the brain to concentrate on one point. During primordial post standing first concentrate on breathing. Regulate the breath to consciously use your breath. Change your normal, natural, unthinking breathing to intentionally regulated breathing that is slow, even, and deep.

- During primordial post standing the head should be lifted slightly upward and the jaw tucked slightly in to maintain the neck in a straight position. The shoulders should be settled down, the chest held slightly in, the arms slightly bent in front of the body in a circle, the elbow tips pointing down, the wrists slightly bent, the fingers open naturally with the thumbs pointing slightly up, and the palms slightly concave. The lower back should be naturally straightened, the buttocks naturally tucked, the hips relaxed and the knees bent to about 160 degrees. The knees shouldn't be overly bent or straight. It takes up too much energy if they are too bent, making it difficult to control the breathing and to stand for a long time. It the knees are too straight they stiffen. When you stand properly in primordial standing you will feel every part of your body is comfortable and unobstructed.

SANTISHI POST STANDING sāntǐshì zhuāng 三体势桩

Introduction to *Santishi*

Three bodies [trinity] post standing [三体势桩 sāntǐshì zhuāng] is also popularly called meridian post standing [子午桩 zǐwǔ zhuāng] and three attributes post standing [三才桩 sāncái zhuāng].

'Meridian' and 'three attributes' are traditional cultural references. The meridians – *zi* and *wu* – usually refer to the two-hour periods around midnight and noon. *Zi* is 11:00 to 1:00 around midnight, when *yang* starts to grow, and *wu* is 11:00 to 1:00 around noon, when *yin* starts to grow. The "Golden Elixir Collection" answers the question "What is the meridian line?" with the response:

> "The meridian line means the central line of heaven and earth. In the heavens the meridians are the sun and the moon. Among mankind – the Heart and the Kidney. In time – the two-hour periods around midnight and noon. Among the eight trigrams the meridians are *kan* [a central *yang* line with top and bottom *yin* lines] and *li* [a central *yin* line with top and bottom *yang* lines]. And among directions – south and north." The "Discussion of the Three Origins" says that *zi* is the head of *yang* and *wu* is the head of *yin*, so *ziwu* form the heads of the *yinyang* 'fish'. It states; "*Zi* is the head of the six *yangs* and the peak of winter, so around the *zi* time one should sit still and collect one's spirit, release all thoughts, focus on one point, and regulate the breath to accord with the season.... *Wu* is the head of the six *yins* and the peak of summer, so before the *wu* time you should sit quietly and collect the spirit, when the peak of *yang* starts to change to *yin*, then the *yin* energy in the mind will naturally settle."

Three attributes also describes many aspects sought in the stance: 1) three attributes refer to heaven, earth and man. They are the attributes of heaven, the attributes of earth, and the attributes of man. 2) The "Book of Changes" says "Each of the three attributes has two aspects: the way of heaven is to have *yin* and *yang*, the way of earth is to have soft and hard, the way of man is to have benevolence and righteousness. These two aspects of each of the three attributes draw the six lines of the changes that form the trigrams. " 3) Chinese medical theory explains the three attributes as the body, spirit and *qi* [internal power or energy and the matter in the body that contains energy]. The "Examination of the Channels" says, "The *qi* houses the spirit and the body houses the *qi*. The spirit gathers in the Heart, the *qi* gathers in the Kidney, and the body gathers in the head. When the body and *qi* intermingle in the spirit, this is the way of the three attributes. " 4) The great martial arts master Sun Lutang said; "The three attributes are the head, hands and feet, that is upper, middle and lower. " He used the concept of three attributes to describe the relationship between the head, hands, and feet, and extended the meaning to the upper basin [head to solar plexus], middle basin [solar plexus to knees], and lower basin [knees to feet] common in martial arts terminology.

Three bodies post standing, meridian post standing, and three attributes post standing are names for the same stance that emphasize different aspects of the stance. The name 'three bodies' emphasizes the outer structure of the head, hands, and feet, the upper, middle, and lower parts of the body. The name 'meridian' emphasizes the importance of post standing in Xingyiquan, that it is the 'foundation of the foundation'. The name 'three attributes' emphasizes the internal meaning, that it is not just a posture, but even more importantly is a type of training to develop deep ability [*gong*]. The inner meaning of *santishi* post standing is very rich. 'Three bodies' indicates its method and practice, 'three attributes' indicates its theory, and 'meridian' indicates its importance.

Each regional and stylistic branch of Xingyiquan uses the *santishi* post standing as its main post standing method. Each uses essentially the same basic framework, position and requirements for *santishi*, and trains the same functions. There are, of course, differences, since each branch has a different understanding of the classic writings, and each person gains a different understanding through training. This is natural. Great trees never grow quite the same, and leaves are never identical. If one teacher teaches ten apprentices, they will all have different heights, body types, temperaments, characters, preferences and levels of education, so will of course gain different understandings from their training. These ten apprentices cannot possibly be identical.

TRAINING METHOD FOR *SANTISHI*

ACTION 1: Stand upright, looking in the direction to which you will do the stance.

ACTION 2: Gradually lift the hands at either side of the body, arms naturally bent and palms up. Do not extend the arms with force. When the hands reach shoulder height, bend the elbows to bring the palms in to the face, fingers pointing to each other and palms down. (images 2.4A and B)

2.4 A

CHAPTER TWO: POST STANDING

ACTION 3: Bend the legs to sit down slightly, press the hands down in front of the abdomen and press the head slightly up. (image 2.5)

ACTION 4: Clench fists in front of the belly and turn the fist hearts up. Keep the left fist where it is, and drill the right fist up past the solar plexus then forward to nose height, twisting the ulnar side up. (image 2.6)

ACTION 5: Advance the left foot without moving the right, so that the feet are shin length apart with most of the weight on the right leg. The weight balance is thirty percent on the front and seventy percent on the back. While doing this, drill the left fist from the abdomen up past the solar plexus and forward, fist heart up. When the left fist crosses the right fist, open both hands and rotate them inward [thumb towards palm] to chop forward with the left palm. Keep the left arm slightly bent. The left palm is angled forward and down with the wrist set and the fingers at nose height. While completing the move, pull the right hand back to the abdomen with the palm facing down. Press the head up and look forward. (images 2.7 and 2.7 front)

- This is the left *santishi* stance. To stand right *santishi* post standing, drill out the left fist instead of the right at action 4, then step the right foot forward to chop with the right palm at action 5.

Positional Requirements For *Santishi*

Santishi is the opening move to start each of the five elements and each form within the Xingyiquan system. Whatever you are practising you will almost always start from left *santishi*.

Santishi can be done at high level, mid level, and low level. For high level, the feet are two foot-lengths apart. For mid level, the feet are two and a half foot-lengths apart. For low level, the feet are three foot-lengths apart.

1. Feet: The feet should be on either side of a straight line – the toes of the lead foot and the heel of the rear foot are to either side of the line. The feet must not be along the same line, and should certainly not be crossing, as this would be unstable. The lead foot is turned slightly inwards at fifteen degrees or less. The rear foot is turned no more than forty-five degrees from the forward line.

2. Legs: The legs are bent such that a plumb bob dropped from the lead knee would not go forward of the heel of the lead foot. The angle formed by the thigh and the shank of the lead leg is about 150 degrees. The rear leg is quite bent, and holds between sixty to seventy percent of the weight. The distance between the feet depends on the degree of bend in the rear leg and the height of the stance. The angle formed by the thigh and shank of the rear leg is 120 to 135 degrees. What is more crucial is that the angle the rear shank forms with the ground is as acute as possible. Considering the biomechanical structure of the lower leg, the ankle can only flex to fifty degrees and approaching this angle assists the thrust from the rear leg. Some books state that a plumb bob dropped from the rear knee should not fall in front of the rear toes, but I feel that this is not logical. This places you too high, with the legs almost straight with almost all of your weight on the rear leg. The rear knee should be in front of the rear foot, with the amount determined by the height of the stance. It will not be far forward in a high stance, and will be more forward in a low stance. The main criteria to determine the optimum angle of the shank are: how to best store thrusting power in the rear leg, how to initiate action quickly, how to get the most distance, how to stand with stability, and how to thrust into the ground strongly. It is as the classics say: "the key is in the thrust of the rear leg." The speed that the body moves forward and the distance that it travels are entirely determined by the thrust of the rear leg. The angle of the rear leg should place the weight between the two legs in the optimum place to allow for stability and forward thrust, about sixty-two degrees towards the rear. That is, not so far forward that the rear thigh goes forward of a vertical line.

3. Hips: the buttocks, the abdomen, and the hip joints bound the hip area. In *santishi* the hips should be angled a bit, about sixty to seventy degrees from the front. This angle helps support the legs to back and front, and helps the upper body to naturally present an angled face to the front. Some people emphasize that the belly should be straight and the upper body angled, but I

CHAPTER TWO: POST STANDING

feel that this does not allow the body to feel at ease. Keeping the belly straight means that your hips face straight forward, but if you then turn your upper body to present a half-face to the front, then the belly feels uncomfortable and impeded. This position doesn't suit defensive and offensive actions either. The positioning and angle of the hips and legs should give very stable yet agile supporting conditions to the upper body. They should also be comfortable and fit the natural structure of the body.

4. Shoulders: According to the classics, the body position and the angle of the shoulders should be "straight yet appearing angled, angled yet appearing straight. " This is a deliberately vague description. Everyone has a different body type and character, and will interpret this saying differently, so this vagueness allows you to find the best angle for yourself through your training. Differences are unavoidable. From my own experience of training and teaching over many years, I have found when standing in *santishi* that the best position is with the upper body and shoulders at forty-five degrees from the front. This position is practical for fighting, as it decreases the frontal surface. It also suits the body's structure and biomechanical action. When you fit with the body's natural structure and biomechanics you can be comfortable, unimpeded, correct, aesthetically pleasing, and improve your health.

5. Hands and forearms: The angle that the left wrist forms with the forearm is 120 to 130 degrees. The wrist sits down slightly, the fingers are slightly bent, the palm concave, the thumb/index finger web spread, the thumb opened, and the index finger lifted. This increases the strength of the muscles in the web of the hand and stabilizes the wrist. Keeping a certain amount of opening in the fingers creates a certain tension in the extensor muscles of the forearm, which in turn gives a certain degree of resistance to strikes. Turning the palm to face downwards twists the distal end of the forearm, crossing the radial and ulnar bones, which increases the work of the involved muscle groups, increasing the strength in the palm. The twist also gives a stabilizing effect to the forearm. If the wrist is too straight then the hand and fingers cannot withstand the strength of a full body strike. If the wrist is pulled back too far then it is stiff and will not move easily, so the hand cannot grab or change positions smoothly. So, for these reasons, the best angle of the forearm to wrist is 120 to 130 degrees.

6. Elbows: the elbow angle is the angle formed by the forearm with the upper arm. The Xingyi classics have this to say on the angle of the elbow; "If it is too bent then you have no reach, if it is too straight then you have insufficient strength. " This gives you a rough idea, neither straight nor fully bent. In the early 1980s, as I was teaching Xingyi at Beijing University, I used this phrase when teaching *santishi* – neither straight nor fully bent. A student asked me, "What is the angle?" This left a deep impression on me. From that time on, I have looked at the angle of every joint in the body, examined old photos of Xingyi masters, thought about my experiences in training, measured with a protractor, and sought out the optimum angle for

each joint. I found that the optimum angle for the elbow is 150 degrees. Why don't we extend the arm fully in *santishi* or other Xingyi techniques? Don't we have more reach if we extend the arm? First of all, in hitting with the fist or palm in Xingyiquan, we must use its requirements and characteristics, and Xingyi emphasizes the use of whole body power. This degree of extension – neither straight nor bent – enables you to generate and use a great deal of force. Secondly, this degree of extension utilizes a relatively large number of muscles of the arm, stabilizing the elbow joint. Thirdly, being neither straight nor bent enables the elbow to change quickly, giving more options of actions.

7. Upper arm and shoulders: The angle formed by the upper arms and the shoulder joint is very important to the upper limb unit. The angle should be about sixty to seventy degrees measured from the chest to upper arm. The classics say; "settle the shoulders and sink the elbows." Settle the shoulders means that the shoulder unit should be consciously settled down. Sink the elbows means that the distal ends of the upper arms are always below the shoulder joint. The positioning of the shoulders and elbows are interconnected. If you settle the shoulders correctly then the elbows will naturally drop. If you drop your elbows then your shoulders will naturally settle. There is one more key point. The upper arm should be consciously gathered in, to keep the upper arm as much as possible on a plane with the body. This helps you generate whole body power. Whether post standing or practising you must at all times keep the upper arm rolled and tucked in to the correct position. The thumb and wrist of the rear hand is tightly held to the *dantian*.[6] The elbow of the rear arm should be naturally sunken, so you should pay attention that it does not stick out, so that you maintain an integrated force within the body. The fingers point forward and the palm faces down.

8. Head: "The head should press up and the neck should be upright." You should tuck in the jaw a bit, but be sure not to tighten the neck, otherwise you will reduce the agility of head movements. The reason for pressing the head up is that this reminds you to keep the spine straight, which helps the body to stay centered and straight, and helps breathing. You should look forward, but do not turn the head too much to keep the face facing straight on. You may allow the head to take a 22.5 degree angle from the front and look forward with the eyes.

9. Buttocks: The buttocks should remain naturally tucked in so that the pelvic basin is at a slightly greater angle than normal [do not do a pelvic tilt]. This helps you to settle the *qi* to the *dantian,* to form a bow with the lumbar spine, and to set up the lead foot to step forward.

---

[6] Translator's note: One more word that I do not translate, *dantian*, in martial arts refers almost always to the area in the core of the body, the front of which is about three finger widths below the navel. This is the energetic and physical centre of the body, where *qi* is stored, so internal styles emphasize settling the body physically and energetically here.

10. The trunk: The requirement for the upper body is "contain the chest and open the back." These are two sides of the same coin. To achieve a contained chest and opened back, you need to let your shoulders pull slightly forward, relaxing the shoulder blades and the back muscles. While maintaining this position, you must be sure to keep the shoulders set down – never shrug the shoulders. 'Contain the chest and open the back' works together with 'set the shoulders and drop the elbows' to organically connect the whole body. Make sure you do not overdo this action – you should be comfortable. The main reason for relaxing the shoulders and containing the chest is to help the abdomen be solid, that is, to settle the *qi* to the *dantian*. One of the most obvious characteristics of Xingyiquan is that the *qi* is settled to the *dantian*. Keeping the shoulders and chest slightly depressed also helps the upper body's ability to both take a hit and to strike. The root of the hand's power is the shoulders, while the root of the body's power is the core area.

LEARNING PROGRESSION FOR *SANTISHI* POST STANDING

Different varieties of Xingyi differ in the exact shape of *santishi*, some being more expansive and some tighter, some with larger stances and some with smaller, some higher, some lower, but this does not matter. Whichever *santishi* you stand, you need to change your intent concerning the power, energy and spirit at each different stage of internal training. Although there will be hardly any change in the external appearance of the stance, at each stage there is a different requirement and a different emphasis for the internal intent, the regulation of breathing, and the leading of the *qi*. Next I will briefly explain the body structure, intent, and breathing for three stages of training *santishi* post standing: the beginning stage, the intermediate stage and the advanced stage

Beginning stage

At the beginning stage you have just started to learn post standing so have only a rudimentary understanding of the requirements. Although you can imitate your teacher's position, yours is not yet correct. With time and more practice, your position will gradually improve. Often you will concentrate on one thing at the expense of another. This is a natural biological reaction, as your brain is overloaded. During this stage you should work on the following three points:

1. First work on getting an upright and correct position, placing each segment of the body at the required angle and position. Go through the checklist given above, from top to bottom, or from bottom to top, checking that each position is exactly as it should be. First get the overall picture of the legs, trunk, arms, and head, then work on the more refined requirements. Pay attention to feeling your body as you correct it, then you will start to understand the requirements of Xingyi, and the requirements for each body part.

2. Second, pay attention to relaxing as you seek to place the body in the correct position, relaxed but not slack. A relaxed body does not use brute

force, but, for example, places the leading arm in the right place with just enough force. Concentrate on releasing the tension from each segment of the body. The upper body should be relaxed and the lower body should be solid. A solid lower body means that the legs have a supporting strength. Because the legs are bent to different degrees, the back leg will become more tired. This is normal, as it supports more weight.

3. Third, calm down. 'Entering quiet ' means to focus entirely on the post standing, to take all your extraneous thoughts and throw them away. During the beginning stage you should focus entirely on placing your body in the correct posture, on the placement of each angle, on relaxing each body segment, on seeking the kinesthetic awareness throughout your body. Only when you calm your mind can you feel and learn from your body. During the first stage the placement of the body is of primary importance. The structure must be set for the power to develop smoothly. Whether or not the structure is correct has a direct effect on whether or not the power can be smooth. During the first stage breathing should be normal, not emphasized. Once the body is in the correct position and the mind is calm, then you may think of changing your natural breathing pattern to a slower, longer, deeper, and steadier breathing. During the beginning stage you should constantly adjust your posture, constantly improve it, and seek to copy the perfect model.

Intermediate stage

The requirements during the intermediate stage of *santishi* post standing are:

1. Body structure: take your correct position and seek the finer points within it, deepen your kinesthetic awareness to seek the feelings of power flow and to become comfortable.

2. Thoughts: work on two types of thoughts. One is 'looking inside,' and the other is 'looking outside.' Looking inside serves to make the body healthy. Looking outside serves to develop fighting ability. During the intermediate stage of post standing, you should direct your *qi* with your mind so that it circulates throughout your body. First think of circulating through the conception vessel, traveling up the back, over the head, and down the front of your trunk. Once you can follow the circuit of the conception vessel with your mind then gradually and naturally your *qi* will also follow this path. Then it can go through the small heavenly circuit, flowing through your whole body. Do not seek too hard to do this, the *qi* should be allowed to flow naturally. If you feel the *qi* connect, that is normal, but it is also normal if you do not feel it.

3. Breathing: during the first stage the body has learned the correct position and structure, so during the intermediate stage you do not need to focus so much on this. Now you may pay more attention to the breathing technique. In general, during the intermediate stage, you should use reverse abdominal breathing. That is, raise the diaphragm and bring in the abdomen as you

CHAPTER TWO: POST STANDING 17

inhale, and lower the diaphragm and round the abdomen as you exhale. Inhale and exhale through the nose. Consciously control the depth, rhythm and rate of your breathing so that it becomes deep, even, and slow. All of this is under the preconditions of a relaxed body and calm mind.

Higher stage

In the beginning stage the *qi* is lead by the mind. In the intermediate stage the *qi* circulates throughout the entire body. Once this has reached a certain level, then you can attain the higher level and can unite the internal and external, connect the form and sprit, become harmonious, and unite heaven and man. This is the stage spoken of in the Xingyi classics, when you 'wash the marrow and transform your power ' and 'train the spirit to return to emptiness'. At this stage, man's consciousness is transformed and man's temperament is changed. He becomes magnanimous, broad minded, and courteous.

All breathing is done through the nose and not the mouth. Inhaling is continuous, long, and deep and permeates the whole body. Exhaling is fine, slight, and almost nonexistent. Inhaling is long, and drawn into every tiny little space, like swallowing breath. Whether inhaling or exhaling, all breath is fine and slight with no sound. This is what the Daoists call "belly breathing." The higher levels in martial arts have many similarities to the higher levels of Daoist and Buddhist practices. The higher level in martial arts is that in which the fist and the Way are as one.

The outer position of *santishi* post standing is no different than in the first two stages, it is just more relaxed and the mind is more quiet, just as Laozi said in the book Dao De Jing: "on arriving at the utmost emptiness, guard the spirit sincere." The heart and mind attain an empty and calm state.

DESCEND THE DRAGON POST STANDING

jiàng lóng zhuāng   降龙桩

Introduction to Descend the Dragon

The name Descend The Dragon post standing is taken from the Daoist technique of 'descending the dragon '. The belief is that when fire rises in your heart you cannot 'fly', so the technique controls this fire and allows you to build up power in the core of your body. In this technique, the essence and spirit are held in, the water from the Kidneys rises and controls the fire – it lowers, or descends, the 'dragon'. This is the explanation according to *qigong* theory. In Xingyi, 'descend the dragon ' also refers to the outer form that the posture takes: the waist and lumbar area twist into a turned bow stance to turn the body around to face backwards, both arms press out with the lead hand bracing and rear hand pressing. This trains the lower back, arms, and legs of the external system, and the heart, mind, and *qi* of the internal system. First train the outer then train the inner, because "the outer trains the muscles, bones and skin, the inner trains the ability to combine everything with one breath ". First try to get the body

18   DESCEND THE DRAGON POST STANDING

comfortable in the correct position. On this foundation you can then progress to practise the next level within the posture, in which the goal is to focus your thoughts and regulate your breathing.

PRACTISING DESCEND THE DRAGON POST STANDING

ACTION 1: Stand upright, then step the left foot to the side, placing the feet parallel about three foot-lengths apart. While doing this, raise the hands at the sides to shoulder height with the palms up and arms slightly bent. Look forward. (image 2.8)

ACTION 2: Without moving the feet, bend the arms and bring the hands together in front of the face, palms down and fingers pointing to each other. Then rotate the hands to turn the palms out, with the thumbs down, at shoulder height, to brace outward with the arms like holding a ball with the back of the hands. (image 2.9)

ACTION 3: Turn the body 180 degrees to the left by pivoting on the left heel to turn the left toes out, and pivoting on the ball of the right foot to turn the right heel out. Bend the left leg to form a left bow stance, and almost fully straighten the right leg, putting almost all the weight onto the left leg. Gradually brace out with both palms. The right palm finishes to the right of the head with the arm bracing round and the elbow slightly higher than the shoulder. The left palm finishes behind the left hip with the palm facing down, the fingers forward, and the arm bracing round. Turn the head around to the left to look at the left hand. This is the left Descend The Dragon stance. (image 2.10)

ACTION 4: Turn around 180 degrees, pivoting on the feet. Brace out with the palms in front of the chest as you turn. See image 2.9 in action two.

CHAPTER TWO: POST STANDING

ACTION 5: Turn the body one-eighty degrees to the right by pivoting on the right heel to turn the right toes out, and pivoting on the ball of the left foot to turn the left heel out. Bend the right leg to form a right bow stance, and almost fully straighten the left leg, putting almost all the weight onto the right leg. Turn the waist to the right. Bring the hands around as the body turns. The left palm finishes to the left of the head with the arm bracing round and the elbow slightly higher than the shoulder. The right palm finishes behind the right hip with the palm facing down, the fingers forward, and the arm bracing round. Turn the head around to the right to look at the right hand. This is the right Descend The Dragon stance. (image 2.11 and 2.11 back)

ACTION 6: The closing is the same for either side. First return to the position described in action two above. Then turn both hands to face the palms in, holding the arms in front of the chest. Then bring in either the left or right foot to stand with the feet together, bringing the hands down in front of the abdomen. Then complete the closing, bringing the hands down.

Pointers

- The opening of Descend The Dragon standing should be done slowly and softly without any hesitation, completed smoothly as one move.

- When settling into the final position pay attention to the position of the hands and arms. The arm/hand above should have a pressing out power, and the arm/hand below should have a pulling and pressing down power. The waist should have a twisting power. Don't use strength or brute force, but relax and maintain the correct position with the chest slightly contained and the head slightly pressing up.

- When you first start post standing breathe naturally and pay attention to getting the stance settled properly. Once you get the balance and position adjusted then you can gradually increase the length of time that you stand, and alternate sides. If you stand for a long time then you may decrease the distance between the feet to two foot-lengths, taking a higher stance.

- At first you should concentrate on the position of the body, getting each body segment into the correct placement, going through a checklist from top to bottom, concentrating on relaxing each muscle group. Be sure not to let the body go slack, but relax each muscle group such that each one takes part in maintaining the position so that the *qi* can flow. The waist, especially, must relax. That is, relaxed but not lax, settled but not stiff. The twisting should have elasticity, storing a power with the capability to explode, so that within the relaxation there is a buildup to suddenly shoot power.

USE AND MEANING OF THE DESCEND THE DRAGON STANCE

Since the feet are relatively far apart and the stance is relatively low, the Descend The Dragon stance places high demands on leg strength, so is most suited for younger and stronger players. Older or weaker players may adjust the stance a bit higher, and turn a little less. The main goal of this stance is to strengthen the legs and waist, and the bracing power of the arms, to physically develop more than does the *santishi*. It trains the supporting strength of the legs, the twisting elasticity of the waist, and the bracing up and pressing down power of the arms, developing these relatively quickly.

The twist and lean at the waist is like a dragon bending its body. The upward bracing and downward pressing of the arms is like a dragon stretching its body. The bent front leg and the straight back leg with the sitting body and settled *qi* are like settling into the dragon as you ride it. In all these, use the mind and not strength, at all times focus on 'the intent is tight but the strength is loose' so that gradually your body learns the kinesthetic feeling of each segment, with comfort being the best guide.

In the Descend The Dragon stance, the dragon refers to your mind and spirit. Training regulates the body, mind, and spirit, and thus 'lowers', or 'descends' the 'dragon'. So, once you have the correct position, the important thing is to regulate the mind and spirit.

SUBDUE THE TIGER POST STANDING   fú hǔ zhuāng   伏虎桩

Introduction to Subdue the Tiger

This stance is also a traditional Xingyi stance used among the people. Descend The Dragon and Subdue The Tiger use Daoist *qigong* terminology. 'Subdue the tiger' means 'the spirit is enclosed and the heart's fire descends and collects as water'. Martial artists of previous generations took this name and gave it to a posture that resembles a crouching tiger, and used the terminology for the internal training that goes with the stance. 'The heart's fire settles down and collects in the Kidney as water ' means that the mind settles and allows the *qi* and blood to flow throughout the body. In this stance the legs are in a half horse stance with the empty and solid clearly distinguished, which strengthens the legs. The arms are rounded with a bracing and holding power, which increases the primordial power of the whole body.

TRAINING THE SUBDUE THE TIGER POST STANDING

ACTION ONE: Starting from standing upright, step the left foot forward without moving the right foot, so that the feet are two or three foot-lengths apart with the left foot forward. Lift the hands to embrace in front of the chest with the wrists crossed, the palms in, and the arms bent. Contain the chest and open the back, release tension in the shoulders and drop the elbows, press the head up, tuck in the buttocks and keep the body upright. Look ahead. Straighten the legs with the weight between the feet. (image 2.12)

ACTION TWO: Without moving the feet, bend the knees to sit down with the weight more on the right leg, so that the right leg is more bent than the left, the right thigh parallel to the ground. Shift back to form a sixty/forty stance, that it, a half horse stance. Round the groin area and tuck in the buttocks, press the head up and tuck in the jaw, keep the body upright with a very slight lean forward. As the body sits down, brace the hands out, the left forward and the right back, with the palms facing each other. The left arm is slightly bent above the left knee. The right arm is more bent, with the palm at the right ribs. Brace the elbows out so that the palms have a closing in power. Release the shoulder tension and sink the elbows, contain the chest and stretch the back, settle the *qi* to the *dantian*. Look in front of the left hand. This position is the left subdue the tiger stance. (image 2.13)

ACTION THREE: Stand up, cross the hands in front of the chest, bring the left foot in beside the right foot, then step the right foot forward and do the right subdue the tiger stance. The actions and positions are the same as described above, only on the other side.

Pointers

- Keep the whole body coordinated in the move, so that the arms brace out and the body sits into the stance all at once.
- Use intent rather than strength to put power into the grab with the lead foot, embrace with the hands and brace out with the elbows.
- Keep the whole body coordinated as you step the foot forward and cross the hands, doing everything together.
- The Subdue The Tiger stance helps to strengthen the legs, especially

the rear supporting leg. Young and strong players should sit fully into the stance so that the *qi* settles down. Weaker players may sit in a higher stance and gradually settle down as they get accustomed to it.

BREATHING IN THE SUBDUE THE TIGER POST STANDING

1. Put a closing power into the legs as you breathe in, as if you are standing on ice. Roll the hip joints in and close the knees towards the centre of the stance to prevent your feet from sliding out, giving you a closing, pulling in power. At the same time, while breathing in, put an inward, embracing power into the arms.

2. Put a grasping power into the lead foot and drive back into the rear foot as you breathe out. Settle the *qi* into the *dantian* as you breathe out, and sit the body down slightly. These actions are done more with intent, and do not change the outward shape very much. With each breath in and out a rhythmic tautening and releasing of power will develop, releasing when inhaling, tautening when exhaling. This develops a kinesthetic awareness of the muscles throughout the body, so that you can relax without becoming slack, and tauten without becoming tense. Relaxing is the method, tautening is the goal.

3. You need to coordinate the movement of the hands bracing and opening to the back and front with the settling down of the body into the legs. Although the trunk reaches slightly forward, focus on pulling in the buttocks and settling down. Shift the centre of gravity slightly forward and backward with each inhalation and exhalation. The front foot will be training its grasping power with each slight shift forward and backward. When bracing out with the hands, you should feel that you are pulling open a spring, and with each closing in to embrace, you should feel that you are embracing and squeezing a spring. Thinking of this will help you find the whole body power. You should use your imagination, not strength. If you use strength then you will tighten up. If you use your mind then you will remain supple.

POUNDING POST   zá zhuāng   砸桩

Introduction to Pounding Post

The meaning of Pounding Post is that you are pounding your foundation 'post' into the ground to make it even more stable, just as a bridge needs many piles pounded firmly into the ground to make a solid foundation. Making a foundation like this ensures that the bridge will be firm, solid, and lasting.

Pounding Post differs from standard post standing in that stnadard post standing is an unmoving position, and Pounding Post uses movement within a maintained stance. The goals are to master the whole body power of Xingyi and get a feel for Xingyi's requirements more quickly. Standard post standing emphasizes the training of breath. Post pounding trains the connection between breath and

power.

Pounding post is not a traditional training method. It is a method that I developed over many years of training and teaching. It serves to augment the standard post standing, and also serves as a stage between static standing and moving training. More importantly, it is a simple application that takes the whole body power developed within the standard post standing, and enables you to train and gain a feeling for launching power. It increases the power in your body within a short time.

POUNDING POST WITH THE LEAD FOOT

ACTION 1: Almost everything is the same as the *santishi:* the distance between the feet, the height of the stance, the position of the trunk (angled but straight, straight but angled), the head pressed up and the buttocks tucked in, the chest contained and the back open. Only the position of the hands and arms differs. For Pounding Post, the lead hand is clenched into a fist and the lead forearm is bent to cross the body with the fist heart facing in, lower than the shoulders. The lead arm is bent ninety to one hundred degrees. The rear hand is placed at the lead wrist, palm on the forearm and fingers up. Relax the shoulders and sink the rear elbow. Look forward. (image 2.14)

Pointers

- Once you have settled into the preparatory position, take three breaths to settle down into the *dantian*. Relax every muscle not needed to remain standing, paying special attention to releasing the tension in the shoulders and lumbar area

ACTION 2: Shift the centre of gravity back about ten centimetres, lifting the lead foot's heel about three centimetres off the ground, leaving the toes on the ground and bending the knee. Bring the lead forearm and fist in a bit towards the chest, maintaining contact with the other hand. Settle the shoulders and draw them back. Bring the weight back to the rear leg, press the head up, and look forward. Breathe in. This movement is slow, and the breath is long and full. (image 2.15)

ACTION 3: Press into the ground forcefully with the rear foot, so that the centre of gravity moves forward about fifteen centimetres. While doing this, forcefully land the leading foot's heel with a stamping power, landing with a thump. Do not bend the

leading knee too much, it should remain springy, so that it snaps back quickly to its original position. As the heel lands, use the power of the lower back to send the shoulders forward, putting power to the forearm and wrist, so that the leading forearm braces out and the rear hand pushes forward. Coordinate your power launch with an exhalation to gain strength. Exhale quickly and forcefully, settling the *qi* to the *dantian*. Bring the power of the whole body through each segment, to culminate and focus in the forearm. At this time the leading elbow is bent about 120 degrees. Press the head up and look straight ahead. (image 2.16)

- When training the pounding stake, do it about fifty times with the left foot forward, then about fifty times with the right foot forward. The exact number of times you do it depends on your fitness.

Pointers

- The first factor is to coordinate breath with movement. Inhale when storing energy and exhale when launching energy. The second factor is to coordinate the relaxing and tautening of the whole body. Relax tension when storing power, tauten when launching power. Relax as soon as you have completed launching the power. Only by releasing completely, all the way, can you be able to tauten fully and completely, and hit fiercely. The proportion of relaxing to tautening is nine to one. When you relax then your mind tautens, when you tauten then your power can be launched explosively.

- In coordination with the storing and launching of power, the body will have some rise and fall – about one twentieth of the body height. Shift back to load power, and let the body rise slightly. Stomp with a thump, launching power and letting the body drop slightly.

- Once you have set properly into the stance you should press the head up and look into the distance, as if standing on the top of a cliff gazing out, stable as a mountain yourself. As you shift backwards, inhaling and storing energy, it is like an ocean wave drawing back. As you exhale with the power launch, it is like the wave pounding on the shore – with an imposing air, a fierce impulse of power. If you use your imagination in this way as you do the pounding stake exercise it will bring unthought-of results.

- Practise Pounding Post with a progression from light to heavy then back to light, from soft to hard then back to soft. First launch power lightly, softly, and slowly, to regulate the *qi* and the body. Once the *qi* is connecting through the body, the body is comfortable and the power smooth, then launch power more forcefully, to train whole body power. Finally, return to a light and soft practice to regulate the breathing and bring health to the body. Throughout these three phases, maintain correct posture, smooth power, and concentration from beginning to end.

- You must determine your training load according to your strength and conditioning. You must not suddenly put out a lot of power or practise too long because you are feeling good, thus tiring yourself. Post pounding is a method of gaining whole body power quickly, but if you practise it improperly you can develop many problems. If you pound the heel into the ground too hard, or for too long a time, until you become tired, you can cause heel pain. The leading knee takes a lot of stress and impact when pounding, so overtraining can cause problems. The impact of pounding with the foot passes through the whole body, so, although you launch force forward, there can be a slight impact on the head, causing headache or other problems. If you practise according to the above requirements you should not have any problems. Training skill must be done progressively and gradually, it cannot be rushed.

POUNDING POST WITH THE REAR FOOT

ACTION 1: The preparatory stance is the same as described above. (see image 2.14)

ACTION 2: Shift the centre of gravity forward about ten centimetres, without moving the leading foot, lift the rear heel about two to three centimetres without taking the toes off the ground, and lengthen the body upwards slightly. The action of the hands is the same as when doing the lead leg pounding. Pay attention when you bring the leading hand back that you straighten the back a bit and put the chest forward. Prepare slowly and breathe in, looking forward.

ACTION 3: Shift the centre of gravity back and stamp with a thud on the rear heel, supporting yourself on the front leg. Settle the foot forcefully backwards and down. While doing this, forcefully press forward with the leading forearm and wrist, supporting it with the rear hand. Be sure to keep the buttocks tucked down, sit back, round the lower back out, send the shoulders forward, and coordinate the outward breath with the power. Left and right are the same.

Pointers

- The rear foot pounding uses the reaction of the rear foot landing. It quickly transfers up through the waist and shoulders to reach the leading hand, giving an impulse of whole body power.
- The rear foot landing is timed with the power launch to the leading hand.
- Breathe out as you launch power.

THE USE OF THE POUNDING POST

You should practise both lead foot pounding and rear foot pounding, though the lead foot is the main method and the rear foot is the secondary.

You may use this pounding exercise in each of the positions of the five basic techniques to find the power of each one more accurately and quickly, and thus improve your ability. The training is the same as described above, taking the power of the whole body to the leading hand or fist, finding the source of the power and increasing your understanding of the requirements of Xingyiquan. This helps you find the correct postures more quickly and makes the actions more correct.

I have developed this training method after many years of training and teaching, and find that it is a simple means of speeding up the learning process of finding the whole body power.

- You should be comfortable in *santishi* before learning Pounding Post. At least three months of *santishi* post standing is recommended before trying Pounding Post training.

CHAPTER THREE

SPLIT

劈拳

INTRODUCTION TO SPLIT, *PI QUAN* (CHOPPING FIST)

Xingyiquan classic texts say "The element that split relates to is metal, its form is like an axe, and the internal organ that it relates to is the Lung. "[7] This is the common view of all classic Xingyiquan texts, and is the theory respected by all traditional folk Xingyiquan. "Split relates to metal" means that split corresponds to metal from among the five elements. "Split adopts the form of an axe, " means that it splits through objects, copying the action of a metal axe splitting wood. Examining the movements of the hands during split, they really do have the appearance of chopping forward and down while holding an axe – the power is applied from above and descends in an arc towards the front. Therefore, when the old masters said, "split takes its form from an axe, " they meant that the action resembled that made while splitting wood with an axe. This is quite descriptive but still vague enough to encourage students to explore and discover the meaning for themselves through training.

There are many methods of doing split. Post standing must be done to start with. Post standing builds the foundation for split – only by doing post standing can one build the strong foundation that will enable one to get a good grasp of split. Variations in footwork include: *fixed stance split, moving stance split, aligned stance split, reverse stance split, advance to split,* and *retreating split.* A variation in handwork is *pull down split.* Variations in bodywork include: *dodging split,* and *split turn around.*

METHODS OF PERFORMING SPLIT

1. STANDARD SPLIT: ALIGNED STANCE SPLIT WITH MOVING STEP

1a Right Split yòu pī quán 右劈拳

Start from left *santishi*. For a description of the *opening move* into *santishi*, see *santishi* post standing.

ACTION 1: Clench both hands, pulling the left fist back to meet the right fist at the belly. Hug both elbows into the ribs. Advance the left foot a half-step and

---

[7] Editor's note: See Chapter One and Volume II Chapter Four for more details.

28 STANDARD SPLIT

immediately bring up the right foot parallel to the ground beside the left ankle. Keep both legs bent with the knees together. Continue on with the left fist – bring it up past the solar plexus then drill forward and up to nose height. Tuck the left elbow in, by twisting the ulnar edge [the little finger side] of the forearm up so that the fist heart is up. Do not move the right fist yet. Press the head up and look at the left fist. (image 3.1)

3.1

ACTION 2: Stride the right foot forward and follow in with the left foot a half-step. Keep most of the weight on the left leg to take a *santi* stance with the right foot leading and the left foot back. Drill the right fist up past the solar plexus, towards the left elbow, then along above the left forearm, fist heart up. As the right fist approaches the left fist, unclench both hands and inwardly rotate them, turning the palms down and forward. Pull the left palm down and back to the belly. Chop the right palm forward and down to shoulder height to split, sinking the wrist slightly so the palm faces obliquely forward and down. Keep the arm slightly bent and urge the right shoulder into the strike. Press the head up and look in the direction of the right hand. (images 3.2 and 3.2 top)

3.2

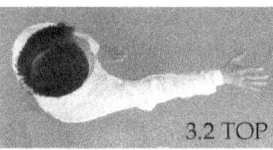
3.2 TOP

Pointers

- During the first movement of action one, the left hand should clench gradually as it moves back, and the trunk should move the left shoulder back slightly to draw the hand in. During the second movement of action one, the left fist should drill out at exactly the same time as the left foot advances, so that they work together.
- The right hand should land its split at exactly the same time that the right foot lands, so that the foot and hand enter together.
- The left foot should follow in quickly. The length of the stance should be appropriate to its height; the feet should be closer together in a higher stance and farther apart in a lower stance.
- Split strides forward into a forward and downward strike, so the stance should be slightly shorter than that of *santishi,* and the hand should finish lower than in *santishi* – at shoulder height.
- Split is a complete movement. Perform it slowly when learning, but once comfortable, actions 1 and 2 should be continuous and completed as a single action.

CHAPTER THREE: SPLIT, *PI QUAN* 29

1b Left Split   zuǒ pīquán   左劈拳

ACTION 1: Following from *right split,* advance the right foot a half-step and bring the left foot up to the right ankle with the foot off the ground. Keep both legs bent and the knees together. Clench both hands and pull the right fist back to the belly, then drill it up past the solar plexus and out to nose height, with the ulnar edge twisted up so that the centre of the fist faces up. Keep the right elbow tucked in, the head pressed up, and the eyes on the right fist. (image 3.3)

ACTION 2: Stride the left foot forward and follow the right foot in a half-step, keeping the weight mostly on the right leg. Drill the left fist up past the solar plexus, out past the right elbow and along the top of the forearm, fist heart up. As the left fist approaches the right fist, turn both hands over and open them, and pull the right hand down and back to the belly as the left hand splits forward and down to shoulder height. The left palm faces obliquely forward and down. Press the head up and look to the direction of the left hand. (images 3.4 and 3.4 front)

1c Split Turn Around   pīquán zhuànshēn   劈拳转身

Starting from the <u>right</u> *split* as example.

ACTION 1: Clench the right hand and pull it back to the belly. Hook-in the right foot, shift onto the right leg, and turn around 180 degrees to the left to face the direction from which you came. Swivel the left foot to get it pointing straight, so that the legs take a *santi* stance. (image 3.5)

ACTION 2: Advance the left foot a half-step and bring the right foot up beside the left ankle without touching down. Drill the left fist up from the belly past the solar plexus and out to nose height, ulnar edge twisted up. Look at the left

fist. (image 3.6)

ACTION 3: Stride the right foot forward and follow in a half-step with the left foot, keeping the weight mostly on the left leg. While doing this, bring the right fist up from the solar plexus to the left elbow then along the top of the forearm to split forward. Press the head up and look forward. This action is the same as *right split*. (image 3.7)

- The action of *split turn around* is the same whether on the right or left side, just transpose the right and left actions.

Pointers

  o Pay particular attention while turning that the weight shift of the body stays stable – hook the foot in and turn the body around quickly.

1d Split Closing Move   pīquán shōushì   劈拳收势

On arriving back at the starting point, do a *split turn around* to face the original direction, and continue on until you arrive in a *left split* – that is, continue until the left foot and hand are leading – then perform *closing move*.

ACTION 1: Clench the left hand and cock the fist to press it down at the belly, fist heart down, beside the right fist, which has stayed at the belly, also clenching the fist with the heart down. Do not move the feet, but press the left foot into the ground as the left fist pulls back. Press the head up and look forward. (image 3.8)

ACTION 2: Shift onto the left leg and bring the right foot up beside the left foot, keeping the legs bent to maintain the body at the same height. Keep the fists at the belly. Press the head up slightly and look forward. (image 3.9)

ACTION 3: Unclench the fists and lower the hands, then raise them in a curved route to shoulder height at the sides of the body, arms slightly bent and palms up. Then bend the arms further and bring the hands in to the face, fingers pointing to each other and palms down. Do not change the flexion of the legs during this action. (images 3.10 A and B)

CHAPTER THREE: SPLIT, *PI QUAN*   31

ACTION 4: Lower the hands past the face, pressing down to the belly, then place them at the sides. Straighten the legs to stand up. Turn the body to face forward, and the closing movement is done. (image 3.11)

Pointers

- Three actions must occur simultaneously, with full spirit: sink and bring in the left fist, press the left foot into the ground, and press the head up.

- Circle the hands up then press them down in one continuous action. Press the hands down as you stand up, so that the hands and legs act in unison.

2. FIXED STANCE SPLIT   dìngbù pīquán   定步劈拳

'Fixed stance' means that there is no half-step advance or half-step follow in. There is only one step for each split, and each action finishes in a *santi* stance. The rear hand comes through with the advance of the rear foot, in one single split action. This is a good practice for beginners, before going on to the standard *moving stance split*.

ACTION 1: Start from left *santishi*. Do not move the feet or right fist. Clench both hands and pull the left fist back to the belly, then bring it up past the solar plexus and drill forward and up to nose height. Keep the left elbow tucked in and the ulnar edge turned over. Press the head up and look forward. (image 3.12

ACTION 2: Advance the right foot but do not follow in with the left foot. As the right foot lands and grabs the ground, let the left foot swivel to forty-five degrees to take a *santi* stance with the right foot leading and the left foot back, most of the weight on the left leg. Drill the right fist up past the solar plexus and out to the left elbow, then along above the left forearm, then, as the right fist approaches the left fist, rotate them inward and unclench the hands. Split the right

hand forward and down to chest height and bring the left hand back to the belly. Press the head up and look forward. (image 3.13)

- Carry on in this way, alternating right and left.

Pointers

  o Do not change the height of the stance while changing position. The split must be completed as the foot lands – hands and feet combining with integrated power and timing.

- *Turn around* and *closing move* for *fixed stance split* are similar to those of the *standard split*, see description 1d.

3. REVERSE STANCE SPLIT àobù pīquán   拗步劈拳

3a Reverse Stance Right Split   àobù yòu pīquán   拗步右劈拳

Start from left *santishi*.

ACTION 1: Withdraw the left foot back to beside the right foot and touch down to shift onto the left leg. Clench fists and pull the left fist back to join the right fist at the belly. (image 3.14)

ACTION 2: Bring the left fist up past the solar plexus then drill forward and up to nose height with the ulnar edge turned up. Step the right foot a half-step forward and follow in with the left foot to nestle it by the right ankle. Press the head up and look forward. (image 3.15)

CHAPTER THREE: SPLIT, *PI QUAN*

ACTION 3: Take a big step forward with the left foot and follow in a half-step with the right foot, keeping most weight on the right leg. Bring the right hand past the solar plexus, to the left elbow, then along above the left forearm to unclench and split forward. Pull the left hand back to the belly. The hand movements are identical to those of *standard split* described earlier. Press the head up and look forward. (images 3.16 and 3.16 front)

3.16

3.16 FRONT

3b Reverse Stance Left Split   àobù zuǒ pīquán   拗步左劈拳

ACTION 1: Take a half-step forward with the left foot and follow in with the right. Clench the right fist, pull it back to the belly, and then drill it forward and up to nose height, ulnar edge turned over. Look forward. (image 3.17)

ACTION 2: Take a big step forward with the right foot and follow in a half-step with the left. Bring the left fist up past the solar plexus and drill forward above the right forearm. As the left fist approaches the right fist, rotate the fists inward [thumb towards palm] and unclench them, chopping the left hand forward and down and pulling the right back to the belly. (image 3.18)

3.17   3.18

Pointers

- Drill the left fist out as the right foot advances a half-step. Split the right hand forward as the left foot lands forward. The upper and lower body act together.
- Keep the lumbar and waist area lively and loose. Urge the right shoulder into the *right split*, and urge the left shoulder into the *left split*.
- The stance should have an appropriate width between the feet for stability – neither on a straight line, nor wider than the shoulders.

34   SPLIT VARIATIONS

4. OLD STYLE SPLIT   lǎoshì pīquán   老式劈拳

This method really is a splitting <u>fist</u>, as it uses fists throughout [although it uses a palm, the name in Chinese of split is 'splitting fist – *piquan* ']. One fist pulls back and the other fist strikes out and down to pound. The footwork is the same as the *standard split*, the main difference between them is in the use of fists.

ACTION 1: The actions of the feet and hands are similar to those of the first action of the standard, or moving stance, *split*, see description 1a.

ACTION 2: Take a big step forward with the right foot and follow in a half-step with the left foot. Bring the right fist up past the solar plexus then drill out along the left forearm. As the fist approaches the left fist, inwardly rotate both forearms slightly so that the fist eyes face up. Pull the left fist back to the belly and split forward and down with the right fist to chest height. Bend the right arm slightly, urge the shoulder forward, settle the elbow, press the head up, and look forward. (image 3.19)

- Carry on alternating right and left.

Pointers

   o   All points to consider are the same as *standard split*, the only difference being that *standard split* uses the palm and *old style split* uses the fist to strike. When you use the fist to split forward and down this gives a hidden pounding and punching power and intent. It uses the fist and forearm to strike, and is a pounding action forward and down. Just as the fist arrives at the point of contact, use the forward drive of the legs, the settled extension of the shoulder and elbow, and the settling of the wrist forward to create a unified whole body power.

- *Turn around* and *closing move* for *old style split* are similar to those of *standard split*, see descriptions Split 1c and 1d.

5. DODGING SPLIT   yáoshēn pīquán   摇身劈拳

Dodging split uses body technique and positioning for evasion while the hands still perform the splitting action to counterattack. Start from left *santishi*.

ACTION 1: Clench the left hand to a fist and pull it back to the belly. Withdraw the left foot to beside the right foot and shift back to the right leg. Turn the body a bit to the right. Press the head up and look forward. (image 3.20)

ACTION 2: Advance the left foot a half-step to the forward right with the toes hooked slightly out. Drill the left fist up past the solar plexus, forward and out with the ulnar edge turned up, arm bent, and fist at nose height. Keep the right fist at the belly. Press the head up and look forward. (image 3.21)

- Follow through with a regular splitting strike. The rest of the actions are the same as the *standard split* described above.

Pointers

- *Dodging split* emphasizes circular footwork. First withdraw the lead foot then step forward.
- Shift the weight back when the lead foot withdraws. At this time the body should turn away and tuck in with an evasive dodging action.
- The actions should link together without hesitation.

- *Turn around* and *closing move* for *dodging split* are similar to those of *standard split*, see descriptions 1c and 1d.

6. RETREATING SPLIT tuìbù pīquán   退步劈拳

Retreating split trains retreating footwork. A characteristic of Xingyiquan's footwork is, "to advance, first advance the lead foot, and when it advances, the other foot must follow in. To retreat, first retreat the rear foot, and when it retreats, the other foot must withdraw." *Retreating split* uses this characteristic footwork – that of first retreating the rear foot then withdrawing the lead foot. Start from left *santishi*.

ACTION 1: Retreat the right foot a half-step and shift back onto the right leg, then withdraw the left foot to touch down beside the right foot. Clench the left fist and pull back to the belly, then drill forward and up past the solar plexus to nose height with the ulnar edge turned up. Press the head up and look forward. (image 3.22)

SPLIT VARIATIONS

ACTION 2: Retreat a big step back with the left foot then withdraw the right foot a half-step to take a *santi* stance with the right leading and the left behind. Perform a *standard split* with the right hand and pull the left hand back to the belly. Press the head up and look forward. (image 3.23)

- Carry on, alternating right and left.

Pointers

- When retreating, the toes touch down first, then the rest of the foot. The retreating step needs to be agile, and the withdrawing step must follow smoothly. The backward weight shift should be stable.
- The first actions must work together – the left fist drills out as the right foot retreats and the left foot withdraws.
- The second actions must work together – the right hand splits as the left foot retreats and the right foot withdraws.
- Do not apply hard power when doing the *retreating split*. Keep the movement soft to work on coordination and smoothness.

- *Turn around* and *closing move* for *retreating split* are similar to those of *standard split*, see descriptions Split 1c and 1d.

- Referred to in some classics as *cat washes its face,* the technique *retreating split* is indeed similar, but emphasizes the footwork. The technique *cat washes its face* emphasizes the hand action.

- There is also another type of *retreating split* that is performed thusly – the right hand splits forward as the left foot retreats back. The left foot lands with a thump. This is just a different personal choice in technique. Everyone may choose from a variety of methods according to their experience and preference.

PROBLEMS OFTEN MET IN SPLIT

PROBLEM 1[8]: A beginner often focuses on the route that the hands and fists take in any technique that involves a drilling action [in most techniques the fists drill as they rise] and neglects to keep the elbows snug to the ribs. This causes partial power delivery because whole body power is inhibited.

CORRECTIONS: The teacher must repeatedly explain the movement requirements and the tracking line of the elbows. The teacher must work physically with the students to help them feel the difference in force between when the elbows are tucked in and when they are not. Do this by leaning into a student's hands or forearms as he holds the different postures. This will help the students to make the correction, to tuck in the elbows and keep them snug to the ribs.

PROBLEM 2: The student allows the body to rise and fall while advancing. He allows his body to come up during the half-step forward, which dissipates power.

CORRECTIONS: The problem arises because not enough attention is paid to the supporting knee. The student is not consciously controlling the height of the stance with the knees. The key lies in controlling the amount of knee flex throughout the action. The student should be sure to bend the supporting leg when advancing into the single leg stance, to keep this stance the same height as the *santishi*. A certain rise and fall cannot be avoided, but it should be limited to five percent of a person's height.

PROBLEM 3: The student's back foot follows in with the heel in a straight line with the lead foot, or even a twisted stance, making the body and stance unstable.

CORRECTIONS: The reason for this problem is incorrect placement of the rear foot as it lands from the follow-in step. As the rear foot lands, the insides of the feet should be on either side of a fist-width line. Any larger lateral distance and the groin area will be open. Any smaller and the stance will be unstable. The base must be just large enough to provide stability. More post standing will make the correct position comfortable and fixed into the body.

PROBLEM 4: The student drags the hip when bringing the back foot in, so that the rear foot lands in a stance that is too open laterally. This causes the groin area to be open.

CORRECTIONS: Weak hip action is usually the result of focusing on the lead foot and hands and forgetting or ignoring the back foot follow-in step. When stepping the back foot up, the teacher must emphasize that the knee

---

[8] Editor's note: Problems 1 through 7 are common amongst beginners, and must be dealt with as they learn the first technique of splitting palm. If not, the same problems will haunt the students as they learn the next four element techniques, and affect all efforts in Xingyiquan.

brings the foot in. Roll the hip in and align the knee to bring the foot forward. The student must also be careful to place the rear foot at an angle smaller than forty-five degrees to the forward line.

PROBLEM 5: The lead foot slips forward as the student hits, when the back foot comes in.

CORRECTIONS: The main cause of this problem is that the student does not use a 'trampling power' when landing the lead foot – the toes do not grip the ground. When the lead foot lands it should combine a 'stamping downward' power with a 'backward raking ' power. The secondary cause is overextension of the lead knee. The knee should always maintain a certain flexion when the lead leg lands, ideally a 150 degree angle between the lower leg and the thigh. The legs should also have an appropriate 'gathering in power ' between them. That is, the lead foot should exert a raking force that pulls it back, which will prevent it from sliding forward. The cause of these mistakes is usually taking too big a step forward and keeping too low. Beginners should take an appropriately smaller step forward at first, and keep the stance relatively high. They can gradually lengthen the step as they improve.

PROBLEM 6: The student is unstable or the feet and hands do not arrive simultaneously.

CORRECTIONS: The cause of instability is often either taking too big a step forward or turning the waist too much to punch towards the midline. Focus on punching forward by using a target. Getting the timing of the feet and hands right needs a lot of practice, focusing on the timing.

PROBLEM 7: The buttocks stick out backwards when the student punches forward.

CORRECTIONS: Leaning the trunk forward and sticking the buttocks out is a big error in most styles. Pay attention to pressing the head up as if hitting the sky, and to sitting the buttocks down solid as a rock, "stable as Mount Tai".

PROBLEM 8: The student allows the lead hand to drop or move back towards the body as the rear hand comes through to drill along the forearm. This is a common mistake among beginners.

CORRECTIONS: At all times focus on keeping the lead fist at nose height with the ulnar edge turned over – keep the three tips lined up (lead hand, lead foot, nose). The fist that is drilling out must have a forward and upward drilling power, creating an oblique upward pressing power. Wait until the rear fist approaches the leading fist before both fists unclench and pull down and back. Emphasize that a clenched fist always presses forward, and that an open hand pulls back.

PROBLEM 9: There is no whole body power in the strike; the hand slaps out with the force of the arm alone.

CORRECTIONS: Snapping or slapping with the hand and forearm results in a weak, shallow force instead of the required whole body power of Xingyiquan. Students must pay attention when applying force to maintain the elbow joint at an angle of about 135 degrees. Urge the arm forward from the shoulder and follow through by extending the elbow slightly. In this way the whole body is behind the strike. Focusing on the shoulder and elbow will keep students from slapping out with the hand alone.

POWER GENERATION FOR SPLIT

The hand action of split "rises with a drill and lands with a turn over." There is no straight line movement as the hands rise and fall and the arms extend and return – the hands follow an elliptical route throughout. Each hand rises with a drilling fist and drops with a turning over open hand. We must focus not only on the route of the hands or fists along this elliptical track, but also on the track followed by the elbows, since the hands are pushed out directly from the elbows. The elbows must hug the ribs, whether extending or returning; they must 'adhere to the ribs,' 'slide on the ribs,' or 'rub the ribs.'

How can Xingyi masters knock someone far away with just one splitting palm? I think that first of all, the old masters had deep skills, high technical ability, and used whole body power. In addition to hitting the right spot, applying force at the optimal angle, and applying the optimal timing, the key lies in applying force in a continuous, unbroken manner at the instant of impact. This increases the length of time of the applied force, thus giving the ability to knock someone far away.

Split should be applied with a wavelike power, but this wave must not be too large or obvious. It is more a matter of synchronizing the hands, eyes, body, and feet and adding focus. The power delivery of split is to chop downward and to push forward, with a very slight upward 'lengthening power' in the body to counterbalance the downward action. The application of these three forces at once with a continuous unbroken energy at the instant of impact at the opportune time is what makes split effective. When using split, first apply the downward forward power. This makes the receiver unwittingly apply an upward countering force. 'Borrow his force to augment your own.' Take the receiver's upward opposition and apply an upward force from your lumbar/waist area. This makes it easy to lift his root. Once his root is lost his body is unstable and his power dissipated. A forceful push forward then will propel him a long way off.

- The downward and forward action of split comes from the settling of the elbow.

- The upward lengthening power comes from the upward press of the head and the lengthening of the lumbar area.

- The forward drive comes from the back heel driving into the ground and the body's forward thrust with the shoulder and waist urging into the move; add a drop of the shoulder and an extension of the arm to push and deliver the

power.

- The integration of these power applications uses mainly the strength of the legs, lower back and shoulder girdle. The resulting force comes largely from the leg force and body technique. You could say that the legs, lumbar/waist area, and shoulders contribute sixty to seventy percent of the force.

- Concentrate your power and force on the last extension, synchronizing the release of force with an expulsion of breath.

Of course, the key to split is whole body power – the hands and feet arriving smoothly together, the whole body's force as one, the power integrated. When hitting with split, be sure to press the head up. When the hand chops forward and down, hold the idea of lengthening the head slightly upward. This gives greater forward and downward splitting power to the hand.

BREATHING CYCLE FOR SPLIT

You must coordinate positional breathing once you are comfortable with the movement, in order to gain whole body power.

- Inhale as the lead hand clenches and pulls back. Move slowly and focus on keeping an imposing manner.

- Pause your breath as the lead foot advances a half-step and the lead hand drills out.

- Exhale as the rear foot steps forward and the rear hand comes through to split.

See Chapter Eleven for more detail on breathing theory and techniques that apply to all Xingyi techniques.

PRACTICAL APPLICATIONS FOR SPLIT

The classic texts say, "learn the set way, but there is no set way in application." You need to act according to the actual situation; you cannot just perform actions as if performing a routine form, but must use techniques flexibly. The key to using split is to apply the power specific to the split technique.

The hands protect the centre line when they drill up. The hands should defend the midline at all times no matter whether you are advancing, retreating, or stepping around.

Analyze the utilization of split according to its structure.

- The implication of the lead hand clenching and pulling in, then drilling out, is: the lead hand grabs and pulls down the attacker's hand, grabbing clothes if they are there, otherwise grabbing 'meat.'

- The implication of the forward drill is: hit the attacker's head or defend by jamming, being aware that you can open the hand to change to a hooking pull.

When advancing, advance the whole body, so when the rear hand comes through to chop down it strikes the attacker's head or chest as you advance, using the footwork to shove the body and the hand to split through, seeking to push the attacker away.

Whether or not you can realize these goals depends on hard practice every day, how matched your strength is to your opponent, and your ability to apply the technique with the proper direction, angle, and timing. As long as you are using a technique or power approximating that of split, that is, if you strike forward and down from above using the split power, then whether you strike with open hand, fist, or forearm, it falls into the range of the 'split' technique.

THE POEM ABOUT SPLIT

劈拳歌诀

劈拳似斧性属金，

起钻落翻细推寻。

拳掌劈落头上顶，

手脚齐到方为真。

Split is like chopping with an axe. Its character is that of metal.

Initiate with a drill and land with a turnover, a little force will push an opponent eight feet away.

The head presses up as the fist or hand lands the strike,

The hands and feet arrive together and go direct to the core.

CHAPTER FOUR

DRILL

钻拳

INTRODUCTION TO DRILL, *ZUAN QUAN* (DRILLING FIST)

Xingyiquan classic texts say: "The element that drill relates to is water; it is like a bolt of lightning, and the internal organ that it relates to is the Kidney. " In describing drill as having the form of lightning, previous generations of Xingyiquan masters were alluding to its speed. Drill has the ability to enter in an instant, to enter before an opponent has time to see it or react to it. Drill is like water because it can bubble up continuously and enter into the smallest gap as does water. When drill launches up, it surges up like a bubbling spring out of the ground, or like waves breaking on the shore. "Drill relates to the Kidney" conforms to the correlation of elements to internal organs found in traditional Chinese medical theory. In this correlation between five elements and internal organs, the Kidney relate to water, so to push this reasoning further, drill relates to the Kidney.[9]

There are many different ways to perform drill, but every region and every style agree on one thing: it drills forward and up from below. This is its common character and wherein lies its key. Variations in footwork for drill include: *aligned stance drill*, *reverse stance drill*, and *retreating drill*. Variations in hand techniques include: *coiling drill* and *pressing drill*. Variations in body techniques include: *dodging drill* and *turn around drill*.

We should first perform the method that is the most representative. As the classics say, "first learn the standard, then refine the variations". By 'standard' they mean the most conventional method, that which uses the standard power, the most common methods and applications. By 'variations' they mean the alternate ways of doing techniques and applications.

---

[9] Editor's note: See Chapter One and Volume II Chapter Four for more detail on the correspondences of the five elements.

Methods Of Performing Drill

1. ALIGNED STANCE DRILL (STANDARD DRILL)

shùnbù zuānquán 顺步钻拳

1a Right Drill yòu zuānquán 右钻拳

Start from left *santishi*.

ACTION 1: First clench the left hand without changing its position relative to the body, and turn the fist heart up. Clench the right hand at the belly. Then advance the left foot a half-step and follow in with the right foot to beside the left ankle without touching down. Turn the left fist over so the fist heart faces down and tuck the thumb in and the wrist down [combine radial flexion of the forearm with dorsiflexion of the wrist]. Bend the left elbow to bring the left fist closer to the chest – one forearm plus a fist away – the fist at shoulder height and the elbow below that. Urge the left shoulder forward into the action, release tension in the shoulders and settle the elbows. Press the head up and look forward. (image 4.1)

ACTION 2: Take a big step forward with the right foot and follow in with the left foot, keeping most weight on the left leg. Drill the right fist up past the solar plexus then along to inside the left fist until it arrives at nose height, ulnar edge twisted up and elbow rolled in. Tuck and press down the left fist and pull it back snug to the belly, fist heart down. Urge the right shoulder into the action and keep an angle of 100 to 120 degrees between the upper arm and forearm. Press the head up and settle the trunk structure slightly [translator's. note: Point the rear knee down and do not allow the leg to collapse, to readjust the trunk structure to settle under the punch.] while lengthening the spine. Look forward. (image 4.2)

1b Left Drill zuǒ zuānquán 左钻拳

ACTION 1: Advance the right foot a half-step and follow in with the left foot to beside the right ankle without touching down. Rotate the right fist and bend the elbow to tuck and press down, fist heart down. The fist should be a distance of one forearm plus a fist away from the chest. The fist is at shoulder height and the elbow settled down below that. Press the head up and look forward. (image 4.3)

CHAPTER FOUR: DRILL, *ZUAN QUAN* 45

ACTION 2: Take a big step forward with the left foot and follow in a half-step with the right, keeping most weight on the right leg. Twist the left fist heart up, and drill it up past the solar plexus, forward, and up inside the right fist. The left fist finishes at nose height

4.3

4.4

with the ulnar edge up and the elbow tucked in. Pull the right fist down and back to the belly, fist down and elbow snug to the right ribs. Press the head up and settle the trunk structure down slightly. Look forward past the left fist. (images 4.4 and 4.4 front and top)

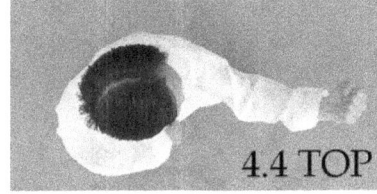

4.4 TOP

4.4 FRONT

- Carry on practicing *left drill* and *right drill*, the number of repetitions determined by the size of the practice area and your fitness.

Pointers

- Work the upper and lower limbs together: the leading foot advances a half-step as the leading fist tucks and presses down.
- Fist and foot must arrive as one, with no time lag. The back foot takes a big step forward as the back fist drills forward.
- On the first move from *santishi*, do not move the feet while the left hand clenches and turns over. After this, press down as you advance.

1c Drill Turn Around zuānquán zhuànshēn 钻拳转身

Using *right* drill as an example.

ACTION 1: Hook the right foot in on the spot and shift onto the right leg, turning the body around to the left to face back in the direction from which you came. After turning around, withdraw the left foot a half-step. Rotate the right fist outward and raise the right elbow over the head. Keep the left fist at the belly. Look forward ['forward' is back in the direction from which you came]. (image 4.5)

46   STANDARD DRILL

ACTION 2: Advance the left foot and follow in with the right to take a *santi* stance with the left foot leading and the right foot behind. Press and cover forward with the right forearm and continue down to the belly with the right fist, fist heart down. Drill forward and up to nose height from the belly with the left fist, fist heart and ulnar side twisted up. Press the head up and look forward (image 4.6)

Pointers

- Lift the right elbow at the same time that you hook-step the right foot in to turn the body around. Hook the foot in as much as possible. The weight shift should be quick and the left foot should withdraw immediately.

- Three actions must happen together, working as an integrated unit: the left foot advances; the left fist drills out, and the right fist covers and pulls back.

- The entire *drill turn around* must be smooth with no hesitation.

1d Drill Closing Move   zuānquán shōushì   钻拳收势

Once you have arrived back at the place and facing the same direction where you did the opening position, continue until you get to a *left drill*. Then you may close the drill practice.

ACTION 1: You are in a *santi* stance with the left foot leading and the right back, so do not move the feet. Tuck and rotate the left fist inward and press it down to the belly, fist heart down. Press the left foot down into the ground. Press the head up and look forward. (image 4.7)

ACTION 2: Shift forward, bringing the right foot up to the left foot. Keep the legs bent and the knees together to maintain the stance at the same height. Keep the fists at the belly with the elbows snug to the ribs. Press the head up and look forward. (image 4.8)

ACTION 3: Unclench the hands, lower them, and then circle them up at the sides with the arms slightly bent. When they arrive at shoulder height with the palms up and elbows dropped, bring the hands together in front of the face, fingers pointing to each other and palms down. Keep the legs bent. (images 4.9 A and B)

ACTION 4: Press the hands down to the belly then place them at the sides as you straighten up the legs. Turn right to face the front to stand at attention, and *drill closing move* is completed. (image 4.10)

Pointers

- The important points to consider for *drill closing move* are the same as those of *split closing move*, see description Split 1d.

2. REVERSE STANCE DRILL   àobù zuānquán   拗步钻拳

The alternative ways of performing drill are just slight changes in footwork or hand technique. Should the leading hand change its technique in a way appropriate and applicable within the drill technique, as long as the rear hand comes through with a drill, then the technique should be seen as drill. Naturally, there will be differences in technique between regions or teachers, so we should look for the similarities. Start from left *santishi*.

2a Reverse Stance Right Drill   àobù yòu zuānquán   拗步右钻拳

ACTION 1: Withdraw the left foot to beside the right ankle without touching down (you may touch down if you need to) and shift back to the right leg. Keep the legs bent to maintain the same height as the *santi* stance. Clench the left hand and pull it back to the belly, then bring it up past the solar plexus and drill forward and up to nose height. Keep the left arm bent and twist the ulnar edge up. Clench the right hand and keep it at the belly. Press the head up and look forward past the left fist. (image 4.11)

ACTION 2: Advance the left foot a big step and follow in a half-step with the right, keeping the weight on the right leg. Turn the left fist over to press down, bend the elbow slightly, and press down to the belly, fist heart down. Drill the right fist up past the solar plexus then forward and up to nose height, passing inside the left fist, and rotating out to turn the fist heart and ulnar edge up. Urge the right shoulder forward, press the head up, release tension in the shoulders, drop the buttocks, settle the elbows, and look forward. (images 4.12 and 4.12 front)

2b Reverse Stance Left Drill   àobù zuǒ zuānquán   拗步左钻拳

ACTION 1: Advance the left foot a half-step and follow in the right foot to by the left ankle. Rotate and tuck the right fist over and to the left to press the forearm down in front, fist heart down. Bend the right arm slightly and keep the fist at shoulder height. Press the head up and look forward past the right fist. (image 4.13)

ACTION 2: Take a big step forward with the right foot and

follow in a half-step with the left, keeping the weight back on the left leg. Press the right fist down to the belly, fist heart down, and drill the left fist up past the solar plexus, inside the right fist, forward and up to nose height, ulnar edge twisted up. Urge the left shoulder forward, press the head up, and look forward. (image 4.14)

Pointers

- o The action of the *reverse stance drill* is: advance the left foot, press the right fist down, step the right foot forward, drill the left fist. The hand technique is the same as the *standard drill*, the only difference is the combination of footwork with hand technique. Make sure to synchronize the right and left, upward and downward actions.

- o When you strike with a drill you must keep the lumbar/waist area lively. Increase your force by turning from below to urge the shoulder into the move.

2c Reverse Stance Drill Turn Around zuānquán zhuànshēn 钻拳转身

From *reverse stance <u>right</u> drill* (image 4.15A)

ACTION 1: First step the left foot forward, hooked in, and turn the body around 180 degrees to the right, shifting onto the left leg. Withdraw the right foot by the left foot, and then step forward in the new direction. Bring the right fist in to the waist then stab out to the rear [in the returning direction], fist heart turned up. Look at the right fist. (images 4.15 A and B)

ACTION 2: Take a big step forward with the right foot and follow in a half-step with the left foot. While doing this, cover and press with the right fist and bring it back to the belly, fist heart down. Drill with the left fist to nose height. Look in the direction of the left fist.

(images 4.16 A and B)

- *Drill turn around* from *reverse stance <u>left</u> drill* is similar, just transposing right and left.

2d Reverse Stance Drill Closing Move   zuānquán shōushì   钻拳收势

From a *reverse stance <u>right</u> drill*, pull the right fist to the belly and turn the body slightly without moving the feet. From a *reverse stance <u>left</u> drill*, step the left foot forward to take a *santi* stance. Then press the left fist down to the belly. The rest of the closing is the same as the *standard split closing*, see description in Split 1d.

3. DODGING DRILL   yáoshēn zuānquán   摇身钻拳

3a Dodging Right Drill   yáoshēn yòu zuānquán   摇身右钻拳

ACTION 1: Clench both fists and advance the left foot a half-step, bringing the right foot beside the left ankle. Rotate the left fist over to turn the fist heart up. Roll the elbow right and drop, circling down to the left. Then circle up, forward and right, to finish with the fist heart facing down, arm bent, and fist at shoulder height. Bring the right fist up with the fist heart facing out, and circle it up and right around outside the left arm, then lower it to the right waist, fist heart up. Do both hand actions simultaneously. Press the head up and look forward. (images 4.17 A and B)

4.17 A   4.17 B

ACTION 2: Take a big step forward with the right foot and follow in a half-step with the left, keeping the weight on the left leg. At this time, tuck and press down with the left fist and bring it back to the belly, fist heart down. Drill the right fist forward and up to nose height, first passing by the solar plexus then inside the left fist. Twist the right arm's ulnar edge up, press the head up and look forward. (image 4.18)

4.18

CHAPTER FOUR: DRILL, *ZUAN QUAN* 51

3b Dodging Left Drill   yáoshēn zuǒ zuānquán 摇身左钻拳

ACTION 1: Advance the right foot a half-step and follow in with the left foot to by the right ankle without touching down. Settle the right elbow down and bring the left fist up across the right forearm, then circle it left and down to the left waist, fist heart up. Bring the right fist down and right, then forward and left to tuck in and press down, fist heart down, at shoulder height. Circle both arms simultaneously without interruption. Press the head up and look forward. (images 4.19 A and B)

ACTION 2: Take a big step forward with the left foot and follow in a half-step with the right to take a *santi* stance with the left foot leading and the right foot back. Tuck and press the right fist down to the belly, fist heart down, and drill the left fist forward and up. The action is the same as that described above in *standard drill*. (image 4.20)

Pointers

- The key to the *dodging drill* is that the hands work together to circle in opposite directions – up and down, left and right, forward and back. The fists and arms must coordinate with each other and with the body technique. The action of the body is intended to give more power to the hands and arms, so you should practise this until you get it.

- Circle the hands as you take the forward half-step, synchronizing the upper and lower limbs. At first make big circles, then once you are comfortable with the action you may gradually decrease the size.

• *Turn around* and *closing move* for the *dodging drill* are similar to those of the *standard drill*, see descriptions in Drill 1c and 1d.

4. RETREATING DRILL   tuìbù zuānquán   退步钻拳

Start from left *santishi*.

4a Retreating Right Drill   tuìbù yòu zuānquán   退步右钻拳

ACTION 1: Retreat the right foot a half-step and withdraw the left foot to in front of the right, touching down the toes. Clench the left hand and place the forearm crossways to press down at shoulder height, fist heart down. Keep the right fist in front of the belly and look forward. (image 4.21)

ACTION 2: Retreat the left foot and settle into it with a thump, sitting back onto the left leg without moving the right foot. While doing this, tuck and press the left fist into the belly, fist heart down. Drill the right fist forward and up to nose height, ulnar edge turned up. Press the head up and look forward. (image 4.22)

4b Retreating Left Drill   tuìbù zuǒ zuānquán   退步左钻拳

ACTION 1: Retreat the left foot a half-step and withdraw the right foot to in front of the left. Cross the right forearm and press down, fist heart down, at shoulder height. Do not move the left fist. Look forward. (image 4.23)

ACTION 2: Retreat the right foot and settle onto it with a thump, sitting back onto the right leg without moving the left foot. Tuck and press down the right fist and pull it back to the belly, fist heart down. Drill the left fist forward and up to nose height, ulnar edge turned up. Press the head up and look in front of the left fist. (image 4.24)

- Carry on, alternating left and right. The number of repetitions depends on the size of the training ground, training time, and your fitness.

Pointers

  o *Retreating drill* is done to train retreating footwork, the hand technique is similar to *standard drill*. To retreat, first retreat the rear foot and then withdraw the leading foot. The retreating step shifts the weight back, giving the impetus of moving back before actually moving the body. Retreat the left foot as you drill the right fist. When the left foot lands the whole foot settles into the ground. Use the reactive force of thumping the left foot to turn the waist and put the shoulder into the right fist's drill. Sit the buttocks down.

  o When the leading foot retreats, press the leading fist down as the rear foot withdraws.

4c Retreating Drill Turn Around   tuìbù zhuànshēn   退步转身

There is no *turn around* when practicing the *retreating drill*. When you want to move forward you may perform the *standard advancing drill*.

4d Retreating Drill Closing Move   tuìbù shòushì   退步收势

Closing move of *retreating drill* is similar to that of *standard drill*, see description in Drill 1d.

5. COILING DRILL   chǎnshǒu zuānquán   缠手钻拳

5a Left Coiling Drill   zuǒ chǎnshǒu zuānquán   左缠手钻拳

ACTION 1: Advance the left foot a half-step and bring the right foot beside the left ankle. Turn the left hand to face palm up, then bend the wrist and circle down. Continue the circle up and right, then clench the fist with the fist heart down, the elbow bent, and the fist at shoulder height. Keep the right fist at the belly.

Press the head up and look past the left fist. (images 4.25 A and B)

ACTION 2: Step the right foot a big step forward and follow in with the left foot a half-step. Tuck and pull the left fist back to the belly with the fist heart down. Drill the right fist forward and up to nose height with the ulnar edge turned up. Press the head up and look forward. (image 4.26)

54 DRILL VARIATIONS

4.26

5b Right Coiling Drill yòu chǎnshǒu zuānquán 右缠手钻拳

ACTION 1: Open the right hand and turn the palm up. Bend the right wrist and wind the hand left and down. Complete the circle right and up and clench the right fist to press left and down, fist heart down, with the forearm crossways and the fist at shoulder height. Keep the left fist at the belly. Advance the right foot a half-step and follow in with the left foot to beside the right without touching down. Press the head up and look at the right fist. (images 4.27A and B)

ACTION 2: Take a big step forward with the left foot and follow in a half-step with the right. Tuck and press the right fist and pull it back to the belly, fist heart down. Drill the left fist up and forward to nose height, ulnar edge turned up. Press the head up and look forward. (image 4.28)

4.27 A   4.27 B

4.28

Pointers

- The key to *coiling drill* is the coiling, trapping circle of the lead hand. Hook the wrist to trap down and in. Use the shoulder to draw the movement of the elbow, and the elbow to draw the arm and hand in the circular movement. Hide a hooked punch in the forward circle when you clench your fist. The palm traps during the back and down action. The fist punches during the forward and up action.

CHAPTER FOUR: DRILL, *ZUAN QUAN* 55

- o You may make the movement large while training the body technique and finding the power of the waist, shoulder, elbow and hand. When you are comfortable with the movement you may make it smaller to do it faster.
- o Move the hands and feet together. The lead hand coils, hits and presses as the lead foot advances. The back hand drills as the back foot steps through.

- *Turn around* and *closing move* for *coiling drill* are similar to those of *standard drill*, see descriptions in Drill 1c and 1d.

PROBLEMS OFTEN MET IN DRILL

PROBLEM 1: The student thinks only of the forward drill and forgets the pulling back hand, so that the two hit with unequal force.

CORRECTIONS: Explain the theory clearly, that the drilling out fist and the pulling in fist are paired forces with equal strength, opposite direction, and along the same plane. The classics say, "Swallow and spit with equal strength, hit out with full force and pull in with full force." It helps to have the students hit themselves in the *dantian* with the returning fist.

PROBLEM 2: The student does not turn up the ulnar edge of the drilling fist, or turns it inadequately.

CORRECTIONS: The ulnar edge needs to turn up to apply power. This action keeps the elbow tucked in, and the elbow needs to be tucked in to defend your midline and to attack the opponent's centre line. This position is needed for both the punch and for the hidden elbow technique. When the forearm is externally rotated this brings the little finger side up. This rotation should be neither overdone nor underdone. If the arm is twisted too much then it becomes stiff and the body gets twisted so that the power won't flow smoothly. If it isn't twisted enough then the elbow technique can't be fully used.

PROBLEM 3: The student thinks only of the line of the fist and not the elbow, resulting in a flicking up power.

CORRECTIONS: Pay attention to the requirements of the movement – keep the elbow snug to the ribs when drilling up. The elbow must close in towards the solar plexus and send the fist forward and up, so that both elbow and fist follow a straight line. Twisting the fist over also aids in tucking in the elbow, which will develop the proper elbow line.

PROBLEM 4: The student punches in a curve or follows a crooked line instead of a straight line.

CORRECTIONS: Pay attention to the straight line. Turn the lumbar and waist area, put the shoulder into the attack, and line up the fist with the elbow to send them both out on a straight line forward and up.

PROBLEM 5: The student applies too much force to the punch without proper focus, dissipating power upwards.

CORRECTIONS: First of all, emphasize that drill hits to nose height. Be sure to loosen up and pay particular attention to releasing and settling the shoulders. The instant before the fist arrives at the point of impact, suddenly tighten and apply power. This makes the muscles involved in extension and flexion contract at the same time, stabilizing the joints and increasing the power application.

Editor's note: Review also problems 1 through 7 described in Chapter Three, Split.

POWER GENERATION FOR DRILL

The elbows must stay snug to the ribs as the drill strikes forward and up. Actively push the elbow in towards the ribs to start the movement of the fist forward, so that the elbow is fully behind the fist as it goes straight down the midline. The fist must follow a straight line forward and upwards following the midline of the body. The angle between upper arm and forearm should be 120 degrees when the drill is completed. The arm must not be too bent or too straight.

The technique of drill consists of one fist doing a forward and upward torquing uppercut from below as the other fist hooks, presses, and pulls back and down from above. The fists must exert equal power up and down. In biomechanics this is called a couple: two actions of equal force and opposite direction exerted along the same plane. The fist that punches out must have a point of focus, so the fist that pulls in should hit the belly with the same force and focus. This helps to settle the *qi* to the *dantian* and to create an explosive whole body force. Hit lightly in early training, then gradually increase the force to develop the ability of the belly to take a hit.

Before drilling out, the fist heart and ulnar edge should twist up to bring the elbow into the ribs. At this time the lumbar and waist area should compress slightly to store power. The elbow should be bent at about a ninety degree angle. Then apply power from the lower trunk area, transfer power to the shoulder, transfer power from the shoulder to the elbow, and transfer power from the elbow to the fist forward. Build a cumulative power from the body core to the shoulder through the elbow and to the fist. The fist continues to twist as it goes forward, like a mechanical drill.

Xingyi's mother fists all use this whole body power instead of segmental power. This whole body power is the most obvious characteristic of Xingyiquan. Xingyiquan's unique positional structure and training methods build this whole body power quickly, better than other styles.

To achieve a strong torquing power all the joints throughout the body need to be adjusted to their optimal state. Since Xingyiquan's power expression is whole body power, you must respect the general principle of "pre-load back to go forward, pre-load right to go left, pre-load left to go right." This is completely in accordance with biomechanical principles.[10] Specifically, this means:

- Urge the left shoulder forward slightly as the left fist circles and presses. This brings the right shoulder slightly back and stores energy in the lower back.

- Then, as the right foot strides forward and the left fist pulls back, urge the right shoulder into the move and turn the waist, sending the right fist forward and up.

- Combine this movement with a settling of *qi* into the *dantian*, and, at the last instant of the hit, settle the buttocks down slightly to increase the drilling force upward. [translator's note: do not necessarily sit lower, but drive the knee down to settle the body under the punch and direct the force up]

BREATHING CYCLE FOR DRILL

You must coordinate positional breathing once you are comfortable with the movement in order to gain whole body power.

- Inhale as the lead foot advances and the lead hand circles to press.
- Exhale as the rear foot steps through and the rear hand drills forward.
- You may gain more power and remind yourself to breathe with the abdomen by hitting yourself in the belly with the root of the returning fist.

See Chapter Eleven for more detail on breathing theory and techniques that apply to all Xingyi techniques.

PRACTICAL APPLICATIONS FOR DRILL

The structure of drill shows it to be a close range technique. Drill attacks by stepping in to bring the body tight to the opponent, attacking by entering to destroy his defensive line. If the opponent approaches, drill defends by directly striking. The key to using drill is to enter to get the body close, and the key to entering is to step in. The classics describe this often:

"To step in and punch, first take the main door.

Stride through the front door to steal your opponent's place, then even

---

[10] Editor's note: This is not a cocking action that telegraphs your attack, but is rather using an aggressive 'defensive' move to set up the attacking move. This quick and short counter movement pre-loads the muscles and enhances their ability to contract instantly, by using the muscles elasticity added to a well timed contraction, thus simultaneously saving energy, remaining more relaxed, and increasing the resultant force. You need to practice slowly to find the coordination and develop the habit of using this movement, then practice quickly to find the optimal speed and angle. In use it must be done quickly, or else the energy will be absorbed and dissipated.

an expert will have trouble defending against you.

To connect with a strike first enter the body, when foot and hand arrive together the technique will work."

The entering footwork must 'steal' the main door – it must take over the opponent's groin area, going through into his rear foot. Get the body tight into the opponent's body. The classics say, "Hit your opponent like an embrace, consider your opponent like common grass." Whether or not you can enter in that close also depends on your courage, so you must develop a win at all costs self-confidence.

The main application of drill is an uppercut, equivalent to the uppercut of boxing or Shaolin style. You must fully utilize the strength of the lower back, turn the waist, and urge the shoulder into the strike. The assisting hand responds to the needs of the moment to block down, block up, knock aside, jam, press down or snap up. As long as the power is drilling then it is drill, whether you drill up, drill obliquely, or drill to one side or another. As long as the strike connects it is a good technique, whether the elbow is a little more bent or extended than is ideal. Your principle is to hit the target, to have an effect. Therefore, "understand techniques without being limited by them, cast off the rules without violating them." You should make full use of your own body factors, particular skills and nature, and do what suits you best.

There is an elbow technique hidden in the traditional drill technique. Drill strikes up from below towards the opponent's stomach, jaw, or other upper body part. If the punch misses, you can bend your arm and thrust your elbow to strike his chest. The key is still to step in to get the body very close.

THE POEM ABOUT DRILL

钻拳歌诀

钻拳似电性属水，
进步近身功在腿。
拧裹钻翻腰肩功，
上钻发劲坐臀尾。

Drill is like lightning and its character is that of water.

The ability to enter to get the body close lies in the legs.

Use the power of the lower back and shoulders to twist, wrap, drill and turn.

Settle down the tailbone to launch the drilling up power.

CHAPTER FIVE

DRIVE, THRUST

崩拳

INTRODUCTION TO DRIVE, *BENG QUAN* (CRUSHING FIST, THRUSTING PUNCH)

Xingyiquan classic texts say, "The element that drive relates to is wood, its form is like an arrow, and the internal organ that it relates to is the Liver. " "Drive relates to wood" means that drive corresponds to wood from among the five elements. "Drive is like an arrow " means that it is swift as an arrow, and that its line of attack is as straight and accurate as that taken by an arrow. "Drive relates to the Liver " is derived from the correlation of the five elements with internal organs found in traditional Chinese medical theory. Since the Liver relates to wood in this correlation, and drive also relates to wood, to push this reasoning further, drive relates to the Liver.[11]

The driving punch is simple and functional, and must be fast and straight. It is said, "Value directness and value speed. " Value 'straightness', or 'directness' does not refer to the straightening of the arm, but to the direction and power application of the punch. Value 'speed ' means that the punch must be fast. The classics say, "The intent flows throughout the whole body, the movement comes from the footwork, the hands come and go, the posture is like bending a bow." Drive must be as fast as an arrow shot from a bow, and shoot out as continuously.

Traditionally, drive was done pushing off only from the right leg, the left leg leading. The left foot always entered – always one foot advancing and the other foot following in – so the skill could become very deep, the power strong, and the technique always perfect. The Xingyi masters Guo Yunshen and Shang Yunxiang were both famous for this punch. It was said of Guo Yunshen that no one could face his half-step driving punch.

The flavour of drive differs by region and among the traditional branches, with different combinations of footwork with hands, and of power use. This is normal, but there is also a common element, and that is to punch with one extended arm. If this isn't done then it isn't considered a drive.

---

[11] Editor's note: See Chapter One and Volume II Chapter Four for more detail on correspondences of the five elements.

METHODS OF PERFORMING DRIVE

Traditionally there are many ways of performing drive. Variations in footwork coordination with hand timing include *rear foot timed drive*, *lead foot timed drive*, *reverse stance (alternating) drive*, and *retreating drive*. A variation in bodywork is *turn around drive*.

1. STANDARD DRIVE: REAR FOOT TIMED DRIVE

hòujiǎo fālì bēngquán   后脚发力崩拳

1a Right [Rear Foot Timed] Drive   yòu bēngquán   右崩拳

Start from left *santishi*.

ACTION 1: Clench both hands. Turn the left fist heart up and lower the fist slightly to solar plexus height with the elbow slightly bent and tucked in. Put the left shoulder slightly forward as the left fist turns. Turn the right fist heart up and lift the fist slightly. Advance the left foot a half-step and settle firmly onto it. Do not move the right foot. Press the head up and look past the left fist. (image 5.1)

ACTION 2: Follow in with the right foot a half-step to behind the left heel, sliding into the landing with a thump. The stance width is about one fist-length, and the weight is mostly on the right leg. Keep the legs bent, the right knee tucked into the hollow of the left knee. Extend the right fist, following the line of the left forearm. As the right fist nears the left fist, turn both fist eyes up. Punch the right fist forward [down the midline] with the fist eye angled slightly down and the elbow bent. Urge the punch forward from the shoulder. Pull the left fist back to the belly, fist heart in, and elbow hugging the ribs. Press the head up, sit the buttocks down and look past the right fist. Punch to solar plexus height. (images 5.2 and 5.2 front)

CHAPTER FIVE: DRIVE, *BENG QUAN*   61

1b Left [Rear Foot Timed] Drive   zuǒ bēngquán   左崩拳

ACTION 1: Advance the left foot a half-step without moving the right foot. Turn both fist hearts up. Lift the left fist to chest height[12] and keep the right fist in position. Look past the right fist. (image 5.3)

ACTION 2: Follow-in the right foot a half-step and shift forward, keeping the weight on the right leg. Do not move the left foot as the right foot slides in to land with a thump. Keep the knees bent, the right knee nestled in the hollow of the left knee. The right foot is beside the left heel, turned slightly out, and about a fist-length away. Punch the left fist out along the right forearm to solar plexus height. Keep the left arm slightly bent and angle the punching surface slightly. Pull the right fist back to the belly, fist heart in. Press the head up and settle the buttocks down. Look past the left fist and urge the punch forward from the left shoulder. (image 5.4)

5.3   5.4

Pointers

- Rotate the fists as you advance the left foot a half-step.
- Punch the right fist as the right foot does the follow-in step. The foot and hand must arrive together.
- The left foot's half-step should advance further than your own shin length. Make sure that the stance does not rise or fall.
- The right foot should slide in, or rake, to thump, not lift to stamp. These techniques have different power applications. The sliding thump transfers power forward, where you want it, while a stamp transfers power upwards, where it is wasted.
- Turn the rear foot less than in it is turned in *santi* stance, so that the tucked-in knee tracks smoothly.
- Use equal force in the punching fist and the pulling back fist. Turn the waist and shoulders, urge the shoulders into the punch and sink the elbows, to punch with whole body power.

---

[12] Translator's note: The book simply says to 'chest height' so that is how I have translated it throughout. The fist at the belly, prior to punching, is actually raised about a fist-length above the navel, no lower than solar-plexus height and no higher than chest height.

STANDARD DRIVE

- o Urge the left shoulder into the left punch and the right shoulder into the right punch to give power and to keep the fist tracking on the midline. The punching arm's forearm is level and upper arm angled, with the elbow bent 140 to 150 degrees. [The elbow is behind the fist throughout the punch, so it must hug the ribs as it drives the fist out.]
- o The punching fist should be tightly clenched at the moment of impact to increase its strength. Keep the wrist line (back of the hand to arm) straight.
- o Be sure not to hook up the fist. This makes it easy to catch, and is a weak punch. Press the fist surface forward slightly with the fist eye angled forward and up, tilting slightly to line the forearm up with the two larger knuckles. Do not overdo the tilt, but keep a comfortable and strong line to the punching surface.

1c Drive Turn Around   bēngquán zhuànshēn   崩拳转身

Drive turn around is traditionally called *leopard cat turns over whilst climbing a tree*. This name comes from the way a leopard cat will, on arriving near the top of a tree, turn over and face down. The name is very expressive of the spirit, intent, and structure of this action.

ACTION 1: Bring the left foot around hooked in outside the right toes, keeping the knees bent. Whichever fist was punching, bring it in to the belly, fist heart in. Shift the weight to the left leg and turn around 180 degrees to the right to face back in the direction from which you came. Press the head up and look forward. (image 5.5)

ACTION 2: Bend the right knee and lift it. Turn out the right foot crossways and do a turned heel kick forward and up to shoulder height. Bend the left leg slightly for stability. Turn the fist hearts up, bring the fists up to the solar plexus, then drill forward. Drill the right fist out on top to nose height and drill the left fist to the right elbow. Tuck both elbows in. Keep the chest closed in, the shoulders settled, the head pressed up, and look at the right fist. (images 5.6 A and B)

ACTION 3: After the kick is completed, stamp the right foot forward and down with the foot turned out. Follow in with the left foot a half-step to bring the thighs together, lowering the body and lifting the left heel to form a high resting stance.  Keep the weight between the feet [slightly to the rear, so that the lead foot is able to step forward into the next punch]. Drill the left fist up along the right forearm, and as it reaches the right fist, unclench both hands and turn the palms down. Split the left palm forward and down to waist height. Pull the right palm back to beside the right hip. Press the head up and look past the left hand. (images 5.7 A and B)

Pointers

- Link up the actions smoothly to hook-step around, pull the lead fist in and turn the body around. Press the head up while turning, do not lower the head or bend at the waist.
- Kick and do the double drilling punches at the same time, working the upper and lower body together. Stand firmly on the left leg.
- Reach forward with the foot to land and turn the foot out to trample. Coordinate the hands and feet so the left hand chops and the right hand pulls back as the right foot lands. Be sure to turn the waist, put the shoulders into the action and press the head up.
- The whole move should be continuous without a break, completed as one action.

1d Drive Closing Move (Retreating Drive and Final Closing)
bēngquán shōushì   崩拳收势

The *closing move* is the same for all types of driving punch. After arriving back at the opening place and turning around, complete a *right drive* and then a *retreating drive*. The *retreating drive* that is within the *closing move* may also be practised separately as another variety of drive.[13]

---

[13] Editor's note: The *retreating drive* trains the ability to strike forward while seemingly retreating. Much of Xingyi emphasizes forward moving techniques, so this technique is vital to having a complete set of skills. The combination of *retreating drive* to *forward drive* – a rebounding attack – within the five elements connected form is also a vital skill.

64   STANDARD DRIVE

After the *retreating drive*, then do the final *closing move*.

Retreating Drive   tuìbù zuǒ bēngquán   退步左崩拳

ACTION 1: Retreat the right foot a half-step and shift back to the right leg, withdrawing the left foot. Turn the right fist heart up and turn the left fist and bring it up to the chest. Look past the right fist (image 5.8)

ACTION 2: Keep withdrawing the left foot steadily, retreating back a full step and landing the full foot solidly. Shift back onto the left leg and withdraw the right foot a half-step with the foot turned out across the stance. Bring the left fist along the right forearm to punch forward, arm slightly bent, at chest height, fist eye up. Pull the right fist back to the belly. Turn the waist and urge the punch forward from the left shoulder. Keep the thighs tightly together, press the head up, and look past the left fist. (image 5.9)

Pointers

- Retreat the right foot at exactly the same time as you turn the right fist.
- The left foot must land with a thump when it retreats.
- Three actions happen at once – the left fist punches, the left foot lands, and the right fist pulls back.
- Exhale to put more power into the action.

Final Closing

ACTION 1: Step the left foot forward without moving the right foot, settling into a *santi* stance. Tuck and press the left fist and pull it back to the belly, fist heart down. Keep the right fist at the belly. Press the left foot into the ground, press the head up, and look forward. (image 5.10)

CHAPTER FIVE: DRIVE, *BENG QUAN*

ACTION 2: Shift onto the left leg and bring the right foot up to the left foot, keeping the legs bent and keeping the body at the same height. Keep the fists at the belly. (image 5.11)

ACTION 3: Lower the hands and unclench them, then lift them at the sides of the body, arms slightly bent, turning them gradually so the palms are up when they reach shoulder height. Bend the elbows to bring the palms together in front of the face, fingers pointing to each other, palms down. Keep the legs bent. (images 5.12 and 5.13)

ACTION 4: Press the hands down to the belly then to the sides and straighten the legs. Turn ninety degrees [optional] and stand at attention. (image 5.14)

Pointers

- Three actions are synchronized together: the left fist tucks, presses, and pulls back in; the left foot presses into the ground; the head presses up. Mental focus must be maintained and shown.

- The hands circle up, come in, and press down in one continuous movement, slowly and evenly. Straighten the legs as the hands press down, as one action.

2. LEAD FOOT TIMED DRIVE

qiánjiǎo fālì bēngquán   前脚发力崩拳

Start from left *santishi*.

2a Right Lead Foot Timed Drive   yòu bēngquán   右崩拳

ACTION 1: Clench both fists. Turn the left fist heart up and lower the fist to solar plexus height. Flex and tuck in the left elbow slightly [keeping the fist forward to put pressure into the forearm]. Release tension in the left shoulder and urge it forward slightly. Turn the right fist heart up and lift it slightly. Do not move the feet. Press the head up and look past the left fist. (image 5.15)

ACTION 2: Advance the left foot a half-step and quickly bring the right foot up to land behind the left heel, with a stance width of a fist-length. Keep the weight on the right leg and the knees bent, tuck the right knee into the centre of the stance so that it nestles near the hollow of the left knee. Bring the right fist along the left forearm to punch forward in a straight line. When the right fist approaches the left fist turn both fist eyes up. Tilt the right fist eye slightly forward as well to line up the punching surface on the first two knuckles. Keep the right arm slightly bent and urge the punch forward from the right shoulder. Pull the left fist back to the belly, fist heart in and elbow snug to the ribs. The right fist is at solar plexus height. Press the head up, settle the buttocks down, and look past the right fist. (image 5.16)

2b Left Lead Foot Timed Drive

zuǒ bēngquán   左崩拳

ACTION 1: Turn both fist hearts up and lift the left fist slightly to chest height. Look past the right fist. (image 5.17)

ACTION 2: Advance the left foot a full step and quickly bring the right foot up near the left heel, keeping the weight on the right leg. Keep the legs

bent and nestle the right knee into the hollow of the left knee. Follow the line of the right forearm with the left fist to punch forward, fist eye tilted forward and up, elbow slightly bent, and shoulder urging the punch forward. Pull the right fist back to the belly, fist heart inward and elbow hugging the ribs. The left fist punches at solar plexus height. Press the head up, sit down, and look past the left fist. (image 5.18)

- Carry on, one step for each punch, punching with the left and right fists without changing the lead foot. The number of repetitions is governed by the size of the training area and your fitness.

Pointers

  o The main difference between the *lead foot timed drive* and the *rear foot timed drive* is the synchronization of the footwork with the punch. The driving punch itself is the same. The *lead foot timed drive* punches as the lead foot lands, and the *rear foot timed drive* punches as the rear foot lands with a thump.
  o The *lead foot timed drive* depends on the thrust from the back leg, so the lead foot must attack forward, the fist leading, the trunk leaning forward slightly, and the back knee pushing down to press the shank down to give good power to drive forward. At the instant of launching the punch, urge the shoulder forward, sink the elbow, and grab the ground with the left foot as it lands. The right foot follows in quickly and lightly.
  o Push the rear knee down as the centre of gravity moves forward to create a small shin-to-ground angle so that the leg thrust directs the force more forward than up. Be careful not to lean forward, but to send the power directly to the centre of the body, then transfer to the fist.

3. REVERSE STANCE DRIVE (ALTERNATING DRIVE)

àobù bēngquán   拗步崩拳

Start in left *santishi*. First do a *rear foot timed right driving punch* as described above. (see images 5.1 and 5.2)

3a Reverse Stance Left Drive   àobù zuǒ bēngquán   拗步左崩拳

ACTION 1: Advance the left foot a half-step and lift the right foot to beside the left ankle. Turn the left fist slightly so the fist heart faces up. Lift the right fist to chest height, fist heart up. Press the head up and look past the right fist. (image 5.19)

DRIVE VARIATIONS

ACTION 2: Take a large step angled to the forward right with the right foot and follow in with the left foot a large half-step, so that there is one foot-length between the feet. Keep the weight back on the left leg. Follow the line of the right forearm with the left fist to punch forward in a straight line. Urge the left shoulder forward and bend the left elbow slightly, punching to solar plexus height with the fist eye tilted forward and up. Pull the right fist back to the belly, fist heart in. Press the head up, settle the buttocks down, and look past the left fist. (image 5.20)

3b Reverse Stance Right Drive   àobù yòu bēngquán   拗步右崩拳

ACTION 1: Advance the right foot a half-step and lift the left foot to inside the right ankle without touching down. Keep the legs bent and the knees together. Turn the left fist slightly to face the fist heart up. Bring the right fist up to the chest, turning the fist heart up and keeping the elbow snug to the ribs. Press the head up and look past the left fist. (image 5.21)

ACTION 2: Take a large step to the forward left with the left foot and follow in a large half-step with the right foot, keeping the weight back on the right leg. The feet should be about a foot-length apart, the knees bent. Bring the right fist along the left forearm to punch forward in a straight line to solar plexus height, putting the right shoulder forward into the punch and keeping the elbow slightly bent. Angle the right fist eye forward and up. Pull the left fist back to the belly, fist heart in. Press the head up, settle the buttocks down, and look past the right fist. (image 5.22)

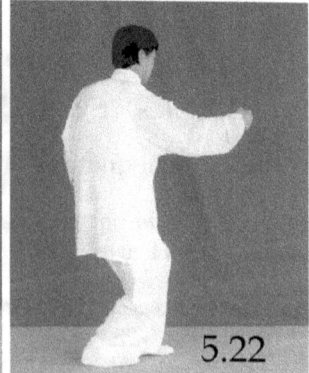

- Carry on to left and right.

CHAPTER FIVE: DRIVE, *BENG QUAN* 69

Pointers

- The actual punch is still the same as that of the *standard drive*.
- The *left and right reverse stance drive* is a driving punch that alternates punches by stepping into a reverse stance, changing lead feet each time. The punch should come with the large forward step, hitting as the lead foot lands, that is, the timing is that of a *lead foot timed drive*.
- The footwork advances in a slight angle to left and right, so pay particular attention that the lead fist stays pointing in the direction to which it will punch. It will then punch straight ahead as the foot comes through. Make sure the body stays stable and does not rise or fall when stepping through.
- For the *reverse stance drive* the action must be tightly coordinated – turn the waist, urge the shoulder into the punch, extend the arm, lead into the fist, drive the lead foot forward and drive hard off the back foot.

PROBLEMS OFTEN MET IN DRIVE

PROBLEM 1: The student's body leans forward and the buttocks stick out. This is an even bigger problem in drive than in the other techniques, due to the shorter stance.

CORRECTIONS: The cause of this is focusing on the forward extension of the arm and moving everything forward into the hit. Correct this by emphasizing pressing the head up and dropping the buttocks like a plumb bob, which will keep the trunk upright.

PROBLEM 2: The student stamps the right foot when doing the *rear foot timed drive*.

CORRECTIONS: Stamping is using force to stamp downward. The *rear foot timed drive* is not a stamp, but is a sliding-in thump, done by rolling in the hip joint and closing the knees to bring the foot forward, shoveling in the right foot to trample forward and down. A shoveling trample has a relatively large forward moving force, which assists transferring power to the punch. A stamp contains only a downward force, which wastes energy.

PROBLEM 3: The student punches with the arms alone, keeping the trunk and shoulders square to the stance. This results in weak spirit and power.

CORRECTIONS: Emphasize using the shoulders to send the punching fist out and pull back the other fist. If the shoulders' power is not used then the body is like a bow without a bowstring – how can it apply its power? The shoulders use the theory of accumulating stretch-tension. Use the lumbar/waist area to draw the shoulders, so that the body technique is played out between the shoulders and body core.

PROBLEM 4: The student loses balance on the hook-step turn around. Three possible reasons for losing balance are: 1) The left foot hooks in too far away from the right foot so that the centre of gravity displaces too far. 2)

The head drops down, making the back bend. 3) The left foot hooks in with not enough angle so the body doesn't get turned around.

CORRECTIONS: Firstly, emphasize hooking the foot around to outside the right toes. The hook-step should hook in a lot to make the next movement easier. Secondly, emphasize pressing the head up while turning, and using the spine as an upright pivot line. Thirdly, be sure not to step too far away, just to outside the right toes.

PROBLEM 5: The student loses balance on the landing of *leopard cat turns over whilst climbing a tree*.

CORRECTIONS: The main cause of this is simply lack of mastery of the technique. The thighs do not grip each other tightly enough, the lower back does not turn enough, the left shoulder does not reach far enough into the movement, and/or the right foot does not press out when it lands. Work on each of these problems individually and the student will gradually be able to cope with the whole move.

Editor's note: Review also problems 1 through 7 described in Chapter Three, Split.

POWER GENERATION FOR DRIVE

In performing drive, the power is mainly an extension of the arm to punch straight forward while stepping forward or bringing the back foot in, achieving unison of foot and hand, combining the whole body into one hit. How does one hit with a complete power? How does one take the strength of the whole body and transfer power through each segment to build up into the fist surface? This is the goal that we seek in our training. Concentrate on the body technique of countermovement to launch power forward into the punch. Before putting the waist and shoulders into the punch, pull the body back a bit so that it builds up kinetic energy.[14] This action of storing energy [in the body] also increases the line of movement [of the punching shoulder]. When directing the fist forward, send the elbow out from the shoulder, and first bend the elbow ninety degrees, then, when the fist and foot move together, extend the arm to the final point.

The part played by the footwork makes up the majority of the action – the forward reach of the lead foot and the backward thrust of the back foot. This is what the classic saying, "The hands contribute thirty percent and the legs contribute seventy percent to the hit" means. The forward reach and backward thrust of the legs moves the entire body forward as a unit. The forward extension of the fist to punch is built on the forward movement of the body. The power of drive comes from the footwork moving the body forward, turning the lumbar/waist area to urge the shoulder forward, pushing the elbow forward from the shoulder, and finally driving forward into the fist. The power moves from

---

[14] Translator's note: The pre-load is the 'defensive' movement, not an empty or extra action. Be sure to press into the leading fist and forearm. This action of the lead shoulder will pull the body back on the other side.

CHAPTER FIVE: DRIVE, *BENG QUAN* 71

the legs to the arms, increasing cumulatively until it reaches the fist surface.

- Before pushing the body forward be sure to press the back knee down, bringing the shank to an acute angle with the ground to increase the horizontal directional force.
- The driving punch must at all times follow the midline of the body.
    - For the *rear foot timed drive,* you can pretend there is a rope attached to your ankles. Push off with the back foot to forcefully break the rope then step up. Roll in the hip joint and close the knees, bringing the foot in with the knee, and sliding in, not stamping. This type of driving punch is heavy and forceful but not very quick. The *lead foot timed drive* uses a direct charge forward, which is much faster though not quite as strong. You should train both types of drive equally and be able to use either one well.

The kick in the *drive turn around,* or *leopard cat turns over whilst climbing a tree*, is an important skill. Make sure that the upper, middle and lower body segments initiate and land the complete action together.

- Within the fist drill, the forearms do an additional forward butting power, and the lower back must have lengthening power upward.
- When kicking, tuck the right hip joint back to let the right foot kick up smoothly.
- When the right hand is up and the left hand down, tuck the waist and close in the chest to keep the body centered. Then stomp the right foot, turning it crossways.
- When the left hand chops down it should have a settling power forward and down. The right hand should pull in like a grappling hook.
- When the right foot lands it should have a trampling power forward and down. Use the weight of the body to press forward, chop and trample.
- The head should press up when the hand chops down.

These types of power can be developed gradually with much thought during repeated practice. No matter how clearly someone explains this, you must practise repeatedly and conscientiously to absorb the skill into your body.

Retreating drive is not just an action within the *drive closing move,* it is another variation of the drive technique. It uses whole body power – power coming up from the ground, from the inside to the outside.

- The weight should move back just before the left foot lands on the ground as it retreats, using the entire back surface to hit backwards, and using the buttocks to settle quickly.
- As the centre of gravity passes the right foot, keep moving back so that the body feels like it will fall backwards, then the left foot retreats back

to support with force, so that the supporting reactive force reaches to the lower back, transfers to the shoulder, transfers to the elbow, and in turn transfers to the fist.
- The left arm extends forward and the right arm pulls back, the shoulders move forward and back creating a couple.

BREATHING CYCLE FOR DRIVE

You must coordinate positional breathing once you are comfortable with the movement in order to gain whole body power.

- Inhale deeply as you move in between the punches.

- Exhale sharply to punch.

PRACTICAL APPLICATIONS FOR DRIVE

Drive is equivalent to the straight punch of Longfist or the jab of boxing, although with a different power application and timing. Drive is a fast straight-line punch that hits when the feet and body enter into the opponent – the body arrives with the feet, the fist punches when the feet arrive. Because the shortest distance between two points is a straight line, drive is the fastest punch in Xingyi. Looking at the statistics in boxing, the straight jab is used most often and scores the most points, suggesting that a quick, straight, punch is a most useful punch to have in your repertoire.

The traditional drive technique is done as continuous punches, containing defensive moves within the attack and attacking moves within the defense, a fast and furious barrage of punches. The classics describe it well;

> "Enter the body [into the opponent] so that the hand and foot arrive together."

> "The hands are like poisonous arrows, the body is like a bow; it all comes from the drive of the back foot."

> "The hand enters like a rasp and lands like a grappling pole."

> "Strike with purpose, retract with purpose. [both in the intent and the technique – always see what can be done]"

The traditional use of drive emphasizes continuous attacking punches, and the key to a continuous attack is the advancing footwork. The 'lead foot half-step advance' is the most effective footwork for this. It is quick, moves the centre of gravity under control, and can change direction easily to react to the opponent.

Other classic sayings point out drive's technique and evoke its fighting spirit, courage, and tactics:

> "Launch like an arrow, land like the wind, chase the wind and the moon without slackening."

"Initiate like the wind and land like an arrow, don't slow down even after hitting."

"Don't turn over or drill, one inch is all you need."

"To step in and launch the punch, first take over the front door."

The target for drive is the head, solar plexus or belly for upper, middle, and lower punches. Do not be content with one hit making contact, but take that opportunity to charge in with more punches, advancing all the time. The classics say,

"Two fists go back and forth, the technique is like continuous shots."

"There is no posturing, no blocking, just one strike, and if need be, ten strikes."

- Xingyiquan emphasizes 'hit to break the attack,' it does not 'block and attack.' The block is the attack, the attack is the block.

To put any and all techniques into use you must ignore the set pattern. Do what it needed to break down the opponent's attack and get in. React flexibly.

THE POEM ABOUT DRIVE

崩拳歌诀

崩拳似箭性属木,

进步近身全凭步。

两手往来连环进,

神技妙法在神悟。

Drive is like an arrow and its character is that of wood,

Count on advancing footwork to get the body in close.

Drive the punches in continuously, one after the other,

The secret to skill lies in gaining intuition through experience.

CHAPTER SIX

CANNON, POUND

炮拳

INTRODUCTION TO CANNON, *PAO QUAN* (POUNDING FIST)

Xingyiquan classic texts say "The element that cannon relates to is fire; its form is like an artillery cannon, and the internal organ that it relates to is the Heart." Gunpowder exploding in a cannon launches the cannonball out instantaneously towards the enemy. Then the cannonball explodes with unstoppable destructive ferocity. The cannon technique imitates this explosive ferocity. The technique enters fiercely, nothing can stop it, and nothing can block it.

Cannon relates to the fire element because of its explosive nature, and relates to the Heart due to the correlation of the Heart to fire in traditional Chinese medical theory.[15] In learning cannon we must first learn the proper movement and pattern, then, on that foundation, seek its explosive and destructive power. Its combination of quickness with heaviness must be expressed in both the body and the spirit.

Looking at the form [structure and movement] of cannon, one fist drills up then deflects out as the other fist punches forward. Different branches of Xingyiquan perform cannon differently, but all use the drilling deflection combined with the punch. We need to analyze the form and goal of a technique because the goal decides the form that it will use, and form serves the goal. There are a variety of forms that are able to serve and reach a goal. But in this case, the form must meet strict criteria: simple movement, fast, able to change, good for protection, an effective attack when used to enter, an effective defense when used to withdraw, biomechanically sound, and effective in combat. Cannon meets these criteria.

The line of action taken in cannon is a Z line, diagonally left and right as it moves forward to hit with the body angled in a reverse stance.

---

[15] Editor's note: See Chapter One and Volume II Chapter Four for more detail on correspondences of the five elements.

METHODS OF PERFORMING CANNON

1. STANDARD CANNON

Start from left *santishi*.

1a   Right Cannon   yòu pàoquán   右炮拳

ACTION 1: Shift forward without moving the left foot. Then take a big step forward with the right foot. Land firmly on the right foot, keeping the leg bent, and quickly follow in with the left foot to beside the right ankle without touching down. Keep the knees together. While shifting, bring the right hand up along under the left and extend it forward. When the hands meet, step and clench to fists and pull them back to the belly with the fist hearts in. Snug the elbows into the ribs, press the head up, and look forward. (images 6.1 A and B)

ACTION 2: Turn the fists hearts face up, then drill the left fist up past the solar plexus and up by the right side of the face at eyebrow height, keeping the elbow tucked in. Lift the right fist to the solar plexus. Step the left foot a big step forward to the left and follow in a half-step with the right, keeping most weight on the right leg. Punch the right fist straight out in the forward left direction at solar plexus height with the arm slightly bent. Turn the waist leftward, put the right shoulder forward and bring the left shoulder back. Fix the angle of the left elbow and rotate the left forearm so the fist eye faces the left temple. The left fist is about a fist-length away from the temple, the elbow hangs down, and the

CHAPTER SIX: CANNON, POUND, *PAO QUAN*   77

forearm is nearly vertical. Press the head up and look past the right fist. (images 6.2 and 6.3, also 6.3 front and top)

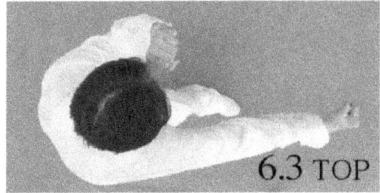
6.3 TOP

Pointers

- In action 1, extend the right hand as the centre of gravity moves forward. Pull the hands back as the right foot advances. Take a long step forward with the right foot and land under control. Bring the left foot in quickly.

- Sit down slightly when the left fist drills up, and pull the right shoulder back to both make the drill solid and store energy for the punch. Coordinate the sitting action of the knees with the shoulder action from the waist. Punch with the right fist when the left foot lands, working together with whole body power.

1b   **Left Cannon**   zuǒ pàoquán   左炮拳

ACTION 1: Advance the left foot a half-step with the foot turned in slightly and follow in with the right foot, lifting it at the ankle. Keep the knees together and the legs bent. While doing this, unclench the hands and lower the left hand to meet the right hand, palms down, and grab and pull forward and down, pulling in to the belly in fists, fist hearts up. Keep the elbows to the ribs, press the head up, and follow the hands with the eyes until they lower, then look to the forward right. (image 6.4)

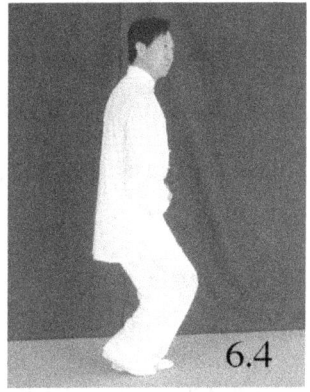
6.4

ACTION 2: Take a big step to the forward right with the right foot and follow in with the left foot a half-step, to finish with the feet about two foot-lengths apart and with most weight on the left leg. Turn the fist hearts up and drill the right fist up the belly to the solar plexus, then up the left side of the face to eyebrow height, keeping the elbow tucked in. Turn the body slightly left and sit down slightly. Lift the left fist to the solar plexus then punch strongly in the forward right direction at chest height, fist eye up. Keep the left arm slightly bent, turn the waist right, put the left shoulder into the punch and bring the right shoulder back. Keep the right elbow angle unchanged and rotate the forearm so that the fist eye faces the temple. The right fist is about a fist-length distance away from the right temple, the elbow dropped, and the forearm near vertical. Press the head up and look to the forward left. (images 6.5 A and B)

78   STANDARD CANNON

Pointers

- Advance the right foot as the hands reach forward and down then pull in. Do not stop the fists at the belly, but continue on to drill up.

- The punch arrives with the footwork, so hands and feet arrive simultaneously, working together. Take a long advancing step and follow in quickly. The body charges forward, the punch is fierce, and the waist is springy and lively.

• Right and left cannon punches are similar, so continue to alternate according to the size of your practice area and your fitness. Make sure to advance in a Z stepping pattern.

1c   Cannon Turn Around   pàoquán zhuànshēn   炮拳转身

Using the *right cannon* as example.

ACTION 1: Settle in a bit after the *right cannon* to prepare for turning around. Hook-in the left foot in front of the right foot, so the feet toe in, taking a character eight [/\] stance. Shift onto the left leg and lift the right foot at the left ankle without touching down. Keep the knees together and bent. Turn around to the right to face in the direction from which you came. While doing this, unclench the hands and circle them up at the left, forward, down and in to the belly, clenching as they move. When circling, the right hand is in the lead and the left hand is behind, palms facing down. As the hands come down, the arms bend slightly, fist hearts turn in, elbows hug the ribs, head presses up, and eyes follow the hands. When the fists arrive at the belly, look forward. (image 6.6)

ACTION 2: Take a big step to the forward right with the right foot and follow in a half-step with the left. Keep most weight on the left leg. Turn the fist hearts up then drill the right fist up, following through into a *left cannon*. (images 6.7 A and B)

Pointers

- The *turn around* is one action, so must be quick and continuous, and the following cannon must hit fiercely.
- In order for the hook-step to bring the body around and allow a smooth forward step, the foot should hook in sharply and step to the outside of the other foot.
- The hands must move in coordination with the body turn, and follow a round circle. The waist must be supple, the shoulders lively, and the elbows settled.
- Press the head up while turning, don't allow it to drop and make the body lean forward. Keep the spine as a vertical pivot line.

1d   Cannon Closing Move   pàoquán shōushì   炮拳收势

Starting from *left cannon*. (image 6.8)

ACTION 1: Withdraw the right foot to land beside the left foot with the legs together and bent, shifting onto the right leg. Bring the left fist back to the solar plexus and turn slightly left. Bend the right arm to cover with the elbow to the left, the right fist turned and at nose height. Look at the right fist. (image 6.9)

ACTION 2: Step the left foot forward without moving the right foot, taking a *santi* stance with the left leading and the right back. Slide the left hand along the right arm and hit forward with a *left split*, bringing the right hand back to the belly, palm down. Press the head up and look forward. (image 6.10)

- Continue on to complete the closing as in *standard split closing move*, see description in Split 1d.

Closing starting from *right* cannon. (image 6.11)

ACTION 1: Withdraw the left foot to land beside the right foot and shift onto the right leg, putting the legs together and keeping them bent. Bring the right fist back to the solar plexus and turn right. Bend the left arm and do an elbow cover by using the movement of the body; press down with the fist hooked in, fist heart down at shoulder height, forearm crossing the body. Look forward. (image 6.12)

ACTION 2: Without moving the feet, press the left fist down and bring it back to the belly with the fist heart in. Drill the right fist forward and up with the ulnar side turned up, at nose height. Look at the right fist (image 6.13)

ACTION 3: Step the left foot forward without moving the right foot, to take a *santi* stance. Split the left hand forward, unclench the right fist and pull it back to the belly, palm down. Press the head up and look forward of the left hand. (image 6.14)

- Continue on the complete the closing the same as in *split closing move*, see description in Split 1d.

Pointers
- In Xingyi the closing moves are always settled and steady. Focus on regulating the breath. The movement may be slowed down, and the spirit must be strong.
- Turn the waist to bring the fist back and coordinate this with the elbow technique – whether the right elbow covering leftward or the left forearm pressing down and rightward. The action comes from the waist, using it as the axis to bring the arms across.
- Use the shoulders to bring the arms across, whether the right elbow covering leftward or the left forearm pressing down and rightward. Transfer power from the waist to the shoulders, to the elbows, and finally to the hands.

2. ALIGNED STANCE CANNON   shùnbù pàoquán 顺步炮拳

Start from left *santishi*.

2a   Right Aligned Stance Cannon   yòu shùnbù pàoquán 右顺步炮拳

ACTION 1: Clench both hands. Turn the left fist heart up and bring it down and back to press the backfist down at the belly, fist heart up, elbow hugging the ribs. Withdraw the left foot a half-step to just in front of the right toes, touching the toes down. Press the head up and look forward. (image 6.15, before the left fist comes in to the belly)

ACTION 2: Advance the left foot a half-step then take a big step forward with the right foot and follow in with the left a half-step, keeping most weight on the left leg. Drill the left fist up past the solar plexus, up the right side of the face to the eyebrow, fist heart in, about a forearm distance from the nose. Lift the right fist to the solar plexus and punch forward in a right cannon punch, fist eye up, at chest height, keeping the arm slightly bent and urging the punch forward from the shoulder. Turn the body left and allow the left shoulder to follow it, the left fist turning inward, the fist eye about a fist-length away from the left temple. Keep the left elbow dropped, press the head up, and look past the right fist. (image 6.16)

CANNON VARIATIONS

2b Left Aligned Stance Cannon   zuǒ shùnbù pàoquán 左顺步炮拳

ACTION 1: Withdraw the right foot a half-step to touch down in front of the left toes. Turn the right fist so the fist heart is up and roll the fist down and back to press the backfist down in front of the belly. Turn the left fist heart up and press the backfist down at the belly past the right elbow. Bend the waist slightly and sit the buttocks down. Press the head up and look forward. (image 6.17)

ACTION 2: Advance the right foot a half-step, take a large step forward with the left foot and follow in a half-step with the right foot, keeping most weight on the right leg. Drill the right fist up past the solar plexus then up to the eyebrows, fist heart in, ulnar side turned. Lift the left fist past the solar plexus and punch out as the left foot steps, fist eye up, arm slightly bent. Put the left shoulder into the punch, punch the left fist to chest height and turn the right fist so the fist eye faces the right temple, about a fist away. Keep the right elbow dropped, press the head up, and look forward. (image 6.18 and 6.18 front)

- Carry on, alternating right and left.

Pointers

  o Press the backfists down timed with the lead foot withdrawal.
  o Step forward quickly and keep the footwork connected. Punch at the same time as the lead foot lands. Turn the waist to urge the fist forward from the shoulder, synchronizing the upper and lower body.
  o The entire move is done as one action, continuously and smoothly.

2c Aligned Stance Cannon Turn Around

shùnbù pàoquán zhuànshēn   顺步炮拳转身

Using the *right aligned stance cannon* as example.

ACTION 1: Hook the right foot in on the spot and step the left foot back in a cross step behind the right leg, turning the body around 180 degrees to the left. (image 6.19 A)

CHAPTER SIX: CANNON, POUND, *PAO QUAN*

ACTION 2: Pivot the feet on the spot and shift onto the left leg. Turn the right fist heart up and circle it up then forward and press the backfist down at the belly. Turn the left fist heart up and press the backfist down at the belly. Press the head up and look forward, back in the direction from which you came. (image 6.19 B)

ACTION 3: Advance the right foot a half-step, take a big step forward with the left foot, and follow in with the right a half-step, keeping most weight on the right leg. Drill the right fist over and punch the left fist forward, in an *advancing aligned stance cannon*. (image 6.20)

- *Aligned stance turn around* is similar starting from the left or the right aligned stance, just transpose left and right directions.

Pointers

  o The *turn around* is one move and should be done smoothly without interruption.

  o The back cross step and pivot turn are synchronized with the fist circle. The advancing step is synchronized with the punch.

2d   Aligned Stance Cannon Closing Move

shùnbù pàoquán shōushì   顺步炮拳收势

Once you arrive back at the starting point and have done the turn so that you are facing in the same direction as at the start, continue until you are in a *left aligned stance cannon*. Pull both fists back to the belly, press the head up and look forward. The rest is similar to *split closing move*. (see images 3.8 though 3.11, description Split 1d)

3. DODGING CANNON yáoshēn pàoquán 摇身炮拳

Start from left *santishi*.

3a Dodge, Left Cannon yáoshēn zuǒ pàoquán 摇身左炮拳

ACTION 1: Advance the left foot a half-step and follow in with the right foot to beside the left ankle. Clench both hands and drill the right fist up in front of the left elbow, fist heart turned out. As they come in front of the right shoulder the left fist is in front of the right fist. Without pausing, take the forearms across to the left, right fist in front of the left fist, both in front of the left shoulder. Sink the elbows dropped, release shoulder tension, settle the chest and keep the waist lively. Look in the direction of the fists. (images 6.21 A and B)

ACTION 2: Take a big step to the right front with the right foot and follow in a half-step with the left foot, keeping most weight on the left leg. Drill the right fist up to the right temple and punch out with the left fist in a *left cannon*. Put the left shoulder forward and punch at solar plexus height. The actions are all similar to those of *standard left cannon*. (image 6.22)

3b Dodge, Right Cannon yáoshēn yòu pàoquán 摇身右炮拳

ACTION 1: Advance the right foot a half-step with the foot hooked slightly inward. Follow in with the left foot to beside the right ankle without touching down. Turn the right fist heart to face out and pull it across leftward to in front of the left shoulder. Turn the right fist heart to face in and roll the forearm towards the left elbow. Turn to the left, with the right fist in front of the body and the left fist behind. Turn the body right and bring the arms across to the right, tucking the elbows, rotating the right forearm inward and the left forearm outward. The left fist is in front of the right fist, which is in front of the right shoulder. Release shoulder tension, sink the elbows, contain the chest, liven up the waist, and look in the direction of the hands. (images 6.23 A and B)

CHAPTER SIX: CANNON, POUND, *PAO QUAN*

ACTION 2: Take a big step to the forward left with the left foot and follow the right foot in a half-step, keeping most weight on the right leg. Drill the left fist up to eyebrow height and punch out to chest height with the right fist in a *right cannon*. All particulars are similar to *standard right cannon*. (image 6.24)

- Carry on, alternating right and left.

Pointers
  o The half-step advance is synchronized with the elbow crosscut roll. The movement of the hands and arms must be quick and the waist must be supple and lively. The fists rotate in opposite directions at the same time so that the fist hearts face each other. Keep the elbows snug to the heart.
  o The punch must come as the foot lands.

3c   Dodging Cannon Turn Around

yáoshēn pàoquán zhuànshēn   摇身炮拳转身

Dodging cannon turn around is similar to the *standard cannon turn around*, see description in Cannon 1c.

3d   Dodging Cannon Closing Move

yáoshēn pàoquán shōushì   摇身炮拳收势

Dodging cannon closing move is similar to the *standard cannon closing*, see description in Cannon 1d.

4. REVERSE STANCE CANNON   àobù pàoquán   拗步炮拳

The footwork of *reverse stance cannon* is the same as that of the *standard cannon*, it advances in a Z pattern. The hand technique is the same as the *aligned stance cannon* – the hands turn over and press down, the elbows tuck and draw in, and then they punch out as the foot advances. So the *reverse stance cannon* combines these two techniques.

Problems Often Met In Cannon[16]

PROBLEM 1: The student's deflecting arm cuts straight across or blocks up, lacking rolling power.

CORRECTIONS: Focus on keeping the elbow down and first drilling the fist up then turning. Turn from the lower back to draw the shoulder into the action, and then turn the fist to deflect. Be sure to turn the body to deflect rather than cutting across or blocking up. If you block up too high the elbow comes up to leave a big gap, making defense difficult.

PROBLEM 2: The student punches too far to the side on completion of cannon.

CORRECTIONS: The punch should be in the same direction that the lead foot points and aligned with the back heel. The punching fist, elbow, and shoulder are on line with the rear foot. The student should train post standing in the cannon posture to understand the angles and directions of the lines of power.

PROBLEM 3: The student shrugs the back shoulder.

CORRECTIONS: The cause of shrugging is not letting the shoulders loosen up, so during practice the student must keep the shoulders loose and settled.

PROBLEM 4: The student straightens the arms when reaching out to pull in, or even straightens and raises the arms up before pulling down.

CORRECTIONS: Remind the student to maintain a bend in the elbows throughout the movement. Be sure to settle the shoulders, close the lower body, sink the elbows and stretch the back to resist extending with the arms. Give a lot of thought to the proper positioning of each body segment.

PROBLEM 5: The student does not hook in the lead foot during the first half-step forward. Since the line of movement is a Z shape, this causes the foot to be twisted during the push off into the punch. This wastes the strength of the leg, twists the supporting knee, and dissipates power.

CORRECTIONS: Remind the students as they take the first half-step to turn the foot in about twenty degrees when it lands. Then, when it is time to push off, they can put good power into it. The knee will track smoothly so they can push it down to get the best shank angle for a forward drive.

Power Generation For Cannon

The classics say; "In the martial way, the postures show visible form and the *qi* or internal strength does not show visible form. The internal power is what moves the postures." 'Postures' mean the structure and form of actions, and 'internal strength' means power (*jin*). Power is shown through the actions, and

---

[16] Editor's note: Review also problems 1 through 7 described in Chapter Three, Split.

CHAPTER SIX: CANNON, POUND, *PAO QUAN* 87

each different action shows a different type of power. If there is no action then no power is created – actions serve power. The kind of action done creates a corresponding type of power – the power is determined by the action.

1. In *standard cannon*, when the hands reach out to grab and pull in as you take a big step forward, it is like you are grabbing a big rope and pulling it back. The strong advance of the footwork is like leaping over a wide gully. The movements are done at the same time with an integrated power.

2. When the hands unclench and reach forward to pull back, the arms should be rounded. When the hands press down, the head should press up. Release shoulder tension, sink the elbows, and close the chest in. Then when the hands press down and pull in, the whole body is tucked in.

3. When the left fist is deflecting it drills up as the body sits slightly down. The body should turn slightly to the right, the chest close in and the trunk tuck in – these small actions all serve to store power. Pre-load back to launch forward, pre-load right to launch left. Sit down slightly by flexing the right knee and pressing it forward. Turn right by moving the shoulders.

4. The forward step in cannon must use the drive from the back leg to its full capacity, the back knee must press down to decrease the angle of the shank with the ground. This increases the forward horizontal force and makes the body's centre of gravity move forward rather than up. This is called 'striding forward and driving back' and enables the forward step to be long with great momentum and power.

5. Turn the lumbar/waist area and urge the punch forward from the shoulder, using the waist to send the shoulder forward, the shoulder to send the elbow forward, and the elbow to send the fist forward. The shoulder, elbow and fist are all aligned on the same plane. Lengthen the spine when you punch, pressing the head up. The angle of the punching arm of cannon is the same as during the drive punch, but the fist has a very slight upward lifting intent. It is important to settle the elbows and release the shoulders.

During the *aligned stance cannon* the fists turn over and pound. They should have both a pressing down power combined with a rolling back power. Develop this power by simultaneously releasing the shoulders, settling the elbows, sitting down with the buttocks tucked in, tucking in the trunk, and pressing the head up. When the fists drill up the shoulder should reach forward slightly, keeping the chest closed, the back open, and the trunk compressed. When you step forward and punch, the shoulders should turn with force.

The key to *dodging cannon* is taking the arms from side to side. When training this, at first turn quite a lot, then gradually decrease the size of the turn to shoulder width. When turning from side to side, first reach the shoulders forward and spread the back, turn the forearms so that they take the fists across. The power of the whole move comes from the lower back, so the key is to keep the waist loose and lively.

BREATHING CYCLE FOR CANNON

Once you are comfortable with the movement you must coordinate positional breathing in order to gain whole body power.

- Inhale as you take the half-step advance and reach the hands to pull down.
- Contain the breath in the lower body as the fists drill up and the body turns slightly, keeping the lower back relaxed.
- Exhale as you drive forward and land the foot and punch, settling the *qi* to the *dantian*.

PRACTICAL APPLICATIONS FOR CANNON

Combat is the true meaning and essence of the martial arts. In training Xingyi the structure of postures, the power line of actions, and specific characteristics of techniques all serve combative applications.

Cannon contains a defensive action in the attack and an offensive action in the block – it combines both defense and offense in the same moves. As the fist drills up, it protects the midline, then the head. As the fist drills up past the solar plexus, it protects the chest, then, as the waist turns the arm rolls to protect the head. As the waist turns this creates an advantageous condition for the other fist to punch forward.

The target for the punch is the chest, belly, solar plexus, or head, but whether or not you can land the punch depends entirely on your footwork. Do you dare to enter in tight with your footwork? Is your footwork quick? Are your movements coordinated with your footwork? It is not too difficult to achieve good footwork while training on your own, but to perform in a combat situation – using footwork to get in and out successfully while keeping in balance at all times and getting yourself into an advantageous position – is another matter. This ability also reflects a person's psychological qualities and combative will.

The placement and action of the defending arm has strict rules in practice, but in a combat situation you have to see the situation and defend yourself flexibly with a deflection out, a deflection up, a press down, a brush aside or a trap. This is what the classical saying "there is no distinction between defense and attack in postures or timing" means. You must learn a fixed posture, but in use there is no fixed technique.

Any punch or palm technique in Xingyi requires a bent arm, not quite fully extended. This type of requirement cannot be separated from the whole body power of Xingyi. All Xingyi hits use whole body power, the strength of every part of the body culminates in the fist or palm. In action, every part of the body, under a high degree of conscious control, follows the form for the specific technique. Once one part moves, all parts move in coordination. Whole body power is created by gathering and settling, then linking from root to tip; the power initiates in the root, and progressively collects, transferring segment by segment to reach the tip. Active and reactive forces are identical. That is to say, the amount of force you apply to the opponent will be reflected back to you. The arms keep a certain flexion to stabilize and protect the arms from this force. The second reason for the arm flexion is for agility, to be able to adjust a technique easily. If the opponent is knocked back when you strike, then you can still straighten the arm to increase the length of time in contact and drive the opponent even faster and farther away. If the opponent is not moved when you strike then the bent arm allows you to adjust your action quickly in any direction.

- The *aligned stance cannon* uses the sideways positioning of the body when advancing, one hand drills and deflects while the other hand hits the chest, stomach or head, using the extension from the turned body. The key is in the footwork.

- The *dodging cannon* uses both arms to knock aside a double armed attack. The footwork can retreat or enter. But when you attack you always enter, keeping the elbows in to protect your midline, the chest, solar plexus and ribs. Your fists protect your head.

No matter what exactly you do with your hands, if one defends while the other attacks it is within the cannon technique. The main point is not the height or forward placement of the defending arm, or whether it deflects upwards or downwards. The key is to effectively defend and attack simultaneously.

THE POEM ABOUT CANNON

炮拳歌诀

炮拳似炮性属火，
进步两手砸带裹。
化钻冲打敌身去，
欲前先后腰要活。

Cannon is like an artillery cannon and its nature is that of fire,

Enter in and use both hands to pound, draw, and wrap.

Deflect and drill, charge and hit, the opponent will be driven away,

Keep the trunk lively to gather back and recoil forward.

CHAPTER SEVEN

CROSSCUT

横拳

INTRODUCTION TO CROSSCUT, *HENG QUAN* (CROSSING FIST)

Xingyiquan classic texts say "The element that *crosscut* relates to is earth, its form is like a shot, and the internal organ that it relates to is the Spleen, the whole body is round. " That crosscut relates to the earth and Spleen is due to the correlation between the five elements and the organs.[17] "Crosscut relates to a shot " should not be understood to mean that it acts like an ammunition shot or pellet, but to mean that it is round like them. It also includes the character's secondary meaning of elasticity.[18] The classics say, "The efficacy of crosscut is that its energy flows smoothly, its shape is round, and its power is harmonious. Only when these three exist together can it be considered a crosscut."

Both the outer structure and the inner power of crosscut are round, even and full. The roundness and fullness of the outer structure helps the *qi* collect and increases the fullness inside. The fullness and collected *qi* inside helps the outer form become fuller, rounder, and more elastic. Internal and external forms support and aid each other. How do you make the outer structure rounded and full? What do you have to do to be considered round and full? When the movement requirements are satisfied, the outer structure is round and full and the whole body – upper and lower, inner and outer – is balanced with no gaps in power, then that is 'round and full'. Not allowing slackening or disconnection of power does not mean to be rigid or to keep the muscles tense. Excess tension in the muscles makes the body awkward, stiff, and uncoordinated. In order for the outer form to be round it is vital that the spirit and energy are full and communicate throughout. Fill the shape with the spirit and control the shape with the will, and a powerful attitude will be shown.

The 'cross' in crosscut has many sayings in the classics; "cross refers to the initial action, aligned refers to the landing, " "initiate crossways without seeing the cross, land alongside without seeing the alignment." The term 'crosscut' means a horizontal action, the opposite of a vertical action. Looking at its form, crosscut is a twisting drill that punches forward from a reverse stance with the

---

[17] Editor's note: See Chapter One and Volume II Chapter Four for more detail.
[18] Translator's note: the character 弹 can be read *dan* as a noun meaning 'pellet, bullet, or shot', and *tan* as a verb 'to shoot' or an adjective 'elastic'.

body turned. Its name would appear not quite appropriate to its action. If it went by its name it should hit side to side horizontally, but why do the classics say that you don't see the cross in the crosscut? Xingyi hand techniques, footwork, positioning and theory are all based on practicality. Hitting is the defense, that is, 'hit to defend,' do not 'defend then hit.' With this theory underlying all training, of course there is the saying "you don't see the cross in the crosscut." If the 'cross' were emphasized then there would have to be a sideways crossing action. Most of a sideways cross would be for defense, as a sideways block. Crosscut has a defensive action hidden within it, but the emphasis is on the attack. What is emphasized is its goal. During the crosscut the twisting roll of the arm is the 'cross' and the forward drill is the hit. The crossing power of crosscut is hidden, so you don't see it in the outer shape.

METHODS OF PERFORMING CROSSCUT

1. STANDARD CROSSCUT: REVERSE STANCE CROSSCUT

àobù héngquán 拗步横拳

1a   **Reverse Stance Right Crosscut**   àobù yòu héngquán   拗步右横拳

Start from left *santishi*.

ACTION 1: Do not move the right foot yet. Withdraw the left foot a half-step to touch the toes down in front of the right foot. Clench the left hand and pull it back to the belly, then drill up and forward from the solar plexus to nose height with the ulnar side of the arm and the fist heart twisted up. Clench the right fist as well and lift it to the solar plexus, fist heart down, elbow tucked in to the ribs, and forearm aligned to the front. Press the head up and look ahead. (image 7.1)

ACTION 2: Take a large step forty-five degrees to the forward left with the left foot and follow in a half-step with the right foot, keeping most weight on the right leg. Bring the right fist from the left elbow, fist heart still facing down, and punch forward while turning the forearm so that the fist heart faces up by the time it reaches its full extent

CHAPTER SEVEN: CROSSCUT, *HENG QUAN* 93

(arm slightly bent) at shoulder height. Turn the left fist over and tuck it, pulling back to the belly, fist heart down. Urge the right shoulder forward and bring the left shoulder back. Press the head up and look forward past the right fist. The right punch is straight forward and the stance is angled forty-five degrees. (images 7.2, and 7.2 front and top)

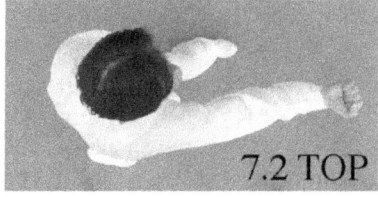

7.2 TOP

1b **Reverse Stance Left Crosscut** àobù zuǒ héngquán 拗步左横拳

ACTION 1: Advance the left foot a half-step with the toes hooked slightly in, and follow in with the right foot to beside the left ankle. Without moving the right fist, bring the left fist, centre still facing down, up to the solar plexus with the elbow snug to the ribs. Press the head up and look forward past the right fist. (image 7.3)

ACTION 2: Take a large step to the forward right with the right foot and follow in a half-step with the left, keeping the weight mostly on the left leg. Drill the left fist out from the solar plexus, under the right elbow, and straight forward, twisting gradually to turn the ulnar edge and fist heart up. The punch finishes with the front arm slightly bent, the fist at shoulder height, both shoulders settled and elbows dropped. Turn the right fist over and pull it back to the belly, fist heart down, elbow snug to the ribs. Urge the left shoulder forward, bring the right shoulder back, press the head up, settle the buttocks down and look forward past the left fist. The left punch is straight ahead. (image 7.4)

Pointers

- In the first action do not pause between pulling the left fist back and drilling it forward. Coordinate this with the withdrawal of the foot.
- Three actions happen with equal timing and power – step the left foot forward, punch with the right fist, and pull the left fist back. Be sure to turn the waist and put the shoulders into the hit, and to twist, roll, drill and turn the fists. These actions are synchronized in timing and launch the same force.
- Be sure to keep the fist hearts facing the way they were while initiating the action – while the lead foot advances, the lead fist does not move,

94 STANDARD CROSSCUT

and the rear fist rises to prepare.

- o Three actions happen with equal timing and power – the right foot lands, the left fist punches and the right fist pulls back. The hands arrive with the footwork, working together. Be sure to turn the waist and put the shoulders into the action, press the head up and drop the buttocks, the segments of the body moving together to perform a single action.

- Carry on the *reverse stance crosscut* to right and left as many times as the training area and your fitness allow.

1c   Reverse Stance Crosscut Turn Around

àobù héngquán zhuànshēn   拗步横拳转身

Using the *reverse stance <u>right</u> crosscut* as example.

ACTION 1: Step the left foot hooked in outside the right toes and shift back, turning around a full 180 degrees to the right to face in the direction from which you came. Shift onto the left leg and lift the right foot by the left ankle without touching down. Hold the hands in position while taking the steps, so that the arms come firmly around with the body. Look forward past the right fist. Lift the left fist to the solar plexus, fist heart still down. (image 7.5)

ACTION 2: Take a big step to the forward right with the right foot and follow in a half-step with the left foot, keeping the weight on the left leg. While doing this, slide the left fist forward along under the right arm drilling and turning it so the fist heart is up at shoulder height. Turn the right fist and tuck it, pulling it back to the belly with the fist heart down and the elbow on the ribs. Press the head up, lengthen the buttocks down and look forward past the left fist. (image 7.6)

- *Crosscut turn around* is the same on the left side, just transposing directions.

Pointers

- o To start the turn, hook the foot in as much as possible – to a T stance or tighter.
- o Stride the right foot out and punch with the left fist in one synchronized action.

CHAPTER SEVEN: CROSSCUT, *HENG QUAN*

1d Reverse Stance Crosscut Closing Move

àobù héngquán shōushì 　　　　　　　　　拗步横拳收势

Starting from a *reverse stance <u>right</u> crosscut*.

ACTION 1: Withdraw the left foot to beside the right without moving the right foot, and shift back to the right leg. Do not move the left fist; unclench the right hand and turn the palm down. Then clench the right hand and pull it back to the belly, then, without pausing, drill it forward and up again to nose height, fist heart up, ulnar edge twisted up. Press the head up and look forward past the right fist. (image 7.7)

ACTION 2: Advance the left foot without moving the right foot, to take a *santi* stance. Bring the left fist up past the solar plexus then along the right arm, to unclench into a split at chest height. Unclench the right hand and pull it back to the belly. Press the head up and look at the left hand. (image 7.8)

7.7

7.8

Closing starting from a *reverse stance <u>left</u> crosscut*.

ACTION 1: Withdraw the right foot back to land beside the left foot and shift to the right leg. Bend the left elbow and press down, fist heart down. Then drill the right fist up and forward to nose height, fist heart up, ulnar edge up. Pull the left fist back to the belly, fist heart down. Look at the right fist. (image 7.9)

ACTION 2: Advance the left foot a step without moving the right foot, keeping most weight on the right leg. Unclench the left hand and split while pulling the right hand back to the belly. Press the head up and look past the left hand. (image 7.10)

7.9

7.10

- *Crosscut closing move* is completed the same as all *closing moves* once you get to the *santishi* stance. See *standard split closing move*, description Split 1d. (see images 3.8 to 3.11)

2. ALIGNED STANCE CROSSCUT

shùnbù héngquán　　　　　　　　顺步横拳

Start from left *santishi*.

2a　　Right Aligned Stance Crosscut　yòu shùnbù héngquán　右顺步横拳

ACTION 1: Advance the left foot a half-step and lift the right foot beside it. Clench the left hand and turn the fist heart up, fist at shoulder height, arm slightly bent. Lift the right fist to the chest, fist heart down. Press the head up and look past the left fist. (image 7.11)

ACTION 2: Take a big step forward with the right foot and follow in the left foot a half-step, keeping most weight on the left leg. Drill the right fist out under the left elbow and along the forearm to shoulder height, turning the fist heart up, keeping the arm slightly bent and putting the shoulder into the punch. Turn the left fist and pull it back to the belly with the fist heart down and elbow snug to the ribs. Turn the waist and urge the shoulders into the hit. Release tension in the shoulders and sink the elbows, press the head up, and look past the right fist. (image 7.12)

2b　　Left Aligned Stance Crosscut

yòu shùnbù héngquán　　左顺步横拳

ACTION 1: Step the right foot a half-step forward and lift the left foot by the right ankle without touching down. Without moving the right fist, bring the left fist up to the solar plexus, fist heart down. Keep the right shoulder forward and the left shoulder back. Look at the right fist. (image 7.13)

CHAPTER SEVEN: CROSSCUT, *HENG QUAN*

ACTION 2: Take a big step forward with the left foot and follow in with the right foot a half-step, keeping most weight on the right leg. Drill the left fist out under the right elbow and along the forearm to finish at shoulder height with the arm slightly bent, rotating as it goes forward so the fist heart turns up. Rotate the right fist and tuck it back to the belly, fist heart down and elbow snug to the ribs. Urge the left shoulder forward and draw the right shoulder back. Press the head up and look past the left fist. (images 7.14 and 7.14 front)

Pointers

- When starting from *santishi*, as the left foot advances a half-step, rotate and slightly drop the left fist, without otherwise moving it in relation to the body.

- The punching fist must hit as the leading foot lands. Coordinate the fists to complete their rotations with the same timing. The key to the timing lies in using the waist and shoulders to do the action.

- Do not turn the right fist or move it in relation to the body when advancing the right foot a half-step – apply pressure into the arm and fist when advancing the body.

2c   Aligned Stance Crosscut Turn Around

shùnbù héngquán zhuànshēn   顺步横拳转身

ACTION 1: Hook the lead foot in and turn the body around 180 degrees in the direction to which the foot has hooked, to face back in the direction from which you came. Bring in what was the back foot to beside the lead foot. While doing this, let the lead arm come crossways around with the body. Look ahead.

ACTION 2: Step the rear foot through into an *aligned stance crosscut*.

2d   Aligned Stance Crosscut Closing Move

shùnbù héngquán shōushì   顺步横拳收势

You may close when you arrive back at your starting place in a *left aligned stance crosscut* after the *turn around* to face the same direction as the original *santishi*. The closing movement is the same as usual, see description in Split 1d.

3. RETREATING CROSSCUT tuìbù héngquán 退步横拳

This is to practise coordinating a retreating step with a forward punch. When training you can use the *aligned stance crosscut* to advance to the limit of the training area, then use the *retreating crosscut* to go backwards. You can also start the *retreating crosscut* after a *right reverse stance crosscut*.

3a Retreating Left Crosscut tuìbù zuǒ héngquán 退步左横拳

ACTION 1: Start with the left foot and right fist leading and the right foot back, in a *reverse stance right crosscut*. Retreat the right foot a half-step and follow by withdrawing the left foot to touch down the toes by the right foot. Keep the legs bent to maintain the same stance height, and keep the legs together. Keep the right fist and arm in the same position and settle the right shoulder forward a bit. Lift the left fist to solar plexus height and keep the fist heart down. Press the head up and look past the right fist. (image 7.15)

ACTION 2: Retreat the left foot diagonally to the left rear and withdraw the right foot, shifting the body back to put most of the weight on the left leg, taking a *santi* stance with the right foot leading and the left foot behind. Do a crosscut with the left fist, coming out from under the right forearm, fist heart up, at shoulder height. Turn the right fist and bring it back to the belly, fist heart down. The basic action of the fists is the same as *standard crosscut*. (image 7.16)

3b Retreating Right Crosscut

tuìbù yòu héngquán 退步右横拳

ACTION 1: Retreat the left foot a half-step and withdraw the right foot back to touch down beside the left foot, shifting back to the left leg and keeping the legs bent to maintain the same stance height. Do not move the left fist and arm, but slightly drop the left shoulder forward. Lift the right fist to solar plexus height with the fist heart down. Press the head up and look past the left fist. (image 7.17)

ACTION 2: Sit back as the right foot retreats to the rear right, so that most weight is on the right leg, then withdraw the left foot a small half-step. Slide the right fist along under the left arm, twisting and drilling forward to shoulder height, fist heart up and arm slightly bent. Rotate the left fist and pull it back to the belly, fist heart down. Put the right shoulder forward into the punch and pull the left shoulder back. Press the head up and look past the right fist. (image 7.18)

Pointers

- The rear foot should take a small step when retreating, and the weight should shift back. The lead fist should not change position relative to the body. The step must be stable, and the other foot should withdraw quickly.

- Be sure to step at a forty-five degree angle when retreating the lead foot. The foot must settle into the ground at the same time that the back fist strikes forward. Turn the waist and urge the strike forward from the shoulders. Press the head up and settle the buttocks down. Release tension in the shoulders and sink the elbows.

- The foot stomps forcibly when landing the diagonal back step, using the backward shift of the weight. The toes should touch down first, then quickly land the whole foot, with a very small time gap. Be careful not to lift the foot too much.

4. REVERSE STANCE INWARD CROSSCUT

àobù lǐ héngquán　　　　　　　拗步里横拳

The *inward crosscut* is opposite to the *standard crosscut*. The *standard crosscut* uses the outer edge of the forearm to twist, roll, and snap in a forward direction. The *inward crosscut* uses the inside edge of the arm to roll and strike crossways. The power, application, and characteristics all differ.

4a　　**Right Inward Crosscut**　yòu àobù lǐ héngquán　　右拗步里横拳

Start from a left *santishi*.

ACTION 1: Shift back and withdraw the left foot to touch down in front of the right toes. Clench the left fst and pull it back to the belly, then, without pausing, drill it up and forward to nose height, fist heart and ulnar edge turned up, elbow tucked in, and shoulder reaching forward into the action. Turn the right fist heart up, lift it by the right nipple, elbow flexed and settled down. Look past the left fist and settle the shoulders. (image 7.19)

ACTION 2: Advance the left foot about twenty-five degrees to the left of straight forward, and follow in with the right foot a half step, keeping most weight on the right leg. Unclench both hands, cross the right hand leftward and forward, rotating out and extending the arm to chest height, palm up, elbow bent, and forearm level. Turn the waist left and put the right shoulder forward and settled down. Rotate the left hand in and pull it back to the belly, elbow hugging the ribs. Press the head up, settle the buttocks down, and look past the right hand. (image 7.20)

4b Left Inward Crosscut   zuǒ àobù lǐ héngquán   左拗步里横拳

ACTION 1: Advance the left foot a half-step and lift the right foot to the left ankle. Do not move the right hand relative to the body, but settle the shoulder forward a bit and clench the fist. Clench and lift the left fist to the left nipple, fist heart down, elbow bent and dropped. Settle the shoulders down and look at the right fist. (image 7.21)

ACTION 2: Take a big step forward and a bit to the right with the right foot and follow in a half-step with the left, keeping most weight on the left leg. Unclench both hands. Strike the left palm out from the left towards the right and forward, rotating the palm up. Keep the elbow bent and tucked in and the forearm horizontal, to strike with the palm to the right. Rotate the right palm in and pull it back to the belly, palm down, elbow snug to the ribs. Press the head up, turn the waist rightward, put the left shoulder forward and bring the right shoulder back, and look past the left hand. (image 7.22)

- Carry on alternating left and right.

Pointers
- o Pull the left fist back and drill out as the left foot withdraws.
- o Strike with the right hand as the left foot lands.
- o The footwork for the *inward crosscut* is: the lead foot advances a half-step, the back foot takes a big step forward, then the lead foot steps out to a twenty-five degree angle.
- o Cut the rear hand across as the rear foot lands. Use the lower back and shoulders and rotate the arm to strike crossways. Use the crossing power of the body, the twist of the forearm, the rotation of the hand plus a forward action. Be sure to keep the lower trunk lively, the shoulders settled and loose, the chest contained, and exhale when you hit. The assisting hand rotates inward and tucks back, or it could also hook and grab to pull back.

- *Turn around* and *closing move* of *inward crosscut* are similar to those of standard crosscut. (see images 7.5 to 7.6 for *turn around*, and 7.7 to 7.10 for *closing move*)

PROBLEMS OFTEN MET IN CROSSCUT (see also in split)

PROBLEM 1: When the student strikes, the power is just a crossing snap done with the arms.

CORRECTIONS: You must search for the meaning of "you don't see the cross in the crosscut." The crossing action is the block; it is a method, while the forward strike is the attack, the goal. Therefore, the crossing action is not enough, you must also have a forward drilling strike.

PROBLEM 2: The student is unstable when turning around.

CORRECTIONS: Instability may be caused by the lack of mastery of the vertical line of the trunk – lowering the head or leaning the trunk. Or it may be landing the hook-in step in the wrong place or at the wrong angle, making the body move too far off line. So first emphasize keeping the head pressed up and the trunk vertical. Next be sure to hook-in to in front of the toes of the rear foot. The degree of the hook-in should be such that the foot can use power to drive off smoothly, so in general, the more the foot hooks in the better.

PROBLEM 3: When the student strikes he focuses on the lead hand and forgets to coordinate the whole body action with both hands.

CORRECTIONS: Make the student practise repeatedly according to the proper method, making sure he focuses on the coordination of the hands and feet and on the different powers of the lead and rear hands, using the power of shoulders and body.

POWER GENERATION FOR CROSSCUT

Crosscut places particular emphasis on the integration of the strength of the whole body. That is what 'being round' means. There is indeed a 'crossing' action within the crosscut technique. This crossing action is seen in the first half of the action, in the lower back and shoulders, upper arm and forearm action. Since Xingyiquan emphasizes attack, and not 'defense then attack', you should emphasize the final goal of the action.

Every branch of Xingyi uses the *reverse stance crosscut* as the standard and primary crosscut technique. Many classics and teaching materials take it as the primary technique, so we should learn the standard technique first and refine the variations later. If you first build a strong foundation with the *standard crosscut* and develop whole body power, it will be relatively easy to learn the variations later.

The legs must have a scissor like force between them in the standard *reverse stance crosscut*. The knees should tuck in slightly and the rear knee should have the sense of stabbing down into the centre of the stance, so the knees have a 'rolling in power' and the legs have a 'closing in' power. It is as if you are standing on ice and want to prevent your legs from slipping out.

The arms have a 'twisting, rolling, drilling, turning' power that is integrated with no slackness. It is as if the hands are twisting a rope – the lead hand rotates inward, turning and rolling to tuck and press down and pull back, and the rear hand rotates outward to twist and roll and drill out. You must pay attention not only to the line of action of the fists, but also to the path taken by the elbows. The lead shoulder draws the elbow back and the elbow protects the heart, pulling the elbow back to the ribs.

When the rear hand hits out the elbow tucks into the solar plexus. Close the chest and shoulders in, settle the shoulders down and send the fist out. The elbows are moved by the shoulders, power is achieved by turning from the lower trunk and putting the shoulders into the strike.

- Crosscut's crossing power is created as the rear fist rolls under the lead elbow and extends, shoved forward by the rear shoulder. The footwork advances at a forty-five degree angle, giving the body a diagonal momentum, while the hand technique hits straight forward, thus creating an angled strike. Overall, the first half of crosscut is crossways, and the second half is a drill forward. The line taken by the fists is curved, and the first half of the arc is large while the second half of the arc is small, almost straight. The crossing power is created during the large initial arc, coming mostly from the shoulders and upper arms. The point of contact is the outer edge of the arm, mostly the upper arm, and secondarily the forearm. The key to the power is in controlling the elbows.

The key to crosscut power is the synchronization of forces coming from the lower back and shoulders to the arms. You must turn the lower trunk and put the shoulders into the action, lengthening the waist and urging the shoulders into the punch, so the power of the whole body reaches the upper limbs.

- o To get the power into the *retreating crosscut* you need to close the chest and lead the *qi*. The key to retreating is to control the weight shift with stable footwork. The power comes from using the stamp as the foot lands to create a rebound force that reaches the whole body, coming from the legs to the lower back and up through the shoulders, through the elbows to the hands.

- o The power of the *reverse stance inward crosscut* is created by the diagonal forward rolling as the front arm rotates and rolls and presses, and the force is applied to the inside edge of the forearm. It has both a diagonal crossing power and a forward power. The power comes from the lower back and shoulders, so the lower back must be relaxed, the shoulders settle then launch, and the power is an instantaneous one inch strike.

- o The *inward crosscut* may also be done with the palms, hitting with the heel of the palm and forearm with the same power. The other hand grabs and pulls back to the belly, the same as the described *inward crosscut*.

It doesn't really matter how many types of crosscut there are, or how they may differ in footwork or movement, they all share the same characteristic whole body force that is also characteristic of all the five basic techniques.

BREATHING CYCLE FOR CROSSCUT

You must coordinate positional breathing once you are comfortable with the movement in order to gain whole body power. The breathing cycle for crosscut is similar to that of cannon.

- Inhale as you take the half-step advance and store power.
- Exhale as you drive forward and land the foot and punch, settling the *qi* to your *dantian*.

See Chapter Eleven for more detail on breathing theory and techniques that apply to all Xingyi techniques.

PRACTICAL APPLICATIONS FOR CROSSCUT

It isn't really correct to speak of a specific application for crosscut. Crosscut trains a certain type of power, not a specific application. Of course the action contains certain implied attacking and defensive moves, but more importantly, training crosscut develops the ability to use a type of power. This is true for all of the five elemental techniques. Long term training of the five techniques gives us a grasp of the characteristics of Xingyi's power. To use the techniques you need to react according to the situation. When you have achieved a high level with the techniques, then "the technique is born in the heart and goes out the hands."

To examine the form of crosscut; the lead hand turns over, tucks, rolls and draws back, which can be seen as defensive, breaking an opponent's punch down the central line. The other hand simultaneously strikes at the opponent's solar plexus or ribs. The hands hit simultaneously, blocking and hitting together, and adding a charging forward footwork. If the lead hand does not succeed in controlling the opponent's hand then the rear hand can roll in and press down, using the power of crosscut to hit the opponent's chest or head. The hands, legs, and body all enter together, sticking to his body with a lengthwise power. Once you have contacted the opponent with your body you can knock him over with a turn of the lower back, shoulders and arm.

- Although the power application of *aligned stance crosscut* differs from Longfist's 'lean' the practical application is similar. If the opponent hits with a left fist, I use my left hand to roll and pull down his left fist or arm, and enter the right foot behind his left foot. I extend my right arm forward and cross hit right to knock him over. I could also hit his ribs with my right fist.

- The use of *retreat crosscut* is essentially the same hand technique as the standard *crosscut*, but the footwork enables you to apply a crosscut forward while withdrawing your body backward.

- While the *standard crosscut* uses a step to the outside to hit in to the centre from the outside, the *inward crosscut* comes from inside and strikes forward. An inward strike is a block, while a forward strike attacks the chest, solar plexus or ribs.

Crosscut uses a crossways action to break a straight line, it uses defense as its attack. Just as the classics say, "use an attack as the defense and no one can see the defense; use a defense as the attack and no one can see the attack."

Crosscut as a defense defends your midline and as an attack breaks your opponent's centre. It moves at an angle to hit straight, and uses a circuitous route to make a straight line.

THE POEM ABOUT CROSSCUT

横拳歌诀

横拳似弹性属土，

斜身拗步气易鼓。

两拳旋拧横破直，

五拳之中它为主。

Crosscut is like a round shot and its character is that of the earth,

The body is angled and the footwork is opposing so the energy expands easily.

The fists twist and cross to break a straight attack,

It is the most vital of the five elemental techniques.

CHAPTER EIGHT

SOLO FORM

FIVE ELEMENTS CONNECTED

五行连环

INTRODUCTION TO THE FIVE ELEMENTS CONNECTED, *WU XING LIAN HUAN* (FIVE TECHNIQUES LINKED)

The Five Elements Connected form is a widespread and popular short traditional form. It is based on the five foundation techniques of split, drive, drill, cannon, and crosscut. The form is also called Advance And Retreat Connected [or Linked]. Characteristics of the footwork are: there are both advancing and retreating steps, emphasizing advancing; stepping is very quick, has side to side movement, and moves back and forth both lengthways and sideways. Characteristics of the hand techniques are: there are both attacking and defensive moves, emphasizing attacking; the techniques combine soft and hard, are hard without stiffness and soft without slackness; the quick moves are not rushed and the slow moves are not slack. Characteristics of the power are: power is full when launched; settled, stable, thick, and fierce; and is always integrated whole body power, emphasizing hard power.

The form goes back and forth once, it goes out with ten moves, and comes back to the same place with the same ten moves. Practising this form helps you grasp the characteristics and flavour of Xingyi. You should pay attention to performing in a continuous manner, getting the power to flow smoothly, getting a good rhythm and spirit, and showing confidence. Long term practice will develop the nervous system, improve coordination, and improve the fighting spirit. It develops the body, trains self-defense, and helps mould character.

NAMES OF THE MOVEMENTS

0. Opening Move
1. Advance Right Drive
2. Retreat Left Drive
3. Right Aligned Stance Drive
4. White Crane Flashes Its Wings
5. Left Cannon
6. Wrap
7. Advance Right Crosscut

8. Leopard Cat Climbs A Tree
9. Advance Right Drive
10. Leopard Cat Turns Over Whilst Climbing A Tree
(the following moves are a repetition back in the returning direction)
11. Advance Right Drive,
12. Retreat Left Drive
13. Right Aligned Stance Drive
14. White Crane Flashes Its Wings
15. Left Cannon
16. Wrap
17. Advance Right Crosscut
18. Leopard Cat Climbs A Tree
19. Advance Right Drive
20. Leopard Cat Turns Over Whilst Climbing A Tree
(the following moves are the closing combination)
21. Advance Right Drive
22. Retreat Left Drive
23. Closing Move

Description of the movements

0. Opening Move qǐ shì 起势

ACTION 1: Stand upright, facing the direction in which you will go. Place the palms on the thighs. (image 8.1)

ACTION 2: Lift the hands at the sides, gradually turning them so that they face up by the time they reach shoulder height. Keep the arms naturally bent and look at the right hand. (image 8.2)

ACTION 3: Bend the arms to bring the hands past the face, palms down and fingers pointing to each other. Look ahead. (image 8.3)

ACTION 4: Press the hands down past the chest to the belly, keeping the arms rounded. Sit down, keeping the knees together. Press the head up and look forward. (image 8.4)

ACTION 5: Without moving the legs, clench the fists and turn the fist hearts up, keeping the elbows snug to the ribs. Drill the right fist up past the solar plexus then out to nose height, ulnar edge twisted over. Look at the right fist. (image 8.5)

ACTION 6: Step the left foot forward without moving the right foot, to sit into a *santi* stance. Bring the left fist up past the solar plexus and out along the right arm, then unclench and split forward at shoulder height, palm facing the front. Unclench the right hand and pull it back to the belly, palm down. Look at the left hand. (image 8.6)

Pointers

- When you lift the hands be sure to keep the arms bent and settle the shoulders and elbows down. Lift the arms on the scapular line, slightly ahead of the trunk, to open up the back.

- Breathe in while lifting the hands. Sit down as you press the hands down. Bend the knees to the height that you will take in *santishi*.

- Strike the left hand as you place the left foot, working together.

1. **Advance Right Drive**　　　jìnbù yòu bēngquán　　　进步右崩拳

ACTION 1: Clench fists and turn the left fist heart up, tucking in the left elbow. Advance the left foot a half-step and follow in with the right foot to ten centimetres behind the left heel, with the weight on the right leg. Slide the right fist along the left arm to punch forward to solar plexus height, fist surface forward and fist eye up, with the elbow slightly bent. Pull the left fist back to the belly, fist heart in. Press the head up and look at the right fist. (image 8.7)

108 FIVE ELEMENTS CONNECTED, *WUXING LIANHUAN*

Pointers

- Punch with the right fist as the right foot lands, working together with a *rear foot timed drive*.

- As they punch out and pull back, each fist's power 'goes out like a steel rasp and returns like a grappling hook.' Settle the shoulders, tuck in the lower back, urge the right shoulder into the right punch, and turn from the body core. The fists work as a paired couple.

- As the right foot lands it uses the power of the whole foot to strike with an impetus forward and down, landing with a thud. Roll the hip in and use the knee to bring the foot forward, as if someone were pulling your right foot back with a rope. Pretend you are pulling him forward and trying to break the rope. Be sure not to lift the foot to stamp.

- Breathe out to shoot power and settle your *qi* to the *dantian*, so that your whole body works as a unit – upper and lower limbs, inner and outer.

2. **Retreat Left Drive** tuìbù zuǒ bēngquán 退步左崩拳

ACTION 1: Take a half-step back with the right foot and shift weight to the right leg. Turn the right fist over so the fist heart faces up, to press down with the forearm. Look straight ahead. (image 8.8)

ACTION 2: Retreat the left foot a large step backwards and place the whole foot solidly on the ground. Shift your weight mostly onto the left leg and withdraw the right foot, turning it crossways so that the thighs press tightly together. Slide the left fist along the right forearm to drive forward at solar plexus height. Keep the left arm slightly bent, the fist eye up. Pull the right fist back to the belly. Press the head up and look at the left fist. (image 8.9)

CHAPTER EIGHT: SOLO FORM

Pointers

- Three actions must happen at once with a complete, integrated power: punch the left fist; land the left foot; pull back the right fist.

- The power of the left fist's punch comes from the weight moving back to the left foot as it lands. The reactive force immediately reaches the lower back and the energy exchange transfers to the shoulder and through the elbow to culminate in the left fist. Co-ordinate the launching power of the lower body turn, shoulder extension, and arm extension, each segment working together to generate power sequentially until the final result reaches the fist surface.

3. Right Aligned Stance Drive yòu shùnbù bēngquán 右顺步崩拳

also called Black Bear Charges Out Of Its Cave
   hēixióng chūdòng   黑熊出洞

ACTION 1: Advance the right foot to the forward right and follow-in a half-step with the left, taking a *santi* stance. Turn the left fist over so the fist heart faces up and roll the left elbow inwards slightly. Drive the right fist along the left arm to punch forward with the elbow slightly bent and the fist eye on top, to solar plexus height. Press the head up. Pull the left fist back to the belly with the fist heart inward. Look at the right fist. (image 8.10)

Pointers

- Land the right punch timed exactly with the landing of the right foot, that is, the power of a *lead foot timed drive*.

- Be sure to keep the elbows snug to the ribs when driving out the punch. When the punch is finished, the forearm should be horizontal, with the elbow on line with, though lower than, the shoulder. Be sure to keep the elbow tucked slightly in.

- At the instant of power launch, land the right foot forward, punch the right fist and pull the left fist back, using the crisp action of turning the lower waist, or body core area and urging the shoulder forward. Co-ordinate this action with an expulsion of breath to create a complete, integrated power. The punch should be strong without being rigid. It should show a spirit capable of pushing mountains into the sea, or surging out ten thousand miles in an instant, with an all-conquering attitude.

110   FIVE ELEMENTS CONNECTED, *WUXING LIANHUAN*

4. White Crane Flashes Its Wings   báihè liàngchì   白鹤亮翅

ACTION 1: Withdraw the left foot a half step, half-sitting into a horse stance. Draw the right elbow across the body and stretch the back to bring the left fist underneath. Then lower the right fist to cross the forearms in front of the belly, and finish bracing out to the sides over the knees. Look towards the right fist. (images 8.11A and B)

ACTION 2: Without moving the feet, but shifting to the left leg and turning, drill the fists up to head height with the fist hearts facing in and the forearms crossed, left inside the right. Look at the fists. Then shift back into a horse stance and rotate the forearms to turn the fist hearts out and open the arms to brace out to the left and right. Keep the arms slightly bent, fists at head height. Look at the right fist. (images 8.12 A and B)

ACTION 3: Shift onto the left leg and withdraw the right foot to beside the left foot, landing with a thump. Bring the fists in together at the belly, striking it with some force. Press the head up, settle the *qi* to the *dantian,* and look forward. (image 8.13)

Pointers

- The actions of *white crane flashes it wings* involve an elbow cover, a low brace, an upward drill, a turning outer brace, a dropping wrap, and a withdrawing embrace at the belly. Be sure to feel the power of each: cover, brace, drill, turn, brace, wrap, and embrace. The whole body must be co-ordinated and

the power smoothly integrated without any slackness.

- When the fists drill up, keep the elbows down, the back stretched, and the chest closed. Breathe in while doing this. When the fists turn over, release the shoulders and turn the elbows out. When the forearms brace out and the arms circle down, they should have a wrapping power. Pulling in to the belly should have an embracing power. The fists should hit the belly timed exactly as the right foot lands, settling the *qi* to the *dantian* to assist in generating power.
- Pay particular attention to the leftward and rightward movement of the body. When the fists drill up, the weight should shift more towards the left leg. When the arms brace out, weight should shift more towards the right leg. When the arms wrap, weight should shift more to the left leg.
- When the right foot withdraws it must rub along the ground. Use a wrapping, gathering force in the hips to bring the foot in, as if you are pulling something along with the foot. Land with a thump – be sure not to lift the foot to stamp.

5. **Left Cannon** zuǒ pàoquán 左炮拳

ACTION 1: Take a big step to the forward right with the right foot and follow-in a half-step with the left. Drill the right fist up past the solar plexus to nose height. Lift the left fist to the solar plexus to prepare. As the right foot advances, punch the left fist forward at solar plexus height with the arm slightly bent, elbow tucked in, fist eye up and shoulder put forward into the punch. Rotate the right fist at the right temple, elbow down. Look in the direction of the left punch. (image 8.14)

8.14

Pointers

- The left punch and the right foot landing are timed together, so that hand and foot hit as a unit.
- Turn the trunk with a counter-movement a bit leftward as you drill up the right fist. Then when the left fist punches, the whole body generates a power turning to the right, launching from the lumbar/waist area to transfer to the shoulders, which in turn transfer to the elbows, which transfer to the fists. Be sure to make full use of the strength of the lower trunk. Be sure also to keep the right elbow down – don't lift it. Keep the right fist in front of the ears but behind the eyebrows at the temple.
- When you launch power, urge the shoulder forward from the body core – the lower back urges the shoulder and the shoulder sends the fist out. Settle your *qi* into the *dantian*. In this way, both upper and lower, and inner and outer, work together, and the resulting force is ferocious.

6. Wrap   bāoguǒ shǒu   包裹手

ACTION 1: Retreat the left foot a half-step, following with the right foot to place it by the left ankle. Pull the left fist back to the belly and turn the torso left. Roll the right elbow in front of the body, so the fist eye faces in. Look at the right fist. (image 8.15)

8.15

ACTION 2: Retreat the right foot and shift back to the right leg. Unclench the hands and pull the right hand back and extend the left hand out along the right arm to brace to the left – right palm facing up, and left palm facing down. Withdraw the left foot to beside the right without touching down. Brace the right hand out to the right, palm down, and circle the left hand down, palm up, bringing it back to the belly. Brace with both arms keeping a rounded structure. Look at the right hand. (images 8.16 A and B)

8.16A

8.16 B

ACTION 3: Advance the left foot and follow in with the right a half-step, taking a *santi* stance. Circle the right hand down to the belly, fingers down and palm forward. Lift the left hand to grab, palm up, and when it gets to in front of the right shoulder, turn the palm over to face down, and brace out to the left and forward. Keep the left arm rounded with the palm at shoulder height. Press the head up. Look at the left hand. (image 8.17)

8.17

CHAPTER EIGHT: SOLO FORM 113

Pointers

- The wrapping technique in the connected form is actually the alligator from the twelve animal forms. When you roll the elbow and retreat, focus on drawing in. Draw the body back and shrink in a bit.
- As the right foot retreats, the right hand knocks and braces out across to the right. As the left foot advances the left hand knocks and braces across to the front. Keep these movement synchronized.
- The hands should draw two circles, using the waist as the axis. The waist leads the shoulders, the shoulders transfer to the elbows, and the elbows send the hands out. Keep the chest closed in and the arms rounded, the waist lively. The entire movement should be rounded with no sluggishness, the power gentle but not lax. The arms and hands should have a rolling embracing power and a knocking away bracing power. Pay attention that the left and right shifting of body weight is coordinated with the hand actions.

7. **Advance Right Crosscut**   jìnbù yòu héngquán   进步右横拳

ACTION 1: Clench the hands and turn the left fist over so the fist heart is up, the elbow rolled in to cover the heart. Take a big step to the forward left with the left foot and follow in a half-step with the right foot. With the fist eye down, bring the right fist up past the solar plexus then along under the left arm, gradually drilling it forward until the fist is at shoulder height and the fist eye is up. Keep the right arm slightly bent. Turn the left fist over and pull it back to the belly with the fist eye down. Press the head up. Look at the right fist. (image 8.18)

Pointers

- Hit the right fist as the left foot advances. The foot steps diagonally to the forward left and the fist hits straight forward.
- To launch force to the crosscut, turn the waist to extend the shoulder. The shoulders must first roll in and then open up and release. The fists should have a torqued rolling force – a rolling, drilling, spiraling force. The legs should have a scissoring force, rolling in the hips and closing the knees, settling the buttocks down and pressing the head up. Settle the *qi* to the *dantian*. Keep focused.

8. **Leopard Cat Climbs A Tree**   límāo shàngshù   狸猫上树

ACTION 1: Unclench the hands and reach forward, palms down, then clench the fists and pull them back to the belly. Advance the left foot straight ahead a half-step and shift forward onto the left leg. Bring both fists up from the belly, past the solar plexus, and drill them forward, the right fist ahead of the left, and the left fist at the right elbow. Both fist hearts slope up and the right fist is at eyebrow height. Look at the right fist. (images 8.19 A, B, and C)

ACTION 2: Lift the right knee, turning the foot out to do a crossways thrust kick forward and up to shoulder height. Keep a forward drilling pressure in the fists. Look ahead of the right foot. (image 8.20)

ACTION 3: After the kick, quickly stomp the right foot forward and down with the foot turned crossways. Follow in a half-step with the left foot, to form a scissors stance. Unclench the hands and turn them over, palms forward. Slide the left hand along the right forearm and chop forward and down, palm down at waist height. Pull the right hand back to beside the right hip, palm down. Look past the left hand. (image 8.21)

Pointers

- Drill the fists up as the right foot kicks up.
- Split the left hand down as the right foot lands crossways.
- The entire movement of *leopard cat climbs a tree* must be continuous, completed as one action.
- Close the shoulders and chest in and settle the elbows down as the fists drill up, to create an embracing power.
- Be sure to turn the waist and extend the shoulders into the double split. Time the right hand pulling back with the left hand splitting down.
- When you kick the right foot be sure to close in the right hip and forcibly lift your knee. This helps give power to the kick. When you land the right foot, use a stamping power as if stomping on a poisonous animal – trying to kill it or prevent it from getting away.
- In the scissors stance keep a bit more weight on the rear leg so that you are able to smoothly advance the lead foot in the following movement.

9. **Advance Right Drive** shàngbù yòu bēngquán 上步右崩拳

ACTION 1: Advance the right foot a half-step then take a big step forward with the left foot and follow in with the right to just behind the left foot – weight on the right leg. Clench fists and do a right driving punch forward from the right waist, following the line of the left arm. The fist eye is up and the punch is at solar plexus height. Pull the left fist back to the belly. Urge the right shoulder into the hit, keeping the right arm slightly bent. Press the head up. Look at the right fist. (image 8.22)

Pointers

- Punch with the right fist exactly at the same time as you land the right foot in the follow-in step, in a *rear foot timed drive*.
- The requirements for the drive punch are the same as usual, but the long forward stride gives it more distance, speed, and power. Put force into both the advancing and pulling back fists. The right leg should thrust the punch forward.
- Be sure to press the head up to prevent the body from leaning forward.

116   FIVE ELEMENTS CONNECTED, *WUXING LIANHUAN*

10. Leopard Cat Turns Over Whilst Climbing a Tree (Drive Turn Around)

límāo dào shàngshù   狸猫倒上树

ACTION 1: Hook-step in the left foot, stepping around so that it hooks in outside the right toes. The more you hook in the better. Bend the knees. Pull the right fist back to the belly. Turn the body around 180 degrees to face back in the direction from which you came. Press the head up. Look forward. (image 8.23)

ACTION 2: Shift onto the left leg and lift the right knee, turning the foot crossways, then kick forward and up to shoulder height. Turn the fists over so the fist hearts are on top, and drill them up past the solar plexus and forward. The right fist is more forward and higher, at nose height, and the left fist is at the right elbow. Look at the right fist. (image 8.24)

ACTION 3: After the kick, stamp the right foot forward and down with the foot turned crossways, and follow-in a half-step with the left foot to form a scissors stance. Unclench the hands and turn them over so the palms face forward. Slide the left hand forward along the right forearm and split down, palm down. Press the head up. Look past the left hand. (image 8.25)

Pointers

- During the turn, three actions are done simultaneously: do a hook-in step with the left foot, pull in the right fist, and turn the body around to the right. Press the head up as you turn around. Do not lower the head or bend at the waist.

- When you hook-in the left foot and turn around be sure to take a good sized hook-in step.

- Then during the kick, two actions are done simultaneously: drill the fists up and kick the right foot.

- When you kick the right foot, be sure to turn the foot out and fully

CHAPTER EIGHT: SOLO FORM 117

extend the leg at the instant you complete the kick. Keep the supporting leg slightly bent to stand firmly. Tuck in the right hip when you kick.

- o When you drill the fists up be sure to keep tightly to the ribs. When you split the hands down, turn the waist, put the shoulders into the action, settle the shoulders and elbows, and put equal force into the forward and backward moving hands. Be sure to press the head up.

- o During the landing, thrust from the left leg to land the right foot forward, being sure to add a stomping force to the crossways landing. Two actions are done simultaneously: split the left hand down and land the right foot. When you form the scissors stance, press the thighs tightly together.

- That is as far as I need to describe, as it is halfway, and you just continue to repeat the moves for the other half of the form. The following section is a repetition of the first section, going back in a returning direction.

11.	**Step Forward Right Drive**	see move 1
12.	**Retreat Left Drive**	see move 2
13.	**Right Aligned Stance Drive**	see move 3
14.	**White Crane Spreads Its Wings**	see move 4
15.	**Left Cannon**	see move 5
16.	**Wrap**	see move 6
17.	**Advance Right Crosscut**	see move 7
18.	**Leopard Cat Climbs A Tree**	see move 8
19.	**Advance Right Drive**	see move 9
20.	**Leopard Cat Turns Over Whilst Climbing A Tree**	see move 10

(Closing section, in the same direction as the opening moves.)

21.	**Advance Right Drive**	see move 1
22.	**Retreat Left Drive**	see move 2

23. Closing Move　　shōu shì　　收势

ACTION 1: Advance the left foot without moving the right foot, to take a *santi* stance. Pull the left fist back to the belly, fist heart down. Press the head up. Look forward. (image 8.26)

118 FIVE ELEMENTS CONNECTED, *WUXING LIANHUAN*

ACTION 2: Advance the right foot to place it parallel to the left foot with the knees together. Do not let the body rise yet. Stand firmly on both legs with the knees bent. (image 8.27)

ACTION 3: Unclench the hands and lift them at the sides of the body, palms up and arms naturally bent, not fully extended. When the hands come up to shoulder height, bring them in towards the face, turning the palms down. (images 8.28 A and B)

ACTION 4: Press the hands down in front of the chest and stand up to attention. (image 8.29)

Pointers

- Do three actions simultaneously: pull the left fist in, press into the left foot, and press the head up.
- Press the palms down and stand up to finish at exactly the same time so that completion is done throughout the body.

RHYTHM AND POWER GENERATION IN THE FIVE ELEMENTS CONNECTED

One clear measure for judging the quality of a performance and the level to which a player has mastered the movements and skills is the coordination of timing and power in the moves and the rhythm connecting the moves. Every form has its own rhythm to differentiate fast and slow, relaxation and tension,

CHAPTER EIGHT: SOLO FORM 119

hard and soft. And each movement within the form has its own rhythm. Only after a considerable period of practice with repeated effort and thought can you find the natural patterns and raise your level of artistry. Each person has a different character and understanding, and so brings a different angle to his appreciation of the movements and the form. Add to this that each teacher passes on the form differently, and it is obvious that each person will have a different rhythm for the same form and movements that shows a personal style and character.

Here is a simple analysis of one possible way to deal with the rhythm of fast and slow within the form.

1. At the start it is vital to show stability, so the *opening movement* must not be rushed. You should be slow and steady, purposefully drawing your focus within yourself and regulating your mind and *qi*. Breathe deeply to the *dantian* to settle your spirit and *qi*. At this time get rid of any emotional tension. Although the movement is slow, your spirit should show a fullness that permeates your whole body. Your slow movement and the gathering of spirit should affect a spectator, creating in him a feeling of stability and quietude. You should settle into the *santishi* with a positive shift and raking power in the front foot, putting power through to the lead hand.

2. The combination of three driving punches (*advance drive, retreat drive, aligned drive*) is called 'three arrows shot from a horse, ' reminding us that drive is 'wood' and acts like an arrow. These three driving punches must have hard power and be heavy as a mountain – fierce, sonorous and forceful. They should not be rushed, but be done with a fullness of power, showing the dense strength and hard power of Xingyiquan. Each punch should increase in strength, culminating in the final *aligned stance drive*. The spirit should be apparent. The power should be first held back then launch. Breathe in slowly and breathe out sharply. Be sure to make the final launch of power fully connected throughout the body, with a vigorous appearance.

3. *White crane flashes its wings* should be quite rhythmic. The beginning and the middle should be fairly slow, showing the intent leading the movements. The drill, turn, brace and roll should show a full, contained energy. The final embracing movement, when the foot and hand hit simultaneously, should be quick and powerful with full power in the *dantian*. Your whole body should show confidence, your elbows should be tucked into the ribs, your fists should hit your belly. You can do this with an expulsion of sound, using sound to show ferocity and to increase power in the *dantian*.

4. You should have an intention to move forward before the *left cannon*, leaning the body slightly to the forward right to build up power for the sudden launch – incline the whole body by driving the supporting knee down, not by leaning at the waist. Stride forward quickly and punch fiercely with a brave spirit. Stop for an instant after the punch with a stable appearance. The punch should be sudden and very quick. Move quickly and stop absolutely – this is the

characteristic of cannon punch.

5. *Wrap*, the alligator form, should be gentle but not lax, with a contained strength, powerful but not stiff. The hands, eyes, body and feet must be coordinated to use the power of the whole body. When the hands circle they should have an unrevealed binding power. The footwork should be light and agile. The waist should be lively and full of elasticity. The speed should be soft and rhythmic, not rushed. Pay attention to the roundness of the movement. The final left hand brace should cut across a bit more quickly, though, with the foot and hand arriving together.

6. *Advance right crosscut, leopard cat climbs a tree*, and *step forward right drive* should increase in speed and be seamlessly connected. They should show an accumulative increase in power, showing Xingyiquan's characteristic attacking spirit of "chasing the wind and the moon." The movements should not be just fast, but should show a brave appearance with a full spirit – quick but unhurried. When practising, pay attention to the integration of the movements and the changing lines of power through the body to get them smooth and flowing.

7. *Leopard cat turns over whilst climbing a tree* is the turn around for drive. Find the pivot point to turn around, pivoting on the left foot and using your trunk to turn. Step the left foot around to hook-in in front of the right foot so that the weight barely moves between the two feet in order to turn with speed and stability. The whole movement should be of moderate speed, showing quick movements within slowness and calmness within speed – the key is to be stable. Kick the right foot up quickly, and turn the waist to split down with the hands quickly. The eyes should be bright and intimidating.

8. The final *closing move* should be stable and fairly slow, giving a feeling that your intentions have not slackened. Although you have completed the form you still show full power. But you should do this for only a few seconds, and show a settling *qi* to come to a satisfactory conclusion.

- The initial movements in the form show a hard and powerful force, the middle movements show softness and coordination, and the speed in the later movements emphasizes the straight line 'chase the wind and the moon ' spirit of Xingyiquan. Throughout the form, the regulation of speed and rhythm should always show Xingyiquan's characteristics and flavour – stressing hard power with softness assisting. You can change the rhythm of the form to suit your own understanding, but it is vital that you not perform at one speed or one unchanging rhythm. If you do that the form will be flat and boring.

CHAPTER NINE

PARTNER FORMS

对练

1. ENTANGLING HANDS, *JIAO SHOU PAO*

jiāo shǒu pào　　交手炮

Introduction

Entangling Hands is the shortest of Xingyi's partner forms. In this form, the stance stays fixed as the hands and arms cross and coil, sticking to each other, entangling the partners arms, so it is called Entangling Hands. Since it contains only split, drive, and cannon it is also called Three Techniques Hit. Traditionally the form is done both as fixed stance and moving stance, but the fixed stance is the more common method.

This form is learned in order to reinforce the understanding of split, drive, and cannon by applying them on a partner. Both partners alternate attack and defense continuously and repetition of the form can help bring mastery of the techniques.

NAMES OF THE MOVEMENTS

1. A: Ready Stance   B: Ready Stance
2. A: Right Drive   B: Left Slap Elbow, Right Driving Punch
3. A: Left Split   B: Left Cannon
4. A: Right Split   B: Right Cannon
5. A: Left Slap Elbow, Right Drive   B: Left Split
6. A: Left Cannon   B: Right Split
7. A: Right Cannon   B: Left Slap Elbow, Right Driving Punch

Description of the movements (fixed stance method)

(A is the author on the left, B is the translator on the right)

1. **Ready Stance**　　　　yùbèishì　　　　预备势

ACTION 1: Partners A and B stand at attention facing each other about a one and a half arm-lengths away from each other. (image 9.1)

122   ENTANGLING HANDS, *JIAO SHOU PAO*

ACTION 2: Both A and B clench their fists and bring them to their waist, fist hearts up. Both step a foot out to the side and sit into horse stances. Partner A steps the right foot out, and B steps the left foot out. The width of the horse stance is three foot-lengths. The partners look at each other. (image 9.2)

2. **A: Right Driving Punch**   yòu bēngquán   右崩拳

   B: Left Slap Elbow, Right Driving Punch

   zuǒ pāizhǒu yòu bēngquán   左拍肘右崩拳

ACTION 1: Partner A shifts weight to the left by pressing into the right leg, to form a left transverse stance. As A shifts leftward, he punches the right fist towards B's solar plexus, with the fist eye up and the arm slightly bent. This is a right driving punch. Partner A looks at the right fist. (image 9.3)

ACTION 2: Partner B stays in a horse stance and unclenches the left hand with the palm facing right and the fingers up, to slap A's right arm at the elbow. Partner B allows the left shoulder to come forward slightly. Partner B hits A's right ribs with a right driving punch, allowing the right shoulder to come forward slightly. The fist eye is up and the arm slightly bent. Partner B looks at the right fist. (image 9.4)

Pointers

- When partner A punches to B's solar plexus he should not suddenly strike out, but should have a stable focus.
- The feet can turn a bit as the weight shifts from left to right. When turning left, the left toes can open out and the right heel can push back. When turning right, the right toes can open out and the left heel can push back. The feet turn with the weight shift. Partners A and B are similar in this action.
- Partner B slaps the elbow first, then punches, but the actions are almost simultaneous. Be sure to move the shoulders into the actions.
- When doing partner forms each partner should focus the hits and not try to hit his partner, to avoid unnecessary injury.

3. **A: Left Split**　　　　　zuǒ pīquán　　　左劈拳
   B: Left Cannon Punch　zuǒ pàoquán　　左炮拳

ACTION 1: Partner A unclenches the right hand and turns the palm down to grab B's right wrist to pull it down. Partner A unclenches the left hand and chops toward B's face, palm forward. Partner A shifts weight to the right to form a right transverse stance and looks at B's face. (image 9.5)

ACTION 2: Partner B bends the right elbow to drill the fist up, drilling out inside A's left arm, rolling the right fist so that the fist eye faces the temple. Partner B shifts to the right while doing this, forming a right transverse stance with the right leg bent and the left leg pushing straight, turning the feet on the spot. At this time, B punches the left fist towards A's solar plexus, the fist eye up and the arm slightly bent, completing the cannon punch. (image 9.6)

Pointers

- Partner A should pull and strike simultaneously, sending the left shoulder forward.
- Partner A should just hook onto B's wrist, not grab it, so that B can continue into the next move. In partner forms the partners need to

cooperate.

- When partner B drills the right fist upwards she must roll it and brace out, sticking to A's right arm. The body should have a drilling in power, and should shift to the right to drill and roll, to complete the cannon punch all at once.

4. **A: Right Split**   yòu pīquán   右劈拳

   B: Right Cannon Punch   yòu pàoquán   右炮拳

ACTION 1: Partner A brings the left fist down to the belly, then drills the fist up outside B's left arm. Partner A then coils around B's arm, grabs the wrist, and pulls it down. Partner A unclenches the right hand and chops towards B's face with the palm forward. Partner A shifts leftward, putting most weight on the left leg, in a left transverse stance. (image 9.7)

ACTION 2: Partner B brings the left fist back, bends the elbow and drills up, drilling up inside A's right arm. Partner B shifts leftward and rolls the left fist so the fist eye faces the temple. Partner B bends the left leg and pushes into the right leg, forming a left transverse stance. At this time B punches the right fist towards A's solar plexus. The fist eye is up, the arm slightly bent, and the right shoulder forward. Partner B looks at A. (image 9.8)

Pointers

- Partner A should bring his left hand down in a circular motion, then circle back up to hook and pull down. He should first turn right then turn left. He should hook and pull quickly, and pull down with a heavy power. He should shift left as he hits with the right hand.

- When doing partner forms, be sure not to grab and hang on, as this prevents your partner from continuing on with the next move.

5. A: Left Slap Elbow, Right Driving Punch

	zuǒ pāizhǒu yòu bēngquán	左拍肘右崩拳
B: Left Split	zuǒ pīquán	左劈拳

ACTION 1: Partner A unclenches the left hand and slaps B's right elbow rightwards with the fingers up. Partner A urges the left shoulder slightly into the movement and shifts into a horse stance. At this time A punches the right fist to B's right ribs, putting the right shoulder forward into the punch. The fist eye is up and the arm slightly bent. Partner A looks at B. (image 9.9)

ACTION 2: Partner B drops the right hand and unclenches it, sliding it along A's right arm, changing to a grab to pull the arm down and back to the belly. At this time B unclenches the left hand and splits towards A's face. Partner B shifts to the right into a right transverse stance and looks at A. (image 9.10)

Pointers

- Points to consider for partner A's *slap elbow, drive* are similar to that done by B in move 2.
- Points to consider for partner B's *left split* are similar to that done by A in move 3.

6. A: Left Cannon Punch

	zuǒ pàoquán	左炮拳
B: Right Split	yòu pīquán	右劈拳

ACTION 1: Partner A bends the right elbow to drill the fist up, drilling up inside B's left arm. Partner A shifts right and rolls the right fist so the fist eye faces the right temple. Partner A shifts into a right transverse stance with the right leg bent and the left leg straight. At this time A punches the left fist to B's solar plexus with a left cannon punch. (image 9.11)

ACTION 2: Partner B brings the left fist back to the belly then drills it out along the outside of A's left arm, unclenching the hand and coiling it to grab A's wrist. Partner B then pulls A's arm down and back. At this time B unclenches the right hand and chops towards A's face with the palm forward. Partner B shifts to the left into a left transverse stance, looking at A. (image 9.12)

126 ENTANGLING HANDS, *JIAO SHOU PAO*

7. **A: Right Cannon Punch**   yòu pàoquán   右炮拳
    B: Left Slap Elbow, Right Driving Punch
                           zuǒ pāizhǒu yòu bēngquán   左拍肘右崩拳

ACTION 1: Partner A drills the left fist up to the solar plexus, turning the fist heart inward, then, as he drills the fist up to nose height, he shifts weight to the left by pressing into the right leg, to form a left transverse stance. As A shifts leftward, he rotates the left fist so that the fist eye faces the left temple and the elbow drops. At this time A punches the right fist towards B's solar plexus, with the fist eye up and the arm slightly bent. This is a right cannon punch. Partner A looks at his right fist.

ACTION 2: Partner B stays in a horse stance and unclenches the left hand with the palm facing right and the fingers up, to slap A's right arm at the elbow. Partner B allows the left shoulder to come forward slightly. Partner B hits A's right ribs with a right driving punch, allowing the right shoulder to come forward slightly. The fist eye is up and the arm slightly bent. Partner B looks at the right fist.

- Partners A and B continue on exchanging techniques. The number of repetitions is determined by the interest and conditioning of the partners.

- The partners should control their speed, maintaining a speed appropriate to their level of mastery. They should go slowly at first, and hold back their punches. Each should give the other the opportunity to block, cooperating fully with each other, to master the pattern and route of the form and learn the defense and attack applications. Once they are comfortable with the form then they can go quicker and link the actions together more, developing a tight coordination. Never go too quickly, as this causes movement to become rushed and sloppy. The partners must work well together because it is important that the moves be done correctly with good timing.

- When doing partner forms you should have full spirit, and show fierceness.

CHAPTER NINE: PARTNER FORMS   127

2. FIVE PHASES CONTEND, *WUXINGPAO*

wǔ xíng pào   五行炮

INTRODUCTION

The Five Phases Contend partner form was created according to the mutual creation and mutual control of the five elements. It is made up of all five basic techniques – split, drill, drive, cannon, and crosscut – and is often called Five Elements Create And Control. One partner performs the five elements as they develop from each other, while the other partner performs the five elements as they control each other. The form practices footwork combined with hand techniques, which makes it more realistic. Partners A and B alternate sides so that they can continue on, making the form long or short, and taking up as much space as they wish.

NAMES OF THE MOVEMENTS

1. Preparation
2. A: Advance, Right Drive   B: Withdraw, Left Press Down
3. A: Advance, Left Drive   B: Step Forward, Right Split
4. A: Retreat, Right Cannon   B: Right Press Down, Left Drill
5. A: Retreat, Left Crosscut   B: Advance, Right Drive
6. A: Withdraw, Left Press Down   B: Advance, Left Drive
7. A: Step Forward, Right Split   B: Retreat, Right Cannon
8. A: Right Press Down, Left Drill B: Retreat, Left Aligned Crosscut

Description of the Movements

(A is in the author on the left, B is the translator on the right.)

1. Preparation   yùbèishì   预备势

ACTION 1: Partners A and B stand facing each other, about three steps away, looking at each other. They salute each other. (image 9.13)

ACTION 2: Both partners simultaneously sit into *santishi*. (image 9.14)

9.13   9.14

2. **A: Advance, Right Drive**   jìnbù yòu bēngquán   进步右本拳
   B: Withdraw, Left Press Down   chèbù zuǒ àn   撤步左按

ACTION 1: Partner A steps the left foot forward, bringing the right foot in just behind the left foot, keeping the weight on the right leg. Partner A moves B's left hand aside to the right with the left hand and punches the right fist towards B's solar plexus. (image 9.15)

ACTION 2: Partner B steps the right foot back a small step, shifting back and withdrawing the left foot back in front of the right foot. Partner B presses A's right fist down with the left hand, looking at A's right fist. (image 9.16)

Pointers

- As partner A punches towards B's solar plexus he should find the proper distancing, as if he could hit B, but he doesn't actually hit.
- Partner B withdraws her feet quickly, but not too quickly – timed neither too early nor too late. The actions should work well together. She should control well and connect accurately with the left hand pressing down.

3. **A: Advance, Left Drive**   jìnbù zuǒ bēngquán   进步左崩拳
   B: Step Forward, Right Split   shàngbù yòu pīquán   上步右劈拳

ACTION 1: Partner A steps the left foot a half-step forward, bringing the right foot up. Partner A brings back the right fist and does a driving punch with the left fist towards B's solar plexus. Partner A presses the head up and looks ahead of the left fist. (image 9.17)

ACTION 2: Partner B turns the left foot out on the spot and steps the right foot forward. Partner B drills the left hand out along the outside of A's left arm. Partner B then turns the hand over to grab and pull A's hand down to the belly, chopping towards A's face with the right hand. (image 9.18)

CHAPTER NINE: PARTNER FORMS

Pointers

o   As partner A advances with the left driving punch he must step the right foot in quickly and extend the left shoulder forward into the punch. His right foot should step in about a foot-length behind his left foot.

o   Partner B must turn her left foot out in the proper place, about a foot-length away from A's left foot. Then B can step her right foot up outside A's left foot. This develops proper footwork. Both sides need to practise to get a feel for the distancing.

o   When partner B drills out and grabs A's arm to pull back, she does not need to hang on, as this is a form, and A needs to be able to continue on.

o   When partner B does the right split she should hold back the hit.

4. **A: Retreat, Right Cannon**   tuìbù yòu pàoquán   退步右炮拳

    B: Right Press Down, Left Drill   yòu yā zuǒ zuānquán   右压左钻拳

ACTION 1: Partner A retreats the right foot a step and withdraws the left foot just in front of the right. Partner A bends the left arm to drill up at nose height to break B's split as it comes. Without stopping the left foot, A then advances a step while doing a right cannon punch towards B's solar plexus. Partner A extends the right shoulder into the punch and looks at B. (image 9.19)

ACTION 2: Partner B retreats the right foot back a step and withdraws the left foot a half- step. Partner B rolls the left elbow in across the chest and pulls the right fist in to cover across from the right, down and leftward to break A's right cannon punch. At this time, B advances the left foot a half-step and punches a drilling fist forward and up towards A's jaw. Partner B looks at the left fist and brings A's right fist down towards the belly. (image 9.20)

FIVE PHASES CONTEND, *WU XING PAO*

9.19

9.20

Pointers

- Partner A needs to perform the retreat, withdraw, and advance quickly and agilely. When retreating he must get the correct foot placement. When doing the right cannon punch, partner A must advance the left foot to the outside of B's right foot, driving it in. Partner A can put his body into the punch a bit. When doing partner forms, the partners should coordinate well together, giving each other space and time to allow each other to break the attacks.

- Partner B should first retreat the right foot, then withdraw the left foot, then immediately advance, connecting the footwork smoothly. The hands should work together with the footwork – the left elbow rolling across as the right foot retreats, the left drill punching and the right fist drawing back as the left foot advances. She should step her left foot in towards partner A's groin. The drill should be held back.

5. **A: Retreat, Left Crosscut**   tuìbù zuǒ héngquán   退步左横拳

    B: Advance, Right Drive   jìnbù yòu bēngquán   进步右崩拳

ACTION 1: Partner A retreats the right foot back a big step then withdraws the left foot a half-step, taking a *santi* stance. Partner A lowers the left fist down the chest to drill and crosscut outside B's left arm, fist heart up, to break B's left drilling punch. Partner A looks at the left fist. (image 9.21)

ACTION 2: Partner B advances the left foot, bringing the right foot in behind the left. Partner B does a right driving punch towards A's left ribs and pulls the left fist back to the belly. Partner B looks in the direction of the right punch. (image 9.22)

CHAPTER NINE: PARTNER FORMS 131

Pointers

- o   Partner A does the retreating step into the aligned stance in order to break B's drilling punch. The concept is to dare to use an attacking move as a defense. The left fist must have a crosscutting knocking power. Partner A must move back quickly with stable footwork.
- When B advances with the right driving punch she then 'becomes A' and repeats what A just did, while A repeats what B just did.

6. **A: Withdraw, Left Press Down**   chèbù zuǒ àn   撤步左按
    B: Advance, Left Drive   jìnbù zuǒ bēngquán   进步左崩拳

ACTION 1: Partner A retreats the right foot a half-step and shifts back, withdrawing the left foot. Partner A presses the left hand down on B's right fist. Partner A turns the body slightly to the right, and looks at the left hand. (image 9.23)

ACTION 2: Partner B advances the left foot and follows up with the right foot. At this time B punches with the left fist towards A's left ribs. Partner B brings the right fist back to the belly, presses the head up, and looks past the left fist. (image 9.24)

7. **A: Step Forward, Right Split** shàngbù yòu pīquán 上步右劈拳

   B: Retreat, Right Cannon tuìbù yòu pàoquán 退步右炮拳

ACTION 1: Partner A turns the left foot out on the spot and advances the right foot. Partner A drills the left hand along the outer edge of B's left arm, then turns the hand to pull back to the belly. Partner A strikes with a right split towards B's face. (image 9.25)

ACTION 2: Partner B retreats the right foot and withdraws the left foot a half-step. Partner B bends the left elbow and drills up to nose height. Without stopping the left foot, B steps to the outside of A's right foot. At this time B does a right cannon punch towards A's solar plexus, looking in the direction of the right fist. (image 9.26)

8. **A: Right Press Down, Left Drill** yòu yā zuǒ zuānquán 右压左钻拳
   B: Retreat, Left Aligned Crosscut

   tuìbù zuǒ shùnbù héngquán 退步左顺步横拳

ACTION 1: Partner A retreats the right foot and withdraws the left foot a half-step. At this time A rolls the left elbow rightward across the chest and brings the right fist back to press down to the left. Partner A advances the left foot a half-step and does a left drill forward and up towards B's jaw. Partner A pulls the right fist back to the belly and looks towards the left fist. (image 9.27)

ACTION 2: Partner B retreats the right foot a big step then withdraws the left foot a half-step, taking a *santi* stance. At this time B circles the left fist down past the chest, then, without pausing, drills it up and out along the outer edge of A's left arm. B's fist heart is up and the arm bent. Partner B looks towards the fist. (image 9.28)

CHAPTER NINE: PARTNER FORMS 133

- Once you have performed to here you have completed a full circuit of the form. The number of repetitions you do depends on your conditioning and the size of the practice area.
- You may do two or three repeats of each person repeating as A and B, or you may switch A and B each time. The partners can agree between them, it doesn't matter.

Closing Move

ACTION 1: Partners A and B touch left arms when they reach an appropriate position, and indicate to each other that they wish to stop. At this time they each retreat the right foot and shift back. They then each withdraw the left foot to beside the right and stand up. While doing this, they unclench the left hand and clench the right fist, holding them out in front of the chest in a salute, looking at each other. (image 9.29)

ACTION 2: Both stand to attention, and the closing is completed.

CHAPTER TEN

THE TWELVE ANIMAL MODELS

ONE: DRAGON MODEL

龙形

INTRODUCTION TO THE DRAGON MODEL, *LONG XING*

The Chinese people venerate the dragon. They consider China the homeland of the dragon and themselves the descendants of dragons. The dragon, a mythical animal with horns on its head and scales on its elongated body, can walk, fly, and swim with equal skill. Indeed, it has the ability to 'mount the clouds and ride the mist'.

Xingyiquan is a style that models the actions of animals. The dragon model in Xingyiquan has developed through combining ancient Chinese traditions and writings about the dragon with the form analysis that previous generations of martial artists have done. The present set model has gradually developed over the years to both imitate the dragon's shape and actions and show its character and spirit. The dragon model imitates the great rising and dropping ability of the dragon in the footwork; its ability to close and open, fold in and expand in its handwork; and its ability to bend and extend in its bodywork. But in Xingyiquan it is not enough to just copy the actions and shape of an animal in order to develop correct actions, lines of movement, and combat effectiveness. It is more important to let the mood and spirit of the dragon direct your actions, to meticulously get a feel for the dragon's essence and grandeur. The dragon can fly to the highest and lowest places, it can coil and turn in all directions, it can suddenly jump up to the clouds, and just as suddenly dive down to the lowest gullies. It can travel in and out of the clouds and the seas and can soar even beyond the earth. Only with this image and mood leading your actions can you really express the dragon model. You must train both form and intent. Your intent gives meaning to your form, and your form physically expresses your intent.

Methods Of Performing The Dragon Model

1.1 Method One: Stomping Dragon Model

tàbù lóngxíng 踏步龙形

Start by settling into *santishi*.

ACTION: Stand to attention and raise the hands at the sides, palms up (image 10.1a). Then bend the elbows to bring the hands to press down in front of the face (image 10.1b). Bend the knees to sit down and bring the hands down to the belly, gradually clenching (image 10.2). Drill the right fist forward (image 10.3). Step the left foot forward and extend the left hand into a split, pulling the right hand back to the belly to settle into *santishi* (images 10.4 and 10.4 front).[19]

---

[19] Editor's Note: See Chapter Two for a more detailed description of *santishi*.

CHAPTER TEN: THE TWELVE ANIMAL MODELS

1.1a Left Stomping Dragon   zuǒ tàbù lóngxíng   左踏步龙形

ACTION 1: Clench the left fist and pull it back to the belly, withdrawing the left foot to in front of the right foot. (image 10.5)

ACTION 2: Shift back to the right leg and lift the left foot with the foot turned out crossways. Drill the left fist up by the sternum and out to nose height. Lift the right fist to the left elbow and do a crossways kick with the left foot up in front, kicking with the heel. Look forward. (images 10.6 and 10.7)

ACTION 3: Land the left foot forward, still turned out, landing firmly on the whole foot. Advance the right foot a half-step, gripping with the ball of the foot and allowing the heel to rise. Squat down so that the right knee is tucked tightly behind the left knee and the buttocks are on the right heel. The left leg is slightly bent and the left foot is turned out and flat on the ground. Slide the right fist forward along the left forearm to chop down, palm down. Pull the left hand back to the left hip. The right hand is in front of the left foot at hip height. Turn the torso leftward and lean forward slightly. Look at the right hand. (images 10.8 and 10.8 front)

1.1b Right Stomping Dragon   yòu tàbù lóngxíng   右踏步龙形

ACTION 1: Clench the right hand and pull it back to the belly. As the right hand comes back, raise the stance and advance the left foot a half-step. Drill the right fist up by the sternum then forward to nose height. Look at the right fist. (image 10.9)

ACTION 2: Quickly lift the right knee and kick the foot forward and up with the flat of the foot, foot turned out crossways. Slide the left fist along the right forearm and, when it arrives at the right fist, unclench both hands. Both palms reach forward with the fingers up, the left above and the right below. Kick no lower than the waist and no higher than the head. Keep the supporting leg slightly bent and grab the ground with the toes for stability. (image 10.10)

ACTION 3: After the right kick, drive the right foot forward and down to land firmly on the ground with the foot turned out crossways, and bring the left foot in a half-step, lifting the left heel. Chop the left hand forward and down and pull the right hand back to beside the right hip. Turn the torso rightward, twist the waist and lower the body, reaching the left shoulder into the move and reaching the torso forward slightly. Sit onto the left heel and bring the belly close to the right thigh. The left hand chops forward of the right foot at hip height, about twenty to thirty centimetres above the ground. Stretch the thumb web and slightly bend all the fingers. Press the head up, keep the neck straight, and look at the left hand. (image 10.11)

Pointers

- The left fist drills out as the left foot kicks.
- The right hand chops as the body drops down.
- The whole rising and dropping action should be done as one movement. There should be no pause in the action, and all segments of the body should rise and fall together.

CHAPTER TEN: THE TWELVE ANIMAL MODELS

1.1c Stomping Dragon Turn Around

tàbù lóngxíng huíshēn   踏步龙形回身

Using the <u>left</u> *dragon* as example.

ACTION 1: Clench the leading hand and pull it back to the belly, standing up. Turn around one-eighty degrees on the spot to face back in the direction that you just came, pivoting on both feet. Drill the fist that you just pulled in up to the sternum and then forward and up to nose height, twisting the ulnar (little finger) side up. Bring the rear fist snug to the lead elbow. (image 10.12)

ACTION 2: Drill the rear fist up along the lead forearm. When it reaches the lead fist, unclench both hands and chop the rear hand forward and down while pulling the lead hand back to the hip. As you split, turn the body and sit down, turning the lead foot out and raising the rear heel. Press the head up, keep the neck straight, and look at the front hand. (image 10.13)

- The *stomping dragon turn around* is the same on the right side, just turn the other way and transpose right and left actions.

Pointers

  o The *turn around* should be quick and stable. The feet must pivot to turn the body.

  o Three actions happen at once: the rear hand comes through to chop, the lead hand pulls back, and the body drops down.

1.1d Stomping Dragon Closing Move

tàbù lóngxíng shōushì   踏步龙形收势

When you practise Xingyiquan you must always start properly and finish properly, or 'have an opening and a closure'. Finish where you started; always begin with *santishi* and come back to *santishi*; always complete any form by getting back to left *santishi* and finishing properly from there.

- If in a <u>left</u> *stomping dragon* position (left foot and right hand forward):

ACTION 1: Push into the right foot to stand up, clench the left hand and pull it back to the belly, drill the right fist out from the sternum to nose height. Look at the right fist. (image 10.14)

ACTION 2: Step the left foot forward to take a *santi* position. Do a splitting action with the hands to settle into a full *santishi*. Look forward. (image 10.15)

ACTION 3: Without moving the feet, clench the left hand and bring it back to the belly. Press the head up, settle and grab into the front foot. Look forward (image 10.16)

ACTION 4: Shift forward to the left leg and bring the right foot up parallel to the left, with the knees together and bent. Do not move the hands. (image 10.17)

ACTION 5: Unclench the hands and raise them by the sides. When they reach shoulder height, bend the elbows to bring the hands in to the face. Do not move the legs yet. Look at the right hand as you raise the hands, then look forward when the hands come in.
(images 10.18 and 10.19)

CHAPTER TEN: THE TWELVE ANIMAL MODELS   141

ACTION 6: Press the hands down in front of the belly and stand up, standing to attention. The form is now completed. (image 10.20)

- If starting from a *right* stomping dragon position (right foot and left hand forward):

ACTION 1: Push into the right leg to stand up, clench the left fist and pull it back to the belly and clench the right hand, which is also at the belly. The legs are still in the crossed stance. (image 10.21)

ACTION 2: Step the right foot slightly forward and drill the right fist out to nose height. (image 10.22)

ACTION 3: Step the left foot forward into a *santi* stance. Slide the left fist along the right forearm and settle into a *santishi*. (image 10.23)

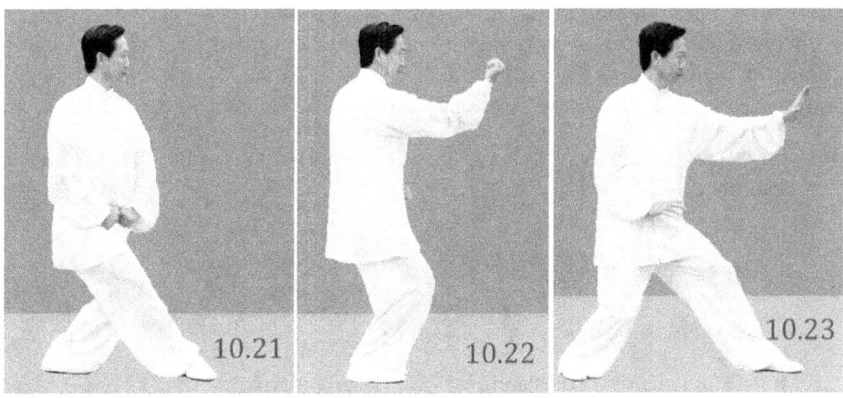

- The rest of the *closing move* is the same as described above in 1.1d from left stance, Actions 3 to 6, see images 10.16, 17, 18, 19, and 20.

1.2 METHOD TWO: LEAPING DRAGON MODEL

yuèbù lóngxíng   跃步龙形

Start from left *santishi*.

1.2a Left Stomping Dragon   zuǒ tàbù lóngxíng   左踏步龙形

This is the same as the *Left Stomping Dragon* described above. (See images 10.5, 10.6, 10.7, 10.8)

1.2b Right Leaping Dragon   yòu yuèbù lóngxíng   右跃步龙形

ACTION 1: Step the left foot a half-step forward and push off forcefully to jump up. Drive the right knee up to give impetus to the jump, turning the foot crossways to kick up with the heel. Clench the right hand and pull it back before jumping, then drill it up and forward above the head while jumping. Put the left fist up to the right elbow. Look forward. You should jump with both feet completely up off the ground. (image 10.24)

ACTION 2: When you land, first land the left foot and squat down, landing the right foot in front with the foot turned out crossways. Land with the legs tightly together, the left knee tucked into the right knee. Chop forward and down with the left hand and pull the right hand back to the right hip, turning the waist and putting the shoulder into the strike. (see image 10.11)

10.24

- All the requirements of the stance are the same as those of *stomping dragon* landing, described above.

1.2c Left Leaping Dragon

zuǒ yuèbù lóngxíng   左跃步龙形

ACTION 1: Clench the left hand and pull it back to the belly. Push back into the left foot to rise, and step forward a half-step with the right foot, then forcefully jump forward and up. Unclench the left hand and drill it by the sternum and up above the head, drilling the right hand to the left elbow. Use the left knee to help drive the power up, doing a crossing kick forward. Press the head up and look forward. (image 10.25)

10.25

CHAPTER TEN: THE TWELVE ANIMAL MODELS   143

ACTION 2: When you land, land the right foot first, bending the knee to squat, then land the left foot crossed out. Sit with the right heel off the ground and the legs tight together, the right knee under the back of the left knee. Chop forward and down with the right hand and pull the left hand back to the left hip, both palms down. Turn the waist and extend the shoulder. (see image 10.8)

- All the requirements of the stance are the same as described above in the *stomping dragon*.
- The number of repetitions depends on personal conditioning and the size of the training area.

Pointers
  o To jump, push strongly off the ground with the left foot, drive the right leg up, and drill the right fist up. These actions must be done together.
  o The jump should go for both distance and height. The landing must be stable. The chop is done at the same time that the body drops down.
  o You may stop for a moment after landing, but you must keep your force and spirit full. Do not take a rest in the squatting posture.

1.2d   Leaping Dragon Turn Around and Closing Move

The *turn around* and *closing move* are the same as those of *stomping dragon* described above.

POWER GENERATION FOR THE DRAGON MODEL

The characteristic of the dragon model is its large rising and dropping action. The body must be springy when rising and tuck in when landing.

In the sitting stance the legs must be pressed tightly together. The rear knee should be tucked in behind, or outside, the lead knee. You must turn your waist and reach with your shoulders to achieve this position. Press the body down on the legs to get power for the strike.

When dropping into the squatting position put power into the hands. This helps the body to gain and hold its position (dropping down from the jump). The lead hand chops forward and the rear hand pulls back forcefully, turning the body and extending the shoulder with a strong exhalation of breath. This coordination helps achieve an explosive power.

Stomping dragon
- The fists drill up as the leg does the crossing heel kick. Keep the body straight and keep the action on the same plane to advance straight forward.

- When doing the crossing heel kick first lift the knee and then thrust into the kick. Press the head up, keep the back straight, and keep the supporting leg slightly bent.

Leaping dragon

- When you jump up from the ground you should press up with your head, reach up with your body, drill up with your arms, and push off strongly from one leg using the other leg to assist the jump. The movement must be coordinated and smooth so that you accelerate throughout to drive the jump up.

- The body technique for the dragon is: when rising, press the head up, straighten the lower back, and expand the belly. When jumping, pull the belly in and close the chest. When landing, turn the waist and put the shoulder into the action. When the landing is completed you should hold the position but the position must remain complete with a fierce attitude and no slackening of power.

BREATHING CYCLE FOR THE DRAGON MODEL

- Inhale when rising. In *stomping dragon*, inhale when drilling the fists up. In *leaping dragon*, inhale when lifting the body.

- Pause your breath at the peak of the action. In *leaping dragon*, use a lifting breath and pause at the peak of the jump.

- Exhale when landing. In *stomping dragon*, exhale when the foot lands, the hands chop and pull, and the body drops. In *leaping dragon*, exhale when the whole stance lands and launches power.

PRACTICAL APPLICATIONS FOR THE DRAGON MODEL

Looking at the structure of the whole action, the dragon model is a technique that uses the feet and hands at the same time, striking two places at once. The hands drill up the midline to protect the head and chest area. Use them to attack if you advance and to defend if you retreat.

Lifting the knee and kicking with the foot turned out can be understood as a defensive action, kicking an attacker's oncoming kick. It can also be understood as an attacking kick, kicking the opponent's belly or leg, then driving forward to stomp. When you land the leg, keep in mind that you could be sliding and stomping onto your opponent's shin and foot. You should land as described in the classics, "The foot lands with a plan of attack."

One hand grabs and pulls while the other hand chops down, intended for the opponent's chest. This contains many possibilities, as the lead hand could then slice up or hit the groin, and the rear hand could come through with a punch.

CHAPTER TEN: THE TWELVE ANIMAL MODELS

The lifted leg can do a heel kick if the opponent is close, and could push off strongly if the opponent is distant, to land and stomp on him.

Training the *leaping dragon* develops the speed and agility needed to rise and drive forward. You can emphasize height or distance. The emphasis is on training the power of the legs and waist.

THE POEM ABOUT THE DRAGON

龙形歌诀

龙形升降缩骨能，

踏跃之法在腿功。

两手钻翻是起落，

伸缩展放意贯通。

The dragon rises and falls with the ability to shrink its bones,

The method of stomping and leaping depends on the skill of the legs.

The technique of rising and dropping depends on the hands drilling as they rise and turning over as they drop,

The intent permeates throughout as the body extends and tucks, expands and releases.

TWO: TIGER MODEL

虎形

Introduction To The Tiger Model, *Hu Xing*

The tiger is a strong and fierce predator, called the king of predators. Xingyiquan's tiger model imitates the tiger's fierceness and skill in pouncing on prey. In training the tiger model, the feet advance right and left in a zigzag pattern. The hands drill when rising and turn over when dropping. The body technique compresses when rising and lengthens when landing. The intent should express the tiger's ferocity. The tiger dominates the mountain regions. It domineers even when still, and when it moves it is like an avalanche. It can jump across gullies and mountain ranges, travelling the mountain regions at will. Its eyes glow like torches, showing the intensity of its spirit. Its power is expressed in its paws. Its cry echoes in the mountains and shakes the forests, terrifying everything that hears it. Its will to kill is strong. The tiger model should express this unapproachable, unbeatable manner and strength. When practising tiger model you should use this imagery to find the tiger's spirit and mood. This will help you to find and express the power within tiger model. When your imagination drives your form, then your form can better express your spirit.

Methods Of Performing Tiger Model

There are six variations of the tiger model: pounce, carry, intercept, trap, brace, and embrace. Each variation develops a specific technique. Although the hand techniques and power application differ, they are all based on the same stance and footwork.

2.1   METHOD ONE: TIGER POUNCES   hǔpū   虎扑

2.1a   Fierce Tiger Jumps over the Ravine   měnghǔ tiào jiàn   猛虎跳涧

Starting from left *santishi*.

ACTION: Take a step forward with the right foot, landing firmly, then quickly lift the left foot to place it beside the right foot without touching the ground. Reach the right hand out along under the left arm. When the right hand reaches the left hand, clench fists and pull both hands back to the belly. Hug the elbows to the ribs, keep the knees together, press the head up, and look forward. (images 10.26, 10.27)

CHAPTER TEN: THE TWELVE ANIMAL MODELS   147

2.1b   Tiger Pounces, Left Stance   zuǒbù hǔpū   左步虎扑

ACTION 1: Take a step forward with the left foot and follow in with the right foot a half-step. Drill the fists up past the chest to about six inches away from the jaw. (image 10.28)

ACTION 2: Unclench the hands and turn them over so that the palms face forward. As the left foot lands, extend the arms to pounce to chest height. Keep the arms slightly bent, the thumbs opposing each other, reach the shoulders, drop the elbows, and look forward. (images 10.29 and 10.29 front)

2.1c   Tiger Pounces, Right Stance   yòubù hǔpū   右步虎扑

ACTION 1: Step the left foot a half-step straight forward and follow in the right foot to beside the left ankle without touching down. Pull the hands down to the belly, clenching them. Look forward. (image 10.30)

148   TIGER, *HU XING*

ACTION 2: Step the right foot a long step to the forward right and follow in a half-step with the left. Turn the fist hearts up and drill them up to the chest. Turn the hands and unclench them to pounce forward to chest height. The thumb web is rounded, the thumbs face each other, the palm centres face forward, and the fingers point up. Look forward. (images 10.31, 10.32)

2.1d   Tiger Pounces, Left Stance   zuǒbù hǔpū   左步虎扑

ACTION 1: Advance a half-step with the right foot and lift the left foot beside the right ankle without touching down. Pull the hands down and back tight to the belly, clenching fists with the fist hearts in. Look forward. (image 10.33)

ACTION 2: Take a long step to the forward left with the left foot and follow in the right foot a half-step. Drill the fists up past the sternum to in front of the jaw, then unclench them and pounce forward to chest height. Look forward. (image 10.34)

- Carry on, doing as many *tiger pounces* left and right as space permits.

Pointers

  o   The first long step forward must cover distance and land very firmly. This step must be completed at the same time that the hands pull back.

  o   The hands pounce as the leading foot lands – at exactly the same time.

CHAPTER TEN: THE TWELVE ANIMAL MODELS   149

2.1e   Tiger Pounce Turn Around   hǔpū huíshēn   虎扑回身

Using the <u>left</u> *tiger pounces* as example.

ACTION 1: Take a hook-in step with the left foot just in front of the right foot, forming a T stance. Shift to the left leg and turn around to the right, lifting the right foot beside the left ankle. Pull the hands down to the belly and clench them. Press the head up and look around to the new direction. (image 10.35)

ACTION 2: Take a long step to the forward right (in the new direction) and follow in a half-step with the left foot. Unclench the hands and pounce forward as before. (images 10.36, 10.37)

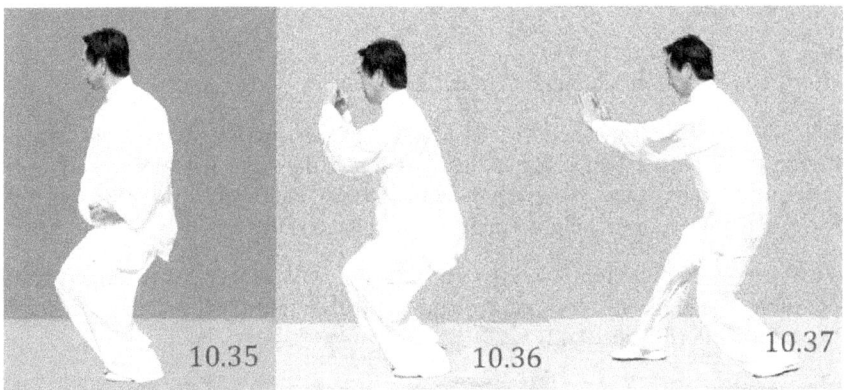

- The action of *tiger pounce turn around* is the same whether on the right or left side, just transpose the right and left actions.

Pointers

- The turn around must be quick and stable. Be sure to hook-in the foot well.
- Keep the body straight when turning around. Be sure not to look down, put the head down, or bend at the waist.

2.1f   Tiger Pounce Closing Move   hǔpū shōushì   虎扑收势

Always wait until you get back to your starting point before doing the *closing move*.

- When your *turn around* arrives in *tiger pounces, <u>left</u> stance*:

ACTION 1: Withdraw the left foot to parallel to the right foot without moving the right foot. Pull the hands back to the belly and clench them. Drill the right fist up to the chest and out to nose height. Look forward. (image 10.38)

150   TIGER, *HU XING*

ACTION 2: Step the left foot forward to take a *santi* stance. Slide the left hand along the right arm to chop forward, and pull the right hand back to the belly. Look forward. (image 10.39)

- When your turn around arrives in *tiger pounces, <u>right</u> stance*:

ACTION 1: Withdraw the left foot a half-step then withdraw the right foot to beside the left foot and place it firmly. Clench the right fist and pull it back beside the waist, then press down with the left hand and drill the right fist forward and up to nose height. (images 10.40, 10.41)

ACTION 2: Step the left foot forward to take a *santi* stance. Slide the left hand out along the right arm to chop forward. Pull the right hand back to the belly. Look forward. (image 10.42)

- Once to here, complete the closing the same as *santishi* closing, fully described in the dragon model. (see images 10.1.15 to 10.20)

Pointers

- The lead foot must withdraw exactly as the hands pull back.
- You must express full power when the feet are parallel and the right fist drills out.

CHAPTER TEN: THE TWELVE ANIMAL MODELS

○ The left foot steps into the *santi* stance as the left hand does the split action. These actions must arrive together. All the requirements of the *santishi* are the same as the usual *santishi*.

2.2 TIGER CARRIES hǔtuō 虎托

Tiger carries does not imitate an action of the tiger at all but is a technique that compensates for a power that would otherwise be lacking if you just practised *tiger pounces*.[20] Both techniques use a power forward and down. Since the hands follow different paths, the power application and combat application are quite different.

Start from left *santishi*.

2.2a Tiger Carries, Right Stance yòubù hǔtuō 右步虎托

ACTION 1: Advance the left foot a half-step, then advance the right foot to beside the left ankle. Slide the right hand along under the left arm. When it arrives at the left hand, circle both hands to the sides then wrap them in to the sides of the waist, palms forward, fingers down. Look forward. (images 10.43, 10.44)

ACTION 2: Take a long step to the forward right with the right foot and follow in a half-step with the left foot. Push forward from the waist with both palms, fingers angled down, palms about a fist-length apart at belly height. Urge the shoulders forward, settle the waist down, and look forward. (images 10.45 and 10.45 front)

---

[20] Translator's note: The English word 'carry' implies a rising meaning, but the *tiger carry* is actually a low technique. 'Carry' is a term for an open palm technique that looks like carrying a tray, but can be applied up, directly forward, or down. When low, the power is like shaking a winnowing basket, so that the rice pops up and the chaff is blown away in the wind.

2.2b   Tiger Carries, Left Stance   zuǒbù hǔtuō   左步虎托

ACTION 1: Advance the right foot a half-step then lift the left foot beside the right ankle. Cross the wrists and drill up with the palms facing in. When the hands arrive at shoulder height rotate them so the palms face out and circle them to the sides then wrap down to beside the waist, palms facing forward and fingers pointing down. Press the head up and look forward. (images 10.46, 10.47)

ACTION 2: Take a long step to the forward left with the left foot and follow in a half-step with the right foot. Push forward to belly height, fingers down, hands a fist-length apart. Look forward. (image 10.48)

Pointers

- The hands must complete the circle as the foot advances.
- The hands must complete the push as the lead foot lands forward.

2.2c   Tiger Carries Turn Around   hǔtuō huíshēn   虎托回身

Using the <u>left</u> *tiger carries* as example.

ACTION 1: Take a hook-in step with the left foot to in front of the right foot and turn around to the right, shifting onto the left leg. Lift the right foot to beside the left ankle. Bring the hands around with the body, crossing them and drilling up. After you have turned around, circle the hands and bring them down to the sides of the waist. (images 10.49, 10.50)

 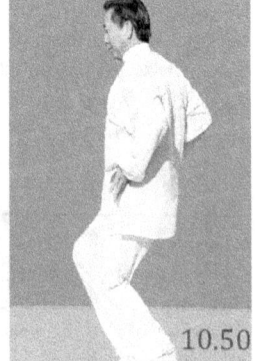

CHAPTER TEN: THE TWELVE ANIMAL MODELS 153

ACTION 2: Take a long step to the forward right with the right foot and follow in the left foot a half-step. Complete the *tiger carries* to push down to the front to belly height. Look forward. (image 10.51)

- The action of *tiger carries turn around* is the same whether on the right or left side, just transpose the right and left actions.

Pointers

  o Do not pause when turning around – move the hands while stepping.

2.2d   Tiger Carries Closing Move   hǔtuō shōushì   虎托收势

From <u>left</u> *tiger carries*:

ACTION 1: Withdraw the left foot to the right foot. Turn the left hand over to press down. Pull the right hand back to the belly. (image 10.52) Clench the right hand, drill up to the sternum and out to nose height, and pull the left hand back to the belly.

ACTION 2: Step the left foot forward without moving the right foot, to take a *santi* stance. Chop the left hand forward and pull the right hand back to the belly. (image 10.53)

From <u>right</u> *tiger carries*:

ACTION 1: Withdraw the right foot to parallel to the left foot, keeping the weight down and the legs bent. Turn the left hand over to cover and press down, and pull the right hand back to the belly, clenching the fist. Then drill the right fist up and out to nose height. Tuck the left hand, clenching it and pressing down to the belly. Look forward. (image 10.54)

ACTION 2: Step the left foot forward without moving the right foot, chop the left hand forward, and pull the right hand back to the belly, to take a *santishi*. Press the head up and look forward. (image 10.55)

- The rest of *closing move* is the same as usual.

Pointers

o Withdraw the left foot, cover with the left hand, and drill the right fist all together. Withdraw the right foot, cover with the left hand, and drill the right fist all together.

2.3   TIGER INTERCEPTS   hǔjié   虎截

Start from left *santishi*.

2.3a   Fierce Tiger Jumps over the Ravine   měnghǔ tiào jiàn   猛虎跳涧

As described above in movement 2a.

2.3b   Tiger Intercepts, Left Stance   zuǒbù hǔjié   左步虎截

ACTION 1: Step the left foot diagonally to the forward left and follow in with the right foot a half-step. Drill the left fist up on the right side and unclench it when it arrives at head height, rotating the palm to face out, fingers up, thumb web stretched as if reaching to grab. Lift the right hand and clench it. (image 10.56)

ACTION 2: Grab and pull the left hand forward and down to the left to the left waist, clenching to a fist. Intercept with the right forearm leftward, fist heart facing in at shoulder height. Keep the elbows settled down, press the head up, and look forward. (images 10.57 and 10.57 front)

CHAPTER TEN: THE TWELVE ANIMAL MODELS 155

2.3c   Tiger Intercepts, Right Stance   yòubù hǔjié   右步虎截

ACTION 1: Advance the left foot a half-step and lift the right foot to beside the left ankle. Pull the right fist back and drill it up to the left side of the head, then rotate and unclench the hand, stretching it in a grabbing action with the palm facing out. Do not move the left fist. (image 10.58)

ACTION 2: Take a long step diagonally to the forward right with the right foot and follow in a half-step with the left foot. Grab forward and pull back to the right with the right hand, clenching it. Lift the left fist at the left side of the body then intercept across to the right with the forearm vertical. The left fist heart faces in at shoulder height. Keep the elbows settled, press the head up, and look forward. (image 10.59)

Pointers

- The lead foot should take a big step, as large as possible, and the rear foot should follow in quickly and firmly.

- One hand hooks and pulls as the other hand intercepts and pounds. These actions need to be coordinated to work together. The upper limbs must also work together with the lower limbs.

156   TIGER, *HU XING*

2.3c   Tiger Intercepts Turn Around and Closing Move

hǔjié huíshēn, shòushì   虎截回身和收势

- The footwork of *tiger intercepts turn around* is the same as that of *tiger pounces turn around*, just change the hand technique to intercept. The action of *tiger intercepts closing move* is the same as that of *tiger pounces closing move*.

2.4   TIGER BRACES   hǔchēng   虎撑

Start from left *santishi*.

2.4a   Fierce Tiger Jumps over the Ravine   měnghǔ tiào jiàn   猛虎跳涧

As described above in movement 2.1a.

2.4b   Tiger Braces, Left Stance   zuǒbù hǔchēng   左步虎撑

ACTION: Step the left foot to the forward left and follow in the right foot a half-step. Lift the fists in front of the chest to just above shoulder height. Unclench the hands and turn the palms out, thumbs down. As the left foot lands, brace forward with both palms. Keep the elbows slightly bent, fingers pointing to each other, and thumbs down. Press the head up and look forward. (images 10.60 and 10.60 front)

10.60   10.60 FRONT

2.4c   Tiger Braces, Right Stance   yòubù hǔchēng   右步虎撑

ACTION 1: Advance the left foot a half-step and follow in the right foot to beside the left ankle without touching down. Lift the palms slightly, then roll them forward, then curl down to press and draw back to in front of the waist or chest. Press the head up and look forward. (image 10.61)

ACTION 2: Take a long step diagonally to the forward right with the right foot and follow in the left foot a half-step. Lift the hands to the jaw and turn the palms out, shoving forward forcefully. Keep the elbows slightly bent, the thumbs down, and the fingers pointing to each other. Press the

10.61

head up and look forward. (image 10.62)

Pointers

- While the lead foot advances the half-step, the hands need to complete all the actions of slicing up, rotating, rolling and drawing back.
- As the rear foot comes through to step forward, the hands need to complete the action of bracing and shoving forward. Hands and feet complete their actions simultaneously.
- There is another way of doing *tiger braces* in which the hands first move down, then back, then up, and finally shove forward. Either method is fine.

2.4d   Tiger Braces Turn Around and Closing Move

hǔchēng huíshēn, shòushì   虎撑回身和收势

- The footwork of *tiger braces turn around* and *closing move* are the same as that of *tiger pounces turn around* and *closing move*, just change the hand technique to brace instead of pounce.

2.5   TIGER TRAPS   hǔlán   虎拦

Start from left *santishi*.

2.5a   Tiger Traps, Left Stance

zuǒbù hǔlán   左步虎拦

ACTION 1: Take a long step forward with the right foot and follow in the left foot to the right ankle. Reach the right hand to meet the left hand, then grab and pull with both back to the belly. Drill the left fist up to the jaw then turn the palm forward, fingers up, thumb web stretched to hook or grab. (image 10.63)

158   TIGER, *HU XING*

ACTION 2: Step the left foot diagonally to the forward left then follow in the right foot a half-step. Turn the right fist eye up and extend it to the forward left as if to catch something in the forearm. Then hook and move it across rightward. The right fist finishes in front of the right shoulder at nose height with the fist heart in. Clench the left hand and turn the fist heart out and knock it horizontally across leftward to in front of the left shoulder. Keep both elbows settled down and look forward. (images 10.64, 10.65, and 10.65 front)

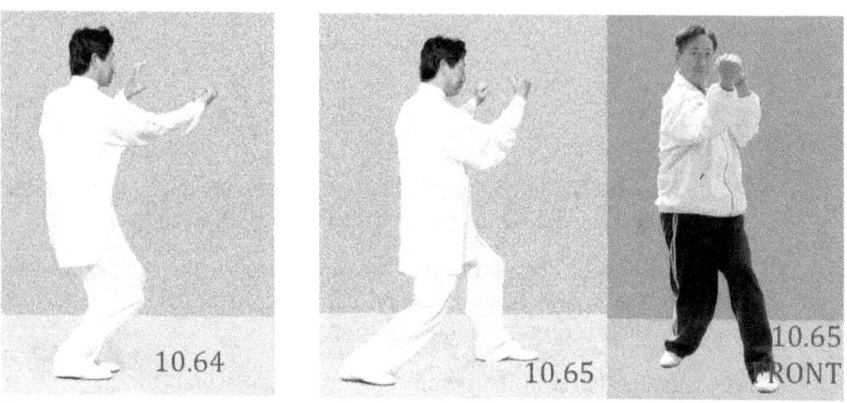

2.5b   Tiger Traps, Right Stance   yòubù hǔlán   右步虎拦

ACTION 1: Advance the left foot a half-step and follow in the right foot to beside the left ankle. Lower the right fist then drill it up to in front of the mouth, then unclench it with the palm in, fingers up, and thumb web stretched in a grabbing shape. As the body moves, lower the left fist to in front of the chest. Look forward. (image 10.66)

ACTION 2: Take a step diagonally to the forward right with the right foot and follow in a half-step with the left. Bring the left fist to the right, bend the elbow to lift up with the forearm, and hook across to the left, finishing with the fist heart in at nose height in front of the right shoulder. Clench the right hand and turn the fist heart out, then knock horizontally across to the right to finish in front of the right shoulder. The forearms are both vertical with the elbows down.

CHAPTER TEN: THE TWELVE ANIMAL MODELS

Look forward. (images 10.67, 10.68)

Pointers

- The right foot steps forward as the hands pull back. Do not stop here, but keep drilling the left fist up to catch.
- The left foot lands as the forearms check across, working together.

2.5c Tiger Traps Turn Around and Closing Move

hǔlán huíshēn, shòushì   虎拦回身和收势

- The footwork of *tiger traps turn around* is the same as that of *tiger pounces turn around*, just change the hand technique to a trap. The actions of *tiger traps closing move* are the same as that of *tiger pounces closing move*.

2.6 TIGER EMBRACES   hǔbào   虎抱

Start from left *santishi*.

2.6a Tiger Embraces, Left Stance   zuǒbù hǔbào   左步虎抱

ACTION 1: Take a step forward with the right foot and follow in with the left to beside the right ankle. Reach forward with the right hand, palm down. When it meets the left hand, clench and pull both hands back to the belly. Press the head up and look forward. (image 10.69)

ACTION 2: Take a long step to the forward left with the left foot and follow in the right foot a half-step. Before stepping, raise the hands to cross the wrists in front of the jaw, unclenching and turning them out. Then circle each to the left and right and lower them to the sides, so that when the left foot advances the palms push forward and up in an embracing posture. The palms face each other at chest height. Tuck the elbows in and look forward. (images 10.70, 10.71, and 10.71 front)

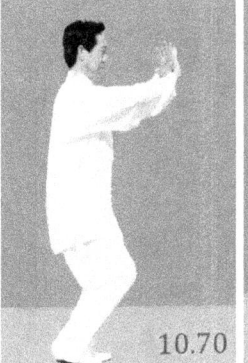

2.6b Tiger Embraces, Right Stance   yòubù hǔbào   右步虎抱

ACTION 1: Advance the left foot a half-step and follow in the right foot to beside the left ankle without touching down. Turn the palms out and cross them in front of the chest. Circle each hand down to either side then open with the palms facing each other. (images 10.72, 10.73)

ACTION 2: Take a long step to the forward right with the right foot and follow in a half-step with the left foot. Push the palms forward and up with the palms facing each other, fingers up, at chest height. Keep the hands shoulder width apart. Look forward. (image 10.74)

Pointers

- The hands should finish their action as the left foot lands.
- The whole movement should be done without interruption, smoothly without a break.

2.6c Tiger Embraces Turn Around and Closing Move

hǔbào huíshēn, shòushì   虎抱回身和收势

- The footwork of *tiger embraces turn around* is the same as that of *tiger pounces turn around*, just change the hand technique to embrace. The actions of *tiger embraces closing move* are the same as those of *tiger pounces closing move*.

PROBLEMS OFTEN MET IN THE TIGER MODEL

Tiger Pounces

PROBLEM 1: The student does not strike as the lead foot lands.

CORRECTIONS: More practice will give the student a feel for this action. While practising, the student must concentrate on landing the technique with the foot landing.

PROBLEM 2: The student does not understand the actions of straightening the lower back and extending the shoulders.

CORRECTIONS: The action of straightening the lower back is to store energy, and the action of extending the shoulders is to release the energy. The lower back should straighten as the fists drill up, sitting the buttocks down. The shoulders should reach forward when the hands pounce forward.

PROBLEM 3: The student straightens the arms when pouncing, or puts the hands too high.

CORRECTIONS: Remind the student to keep the arms rounded when pouncing, urging the shoulders forward and settling the elbows. The heel of the palms should be at chest height, and the fingers should be no higher than the shoulders. Tell the student to think of striking the opponent's chest.

PROBLEM 4: As the student does the half-step forward, pulling the hands back, the hands move along a straight line, or the body rises.

CORRECTIONS: Remind the student to draw a circle with the hands, bending the arms, reaching into the shoulders and keeping the elbows settled, so that the hands come down and then in. Remind the student to press the head up, thinking of doing a head butt.

PROBLEM 5: The student does the move too ferociously, landing without stability, and even sliding forward.

CORRECTIONS: Remind the student to always consciously grip the ground with the landing foot. This will prevent slipping.

Tiger Carries

PROBLEM 1: The student does the carry too high, or straightens the arms.

CORRECTIONS: Remind the student to strike to his own belly height, keeping the arms bent. The hands should be about a foot away from the belly.

PROBLEM 2: The student does the carry with the hands too far apart.

CORRECTIONS: Remind the student that both hands should be able to contact an opponent's body, so are about five to six centimetres apart. Pay attention to keeping the elbows close together, as this will keep the hands close as well.

PROBLEM 3: The student does a slicing up action.

CORRECTIONS: Remind the student of the correct line that the hands should be taking. *Tiger carries* is not a slice or a scoop. The palms should move forward and down with a pushing, 'carrying in the palms' action.

POWER GENERATION FOR THE TIGER MODEL

Tiger Pounces

First of all, you must put the spirit of the tiger into all your actions, so that its ferocity pervades all movement.

The tiger model emphasizes the saying, "The hands drill as they rise and turn over as they land. The hands and feet work together. Straighten the lower back and reach through the shoulders."

Make sure that the elbows hug the ribs as the hands drill to rise, so that the elbows lead the hands up. When the elbows reach the chest, then contain the chest and lengthen the lower back, sitting the buttocks down. This is how the pouncing action pre-loads in order to launch power.

The whole movement is one action, it must continue without hesitation. You must step forward quickly and not stop in the middle. Especially, after the lead foot advances a half-step, the rear foot must come through quickly to take a long step forward. You must not pause in your footwork.

When the hands clench and pull back to the belly, be sure to circle them down and back, do not pull them in a straight line. Keep the thumb web stretched and the palm rounded. Brace out slightly with the elbows and settle the shoulders down. Press the head up and hold a charging forward intent.

When the hands pounce forward, settle the buttocks down and urge the shoulders forward. Fold in the waist and contain the chest. Coordinate your breathing to settle the *qi* to the *dantian* to aid your power release.

When practising repetitive lines, be sure to turn the lead foot in slightly when it advances the half-step. This will help the zigzag line stepping.

Tiger Carries

The carrying action of the hands must come as the lead foot lands.

When you launch power to the hands, press the elbows snug to the ribs in order to send the hands forward with the carrying action. Settle the shoulders down and sit the buttocks down. This settles the torso down. Exhale to assist power output.

When circling the hands in front of the body, the wrists cross as the hands drill up with the palms in. When they reach head height turn the palms forward. Brace out, keeping the arms rounded, and roll down, drawing a circle, roll until the hands reach the sides of the waist, palms out so that they face forward. The elbows should draw back a bit. When the hands drill up, the chest should be contained and the upper back stretched, the lower back flexed and the torso tucked. When the hands lower the head should press up, the lower back should lengthen, the chest should widen, and the shoulders should settle.

The turn around must be quick and stable, turning on the body's pivot point. Be sure to hook the lead foot in to in front of or on the outside of the rear foot.

Tiger Intercepts

Watch your hand shapes as they drill up then hook and pull. Rotate to drill and turn over to pull. The body should pre-load back to assist the forward movement and pre-load right to assist the leftward movement.

When doing the crossing intercept turn the waist and urge the shoulders, settle the elbows, in order to get the power launch from the lower back and shoulders to reach the forearms. The forearms should have a twisting, checking power.

Tiger Braces

The hands may do a rolling circle up and back while the lead foot takes the half-step forward. The hands may move forward and down, then lift to in front of the chest while the lead foot advances a half-step. Either way is fine for *tiger braces*.

When the rear foot comes through to step forward, the hands must complete the pushing and bracing action as the foot lands.

The hands must move in a circular action, whether lifting and rolling forward or reaching forward and pressing down.

When bracing forward the palms must rotate so that they face out. The arms are rounded, the shoulders settled and extended, the chest contained, the abdomen pulled in, and the buttocks settled. Exhale to assist the power release.

Tiger Embraces

> All the varieties of the tiger model use the same footwork, only the hand techniques differ. The handwork must always be timed exactly with the footwork. The power output and breathing must be coordinated. This type of power is whole body power.

Tiger embraces has an inward pressing power, there is a closing in as the palms push forward. This combines with a forward checking power. The elbows must urge the elbows forward, keeping a closing in power, so that the palms twist as they check forward.

Tiger Traps

One hand drills then turns to grab and pull while the other hand traps to the back. The forearms use a scissoring checking power.

The lead foot advances while the hands circle forward, down, then drill up and turn to catch. This action should store power, preparing to launch the strike, so the chest closes and the abdomen tucks in.

When the forearms hook and trap, crossing, use the shoulders to close then open, storing then launching power.

BREATHING CYCLE FOR THE TIGER MODEL

You need to coordinate breathing for all movements to assist in storing and launching power.

- Inhale. Generally, inhale when doing the preparatory storing of power, pre-loading, or initiating the movement. Inhale as you advance the lead foot a half-step, pull the fists back and drill up. Inhale as you circle the hands to the sides before the *tiger carries*.

- Exhale. Generally, exhale when launching power, or landing the technique. Exhale as you step the rear foot through a big step, following in with the other foot, and pounce, carry, or strike out.

PRACTICAL APPLICATIONS FOR THE TIGER MODEL

Tiger Pounces

This is like a tiger pouncing on its prey. You can dodge out of the way and then advance to pounce, or you can knock the opponent's attack and get in close to pounce. If going straight in, hit directly on his chest. If going in from the side, hit his shoulders or ribs. You need to get the body in with the footwork, hitting as the foot enters. It is just as the classics say:

> "Your head should barge into the enemy, your torso should press into him, your footwork should chase him, your hands should strike him, your spirit should threaten him, your *qi* should harass him, your power should surpass his."

Tiger pounces is the most important of the tiger techniques and the most dangerous. When done as a single hand technique it is a splitting palm, and as a double handed technique it is *tiger pounces*. The hands protect the torso and head, and both hands attack as the footwork enters.

Tiger Carries

This is a low strike to the opponent's belly. The hands first circle to open out the opponent's hands, then the feet can drive in to allow the strike to the belly, knocking him over. This is a close range attack; you must drive the feet in to get the body close. The head should barge in, the body press in, the feet enter, and the spirit threaten. It is not effective if done at a distance. The key to this attack is to use both hands to open out the opponent's hands, giving you the opening to get your strike in.

Tiger Intercepts

One hand hooks and pulls the opponent's wrist or forearm while your other fist or forearm strikes it. This is meant to break the opponent's elbow or upper arm so that he cannot continue the attack. The key is that once the hook is made, the intercepting fist must be forceful. In addition, once the interception is done, your action can smoothly change to a drill, a driving punch, a cannon punch, or a crosscut. Your following strike is determined by your preferences and the situation.

Tiger Traps

This knocks and controls the opponent's elbow, using the connected power of your shoulders, one forward and one back, one left and one right. If the opponent strikes at your face with his right fist, you hook his arm with your left hand and pull out, using your right hand to knock his elbow up, knocking it crossways to the right. This will break his elbow. If you don't succeed with this and the opponent is able to continue with a left punch, hook his arm to the right with your right forearm and quickly strike to his face. You must react to the situation and change your techniques to take whatever opportunity presents.

Tiger Braces

This knocks the opponent's arms open to gain an opportunity to strike to the chest with both palms, knocking him away. The key is daring to step in close, using your body for the technique. This is easy to say but hard to do. You need to practise this technique a lot to find the proper way to apply power, and then you need to practise drills with a partner and practise fighting until you can use this technique with spontaneity.

Tiger Embraces

This sticks to the opponent's upper arms, forcing them back as you step forward to strike his chest or ribs with a short forward and inward strike. It looks like you are tying him up in a package. Actually you are pressing into his ribs and using your whole body to shove him away.

- The six methods of doing the tiger model train six types of power and six combat techniques. *Tiger pounces* and *tiger carries* are common, but the other four are seldom seen. The six are called 'tiger model's six matchless techniques.' I have written them out here according to traditional training and my own years of experience, to expand on tiger model's contents and fighting methods.

The Poem About The Tiger

虎形歌诀

猛虎扑食气势雄，

意贯周身卷地风。

腰肩之力在臀尾，

挺伸两字显其功。

The brave tiger pounces on its prey with a fierce mien,

Its will courses through its entire body like a tornado.

The strength of the back and shoulders comes from the tailbone,

Its skill is expressed in two words: straighten and extend.

THREE: MONKEY MODEL

猴形

INTRODUCTION TO THE MONKEY MODEL, *HOU XING*

The monkey model references monkeys and apes. Although humans resemble monkeys and apes to some extent, we lack their agility. Many animals surpass humans in their natural abilities, which is why Xingyiquan imitates them – to practise certain aspects of these abilities, both for health and combat purposes. The monkey model imitates the monkey's skills at leaping, its overall nimbleness, the strength of its arms, its ability to kick branches, to 'pick and present peaches,' to 'climb up poles' and to 'pull on ropes.'

When you practise the monkey model you should express a monkey's characteristics: quick-wittedness, alertness, bravery, and agility. Its eyes flash like lightning, it spins like the wind, leaps as if flying, and is light as a floating feather. Its scream haunts the mountaintops like the clouds and mist that encircle them. It can go into the deepest gullies and remotest caves. It can compress its body, dodge and tumble. It is capable, energetic, nimble, light and lively – suddenly up, suddenly down, suddenly left, suddenly right, suddenly forward and suddenly back. It can change instantaneously between substantial and insubstantial. It can stare fixedly with rapt attention, or can shift its gaze at will. Its spirit shows in its eyes. It is light and agile, combining hard and soft. When training monkey model, imitate its postures and movements, its spirit and attitude. Don't try to copy 'monkeyness', but to do what makes the monkey effective. Take your ideas from the form of the monkey, and use these ideas to develop your form. In this way the idea comes from the form, and the form flows from the idea.

METHODS OF PERFORMING THE MONKEY MODEL

There are two main ways to practise the monkey model. One is to four corners, and the other is in a straight line. The techniques are not quite the same but the ideas and mood are the same.

3.1 METHOD ONE: MONKEY MODEL TO FOUR CORNERS   sìjiǎo hóu xíng   四角猴形

168 MONKEY, *HOU XING*

3.1a Monkey Scratches its Mark (left)   yuánhóu guà yìn   猿猴挂印

Start from left *santishi*.

ACTION 1: First turn the body thirty degrees to the right and lower the left hand, clenching it and drawing it in to the belly. Withdraw the left foot to beside the right foot. Look at the left hand. (image 10.75)

ACTION 2: Step the left foot in front of the right foot, circling it around and hooking the foot out, turning the body leftward. Drill the left fist up to in front of the jaw, turning it so the fist heart faces out, to hook and knock away in an outward blocking action at shoulder height. Do not move the right hand. Look at the left hand. (image 10.76)

3.1b Monkey Drops Back on its Haunches   chèbù hóu dūn   撤步猴蹲

ACTION 1: Shift forward to the left leg and step the right foot in front of the left toes, hooking it in to take a character eight [/\] stance. Continue to turn around to the left to face in the direction from which you just came, and shift onto the right foot, withdrawing the left foot behind. Slide the right hand forward on top of the left arm to eye height and pull the left hand back to the left side of the belly. Both palms face down. Look at the right hand. (images 10.77, 10.78)

ACTION 2: Withdraw the right foot to in front of the left foot and touch the ball of the foot down, shifting onto the left foot. Squat down to a ninety degree angle of the knees. While doing this, bring the right hand back to the belly and lift the left hand in front of the right shoulder. Keep the elbow set down, the palm down, and the hand at shoulder height. Look to the forward right. The body may lean into the right shoulder a bit. (images 10.79 and 10.79 front)

CHAPTER TEN: THE TWELVE ANIMAL MODELS

3.1c   **Monkey Pulls at its Leash**   hóu dáo shéng   猴扌到 绳

ACTION 1: Lift the right hand then extend it along above the left arm, circling the left hand down to pull it back to the belly. Then lift the left hand and extend it out on top of the right arm to eye height, while circling and pulling the right hand back to beside the belly. Don't move the feet yet. (image 10.80)

ACTION 2: Advance the right foot a half-step and follow in the left foot. Do a splitting palm with the right hand to shoulder height. Pull the left hand back to the belly. Look past the right hand. (image 10.81)

3.1d   **Monkey Scrambles up a Pole**   yuánhóu pá gān   猿猴爬竿

ACTION 1: Step the left foot forward and, as soon as it lands, push off to hop forward. Lift the right knee as the left foot pushes off, to help drive the jump forward. As you hop, thread the left hand forward along on top of the right hand to eye height and withdraw the right hand to in front of the chest. The palms are angled downward. Look at the left hand. (image 10.82)

170   MONKEY, *HOU XING*

ACTION 2: After the left foot lands, advance the right foot, then follow in a half-step with the left foot. While landing, thread the right hand forward along under the left hand to chest height, fingers up, palm forward. Pull the left hand back to in front of the belly. Look past the right hand. (image 10.83)

Please refer to images 10.84 a, b, c, d, e, f, g, h (the photo g is taken at slightly different angle from the others, it follows the same line, though) to see the monkey model from the other side.

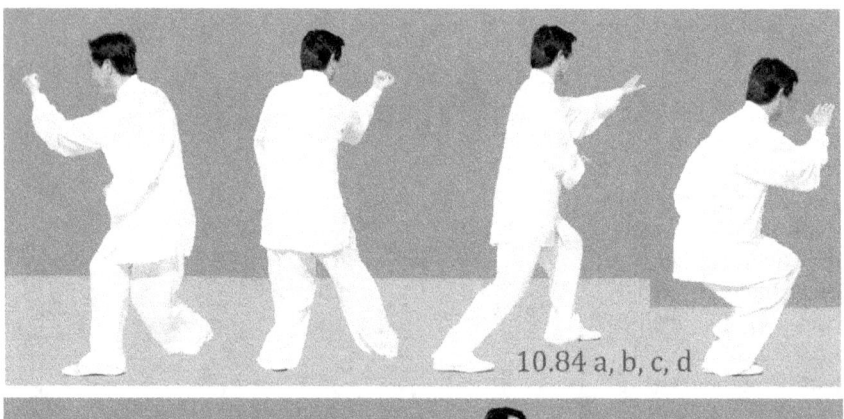

10.84 a, b, c, d

(g from angle)   10.84 e, f, g, h

CHAPTER TEN: THE TWELVE ANIMAL MODELS 171

- The key to the *four-cornered monkey model* method is to use the hook-in step to turn the body around to face the correct direction.

    Starting facing south, the first *monkey scratches its mark* turns to face northwest. Advance with *monkey scrambles up a pole* to the northwest.

    The second *monkey scratches its mark* turns around one-eighty to face southeast. Be sure to hook-out and hook-in well to get the body turned around to face southeast. Advance with *monkey scrambles up a pole* to the southeast.

    The third *monkey scratches its mark* turns to face southwest. Advance with *monkey scrambles up a pole* to the southwest.

    Then the fourth *monkey scratches its mark* turns to face northeast.

    The last *monkey scratches its mark* turns to face south for the closing.

- The *four-cornered monkey model* depends on getting the *monkey scratches its mark* turning to the correct angles, and this depends on the hook-out and hook-in steps.

- The monkey model alternates left and right sides, and the actions are the same as described, just transposing left and right. There is no limit to how many you do, just wait until you are back at the starting point facing in the starting direction in a left *santishi* to close the form.

Pointers

- To start from *santishi*, withdraw the left foot and pull back the left hand together, then do a hook-out step with the left foot and drill and hook the left hand together.

- Hook-in the right foot to turn the body around with it. Retreat the left foot a long step, and be quick. Withdraw the right foot quickly as well, and land firmly.

- The hand action of *monkey pulls at its leash* must be fast, with the hands and feet working together.

- Push off strongly with the hopping leg to cover distance. If pushing off the left leg, drive the right leg forward and thread the left hand forward at the same time, so that the upper and lower actions work together.

- As the right foot lands the right hand should strike. The whole action should be continuous without any pause.

3.1e   Monkey Closing Move   shōu shì   收势

ACTION: Once you get back to the starting place in left *santishi*, close as you would normally.

3.2 METHOD TWO: STRAIGHT LINE MONKEY MODEL

zhí tàng hóu xíng   直趟猴形

This method is made up of *present fruit, push a boat, pluck a peach, drop off a branch, kick, sit on haunches,* and *pull a rope*. The actions differ from the *four-cornered monkey model*, but the intent and mood are the same. Start from left *santishi*.

3.2a   White Ape Presents Fruit   bái yuán xiàn guǒ   白猿献果

ACTION: Advance the left foot a half-step and follow in the right foot a half-step. Extend the right hand forward under the left hand, both palms angled down. Draw a small circle with each hand outward and then bring them in front of the chest with the wrists sticking together, palms forward. As the left foot advances, carry with the palms forward and up to jaw height. Look forward. (images 10.85, 10.86)

3.2b   Push a Boat Downstream   shùn shuǐ tuī zhōu   顺水推舟

ACTION 1: Take a step forward with the right foot without moving the left foot, turning the right foot out as it lands. Turn the palms down and pull down and back, the left hand stopping in front of the body and the right hand pulling back to beside the waist. Press the head up and look forward. (image 10.87)

ACTION 2: Step the left foot forward and follow in a half-step with the right foot. Close the elbows together and push forward with the left hand leading and the right hand at the left elbow. Push to chest height with the palms forward and the fingers pointing up. Look forward. (image 10.88)

CHAPTER TEN: THE TWELVE ANIMAL MODELS

3.2c Ape Plucks a Peach yuánhóu zhāi táo 猿猴摘桃

ACTION: Advance the left foot a half-step and follow in a half-step with the right foot. Do a covering press forward and down with the left hand, palm down and turned crossways. Turn the right hand's thumb web forward and extend it forward above the left hand to neck height with the fingers closed slightly. Keep the arm slightly bent. Look at the right hand and reach with the body forward slightly into the action. (image 10.89)

3.2d Ape Drops off a Branch yuánhóu zhuì zhī 猿猴坠枝

ACTION: Step the right foot forward with the foot turned outward crossways, lifting the left heel in place. Turn the right hand palm out, thumb down, and stretch the thumb web to grab and pull back at the right side of the head. Turn the left hand palm up to carry until the left elbow is in front of the chest. Keep a backward drawing action towards the right with both hands. Sit down slightly. Look past the left hand. (image 10.90)

3.2e Ape Kicks a Branch yuánhóu dēng zhī 猿猴蹬枝

ACTION: Shift forward onto the right leg and lift the left knee to kick forward with the ball of the foot. Kick to chest height and keep the supporting leg slightly bent. Do not move the hands. Look in the direction of the kick. You may also kick with the heel. (image 10.91)

174   MONKEY, *HOU XING*

3.2f   Monkey Turns and Sits on its Haunches

zhuànshēn hóu dūn   转身猴蹲

ACTION: Bring the left foot back quickly, as soon as it completes the kick, landing hooked in just outside the right foot to turn around two-seventy degrees to the right. Shift onto the left foot. Lift the right foot with the ball of the foot on the ground and sit down slightly. When you turn around, swing the arm to chop with the right hand then pull the hand back to the right side with the palm down. Extend the left hand to reach forward as the body turns around, with the left elbow at the sternum and the palm down. Angle the right shoulder to the front. Look past the left hand. (images 10.92, 10.93)

3.2g   Monkey Pulls at its Leash   yuánhóu dáo shéng   猿猴才到 绳

ACTION: Advance the right foot a step and follow in the left foot a half-step. Extend the left hand to the front, then do a covering press down and pull it back. Lift the right elbow and thread it forward over the left hand, then hook and pull it back to the belly. Chop the left hand forward to chest height. Press the head up and look forward. (image 10.94)

3.2h   White Ape Presents Fruit   báiyuán xiàn guǒ   白猿献果

ACTION: This is similar to movement 3.2a, just transposing right and left.

- Continue on, doing the movements on the other side.

Pointers:

  o   The hands and feet work together. As the foot advances a half-step the hands need to complete their action. As the right foot steps forward the hands need to complete the action of pulling back. As the left foot steps forward the hands complete the push forward.

- o The left hand completes the covering press down as the right hand strikes forward and the feet advance and follow-in.
- o *Monkey drops off a branch* and *monkey kicks a branch* are completed as one move with no pause in between.
- o To do the turn around, the hook-in step needs to turn well in. Turn the body quickly. Move the hands as the turn is being done.
- o All the moves should be linked together smoothly without undue pauses between them.

3.2i   Straight Line Monkey Model Turn Around

hóu xíng zhuànshēn   猴形转身

This is a *monkey turns and sits on its haunches*.

- If the left foot has just kicked, quickly withdraw it and land it hooked-in inside the right foot, turning the body around one-eighty degrees. Then go back with *monkey pulls on its leash*.
- If the right foot has just kicked, quickly withdraw it and land it hooked-in inside the left foot, turning the body around one-eighty degrees. Then go back with *monkey pulls on its leash*.

3.2j   Monkey Model Closing Move   shōu shì   收势

Continue with *straight line monkey model* until you are at your starting place in *monkey pulls at its leash*. If the right foot and hand are forward then move forward to form a left *santishi*, then close the form. If the left foot and hand are forward then simply close the form.

PROBLEMS OFTEN MET IN THE MONKEY MODEL

Monkey to Four Corners

PROBLEM 1: The student goes in the wrong direction.

CORRECTIONS: The key to advancing in the correct direction is to get the feet to hook-out and hook-in to the correct angles.

PROBLEM 2: The student does not coordinate the feet and hands when doing the *monkey drops back and sits on its haunches*.

CORRECTIONS: More practice, reminding the student that when the foot reaches back the hand stretches forward. The move should be light and agile.

PROBLEM 3: The student does not coordinate the hands and feet well during *monkey pulls at its leash*.

CORRECTIONS: Have the student do some hands only practice. For example, left, right, left. Then add the footwork; remind the student that when the right hand reaches forward the right foot steps forward.

PROBLEM 4: During *monkey climbs a pole*, the student doesn't jump very far or doesn't land firmly.

CORRECTIONS: The cause of a short jump is not getting the correct angle at takeoff. Be sure to press the knee of the push-off leg forward and down, bringing the shank to a tight angle to the ground. Move the weight forward and then jump. Use the other knee to forcefully drive forward. Have the student practise just the jump for a while to gain more distance. Bend the knee when landing and grab the ground with the toes to maintain good stability.

Straight Line Monkey

PROBLEM 1: The student makes too big a circle with the hands for *ape presents fruit*.

CORRECTIONS: Remind the student to first cross the wrists. When each hand does its circle, the forearms should move only a little. The fingers circle out, and the circle is only a twenty centimetre diameter.

PROBLEM 2: The student places the hands too far apart for the carry action in the *ape presents fruit*.

CORRECTIONS: Remind the student to keep the wrists close together, no more than ten centimetres apart. The key lies in closing the elbows in. The wrists may touch, but this depends on the flexibility of the student. The movement needs to be natural and strong.

PROBLEM 3: When doing *push the boat*, the student leaves too long a time gap between the pull back and down and the push forward and strike.

CORRECTIONS: Remind the student that the pull down is the power gathering movement in order to launch force forward. When loading back to launch power forward, the action needs to be continuous or else the energy will dissipate.

PROBLEM 4: The student pushes with straight arms or hunches the shoulders when doing *ape plucks fruit*.

CORRECTIONS: Remind the student to keep the elbows bent slightly and to settle the shoulders down. Urge the shoulders forward into the push.

PROBLEM 5: The student lets the hip go forward on the kick, or the supporting leg is unstable.

CORRECTIONS: To do the kick, the student should first lift the knee and then snap the kick from the knee as a snap kick or a thrust kick. If the student

CHAPTER TEN: THE TWELVE ANIMAL MODELS

grabs the ground with the supporting foot and keeps the knee bent, then he will be more stable.

PROBLEM 6: The student is unstable on the *monkey turns around and sits on its haunches*.

CORRECTIONS: The first thing to check is that the hooking-in foot is placed in the correct position and at the proper angle. In addition, check that the turn around movement is not too forceful, and that the centre of gravity does not move about too much. To be stable on the squat, flex the waist and tuck in the body, lowering the buttocks and flexing the knees. The non-supporting leg's foot should touch the ground in the correct place to help maintain stability.

POWER GENERATION FOR THE MONKEY MODEL

Monkey to Four Corners

- In training the monkey model you should seriously consider what I stated earlier – that you should seek the mood and the actions of the monkey. You should express the monkey's agility and lightness, its ability to spin quickly and leap, the speed and agility of its body and hand actions.

Monkey scratches its mark: For the first move, the lead hand comes back then drills up, and then turns out, all actions done as the lead foot comes in then does the hook-out step. The body technique uses integrated body action with no slackness – pre-load right to go left, pre-load left to go right, and pre-load back to go forward.

Hook-in step, turn around: Use the waist to draw the shoulders around. Withdraw the foot to the rear with a large jump, by shooting back the rear leg and pushing off strongly with the lead foot. Land firmly and squat down. Reach the hand forward as you withdraw the foot.

Monkey pulls at its leash: The hands draw vertical circles continuously in front of the body – one back and the other forward, one up and the other down – so they need to be coordinated. The last palm action is a forward split, and it must land exactly as the foot lands.

Monkey climbs a pole is done with continuous power. The advancing footwork and the hand actions are fast. The hop goes for distance, and the landing is stable. As one leg pushes off, the other leg needs to drive the knee to put more power into the hop. When the hands thread forward, the palms should slide against each other with some friction. They strike to eye height, focusing on the face.

Straight Line Monkey

White ape presents fruit: As the hands circle in front of the body, the movement should be small and the body should tuck in a little by closing the chest. Keep the arms rounded. The movement has a hidden wrapping and bracing power. When the forearms rotate, they lift up as they turn, and this action is done as the foot steps forward. When the hands push and carry up, settle the shoulders and bring the elbows together with a wrapping power. Press into the lower back to urge the shoulders to send the carrying action up.

Push a boat downstream: The hands pull and lead back as the rear foot steps forward. When the foot lands with a stomping action, press the head up to get a charging forward power. The step forward and push uses a closing power in the hands, bringing the elbows together and lengthening the lower back to urge and release power forward. The forward step goes for distance, and the follow-in step needs to be quick.

Monkey picks a peach: The lead hand does a cover and a press down as the rear hand extends forward. The rear shoulder should urge forward into the action and the weight should shift forward. The thumb web reaches forward, with the thumb and fingers hooked as if grabbing someone's neck.

Monkey kicks a branch is also called *monkey moves a branch*. The lead hand turns and draws a small circle, which is a hooking and pulling action as it twists. The rear hand does a lifting carry upwards, so the elbow must stay tucked down. The feet and hands must advance together in order to fully use the power of the waist and shoulders.

To do the kick first lift the knee. Kick with either the ball of the foot or the heel. Keep the supporting leg slightly bent and grab the ground with the foot to stand steadily.

Monkey turns around and sits on its haunches: This turns sideways to the line of action. One leg is bent to ninety degrees and the other touches the ball of the foot on the ground just beside the supporting leg. Flex the lower back and tuck in the torso, close in the chest and shoulder area. When the hand chops towards the back, relax the shoulders and use the shoulders to lead the elbows, the elbows to lead the hand. The key to turning to the correct direction lies in the amount of hook-in that the foot does and the placement of the foot on landing after the kick. If the foot lands hooked-in just inside the supporting foot, then the body turns around to the direction in which you just came. If the foot lands hooked-in outside the supporting foot, then this is a 'big turning' that allows you to continue on in the same direction. The 'big turning' can also be done as a jump, and should be light and agile.

BREATHING CYCLE FOR THE MONKEY MODEL

It is vital to coordinate breathing with the actions. Mastery of correct breathing directly affects the quality of movement.

- Inhale during non power-launch actions.
- Exhale on power launching actions.
- The monkey model uses a number of breathing techniques to complete the actions with power. On turning, lead with the breath. On squatting, settle

CHAPTER TEN: THE TWELVE ANIMAL MODELS 179

the breath. On kicking, gather the breath. On pushing off to jump, lift the breath. During a jump, hold the breath. On landing, breathe out.

PRACTICAL APPLICATIONS FOR THE MONKEY MODEL

All of the techniques in the monkey model contain practical applications. These techniques can be practised separately to find how to use your power and to increase your combat effectiveness.

The small circle in *monkey presents fruit* is to release the grip of your opponent so that you can then use both hands to strike upwards into the jaw. The key is to get in close with your whole body.

Push the boat first draws the opponent down and back with both hands so that his oncoming punch loses its target and effectiveness. When the opponent then tries to pull his hand back, time your strike to use this action to push forward with both hands to drive him back. Push between the chest and the belly and step forward, lengthening the spine to launch full power.

Pluck fruit uses one hand to cover and press the opponent's hand down while the other hand grabs his throat. Close the fingers to choke and push forward with a pressing down power.

Drop off a branch uses both hands to hook onto the opponent's arm and pull along with his line of action to one side. The technique is meant to break his arm.

Kick the branch is a kick to the chest or ribs. It works best when combined with the arm controlling technique of *drop off a branch*.

Scratch a mark is a dodging action that hooks with one hand while finding an entrance for the other hand to strike the opponent's face. If there is a chance, then strike. If there isn't, then quickly retreat and try again. So the power is first contained then launched, waiting for an opportunity and adapting. The squat is a defensive move that stores the power, so be sure to use it in that way – to prepare for the attack.

Monkey pulls at its leash alternates both hands to pull down, and then to chop and push forward. Attack by entering the feet with the hands, going for the chest or face.

Climb the pole chases after the opponent. If he is backing up then take the opportunity to advance. Go for his eyes with the hands and for his groin or belly with the feet. Use the hands and feet together, hitting high and low.

- The monkey model often uses a threading action, attacking the eye area. It doesn't use a lot of power, but the speed and agility attacking to the eyes is sufficient to put an opponent off. This creates the opportunity to finish off more strongly with a heavier power.

MONKEY, *HOU XING*

THE POEM ABOUT THE MONKEY

猴形歌诀

猴形练灵起纵轻,

挂印倒绳爬竿能。

摘桃献果蹬枝法,

机警敏捷快如风。

The monkey model trains agility for leaping lightly, both high and far,

With the techniques of *scratch your mark*, *pull a rope*, and *climb a pole*.

The techniques *pluck a peach*, *present fruit*, and *kick a branch*,

Are all methods of creating opportunities and then taking advantage of them by being as quick as the wind.

FOUR: HORSE MODEL

马形

INTRODUCTION TO THE HORSE MODEL, *MA XING*

The classics say, "The horse has the skill of striking with its hooves. 'Striking with its hooves' means that as the horse gallops, its rear hooves overtake its front hooves. This is what it excels at." When training horse model, you need to push off the rear foot to drive the front foot forward, and then advance the rear foot with force. This footwork is called a gallop. To find the intent and mood of the horse, remember that when one horse takes the lead then all the horses in the herd will take to the gallop. A wild horse gallops forward fearlessly, there is nothing that it won't charge – it 'gallops through the mountain ranges like the wind.' When wild horses fight they kick with their hooves and charge straight in regardless of the consequences. They glare with eyes wide open. So when training horse model, you should express this gallop – charging in for distance – very fast and powerful. Moreover, your hand technique should express the charging in to hit. Your intent and power must be charging and penetrating. The hands and feet arrive together, working together with the power of the whole body.

METHODS OF PERFORMING THE HORSE MODEL

4.1 METHOD ONE: SINGLE HORSE   dānmǎ xíng   单马形

4.1a   Single Horse, Right Stance   yòubù dānmǎ xíng   右步单马形

Start from left *santishi*.

ACTION 1: Advance the left foot a half-step and lift the right foot beside the left ankle. Clench the hands and turn the fist hearts up in place. Thread the right fist forward under the left arm. Sink in the chest and settle the elbows. Look forward. (image 10.95)

ACTION 2: Take a long step forward with the right foot and follow in a half-step with the left foot. When the right fist reaches the left fist, turn both up and in so the fist hearts face down. Bend the elbows so that the right fist is in front of the right shoulder.

10.95

182 HORSE, *MA XING*

Step the right foot forward and strike forward with the right fist to chest height. Withdraw the left fist to behind the right elbow. Keep the elbows up, slightly lower than the shoulders. Keep the arms slightly bent. The fist hearts are down, the right fist surface is forward with the wrist slightly cocked. Look past the right fist. (images 10.96, 10.97, and 10.97 front)

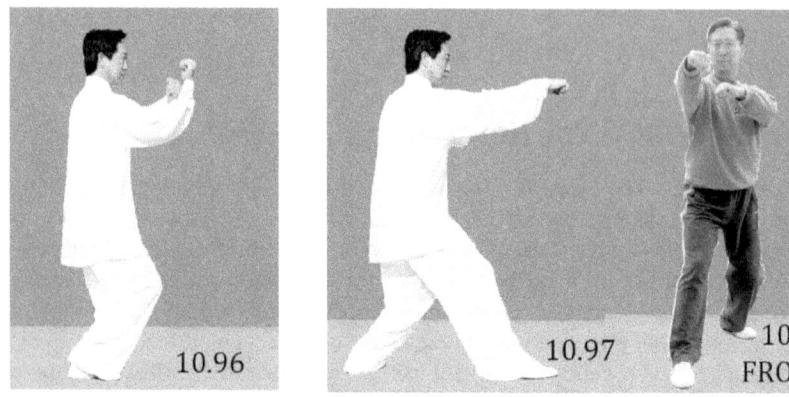

4.1b   Single Horse, Left Stance   zuǒbù dānmǎ xíng   左步单马形

ACTION 1: Advance the right foot a half-step and lift the left foot to beside the right ankle. Turn the fist hearts up, and bring the elbows in. Thread the left fist forward under the right arm. Sink in the chest and settle the elbows. Look forward. (image 10.98)

ACTION 2: Take a long step forward with the left foot and follow in a half-step with the right foot. When the threading left fist reaches the right fist, turn them up and in so the fist hearts face down in front of the left shoulder. Step the left foot forward and strike forward with the left fist to chest height. Pull the right fist back behind the left elbow, in front of the left shoulder. Keep the arms slightly curved. The left fist surface is forward with the wrist slightly cocked. Look at the left fist. (images 10.99, 10.100)

CHAPTER TEN: THE TWELVE ANIMAL MODELS

Pointers

- As you advance the lead foot you must complete two actions with the hands; threading the rear fist through and also rolling the fists.
- As the rear foot comes through to charge forward, you must charge forward with the hand strike, hitting with full, integrated power.
- Keep the elbows tucked in on the midline throughout the whole movement.

4.1c   Single Horse Turn Around   dānmǎ huíshēn shì   单马回身式

ACTION 1: If you are in the *right stance single horse*, with the right foot forward, first take a half-step forward with the right foot, hooked in, and shift to the right leg. Turn around to the left, lifting the left foot by the right ankle. Turn a full one-eighty degrees to face back in the way from which you came. Bring the left fist down to the chest and lift the right fist to nose height with the elbow bent. Both fist hearts face in, hooking and knocking across to the left with the body turn. Look forward. (image 10.101)

ACTION 2: Step straight forward with the left foot and follow in a half-step with the right. Keep moving the left fist around with the turn, bringing the fist in to in front of the shoulder, fist heart down. Then strike forward to chest height as the left foot steps forward. The right fist finishes just behind the left elbow. Both fist hearts are down, and the elbows are bracing slightly outward with the arms forming arcs. Look at the left fist. (image 10.102)

10.101   10.102

- To turn from the *left stance single horse*, just transpose right and left while following the directions.

Pointers:

- When taking the hook-in step to turn around, be sure to take a half-step forward. Hook in the foot as much as possible. The body turns around by using the hooking footwork and turning the waist.
- Turn around quickly and bring the fists and arms around with the body.

4.1d Single Horse Closing Move   dānmǎ shōushì   单马收势

- From *single horse, left stance*.

ACTION 1: Withdraw the left foot a half-step to in front of the right foot. Bend the left wrist to cover and press down, pulling back to the belly. Drill the right fist forward and up to nose height. Look forward.

ACTION 2: Advance the left foot forward without moving the right foot, to take a *santi* stance. Do a splitting palm with the left hand and pull the right hand back to the belly. Look forward. The rest of the move is the same as *closing move* from left *santishi*.

- From *single horse, right stance*.

ACTION 1: Withdraw the right foot a half-step to beside the left foot and shift onto the right leg. Pull the right fist back to the belly then drill forward and up to nose height. Cover and press down with the left fist, pulling back to the belly. Press the head up and look forward.

ACTION 2: Advance the left foot forward without moving the right foot, to take a *santi* stance. Do a splitting palm with the left hand and pull the right hand back to the belly. Look forward. The rest of the move is the same as *closing move* from left *santishi*.

Pointers

- Withdraw the lead foot at exactly the same time as you drill the right fist forward.
- Land the left foot at exactly the same time as you split with the left hand.

4.2   METHOD TWO: DOUBLE HORSE

shuāngmǎ xíng   双马形

Start from left *santishi*.

4.2a   Double Horse, Right Stance

yòubù shuāngmǎ xíng   右步双马形

ACTION 1: Clench the left hand and pull it back to the belly, clenching the right hand as well. Turn the fist hearts up and lift them to the sternum, then drill forward to nose height. Do not hesitate after drilling up, but pound down with the fist hearts up, and lead them back to beside either hip. Advance the left foot a half-step and lift the right foot beside the left ankle.

10.103

Press the head up and look forward. (images 10.103, 10.104)

ACTION 2: Take a long step forward with the right foot and follow in a half-step with the left foot. Bend the elbows to bring the fists up in front of either shoulder, turning the fists so the fist hearts are down, fist surfaces forward, wrists slightly tucked, and elbows raised. Strike forward from in front of the face to chest height. Keep the arms slightly bent, the fists about an inch apart. Press the head up and look forward. (images 10.105, 10.106)

4.2b   Double Horse, Left Stance   zuǒbù shuāng mǎ xíng   左步双马形

ACTION 1: Advance the right foot a half-step and lift the left foot beside the right ankle. Turn the fists over so that the fist hearts face up and tuck in the elbows. Circle the fists forward and down to either hip with the fist hearts up. Press the head up and look forward. (images 10.107, 10.108)

ACTION 2: Take a long step forward with the left foot and follow in a half-step with the right foot. Raise the fists from the hips to in front of the shoulders by bending the elbows and turning the fists so that the fist hearts face down and the fist surfaces face forward with the wrists slightly cocked and the elbows out at shoulder height. Strike forward to chest height, keeping the arms slightly bent, the fists about an inch apart. Press the head up and look forward. (images 10.109, 10.110)

Pointers

- Pound down with the fists as the lead foot advances.
- Strike forward with the fists as the foot lands, using whole body power.

4.2c   Double Horse Turn Around   shuāngmǎ huíshēn shì   双马回身式

Using the *right double horse* as example.

ACTION 1: Hook-in the right foot and turn the body around to the left to face around in the opposite direction. Shift onto the right leg and lift the left foot beside the right ankle. Turn the fists over so the fist hearts face up, and tuck the elbows in. Circle the fists forward and down to beside either hip, fist hearts up. Press the head up and look forward. (image 10.111)

ACTION 2: Step the left foot forward and follow in a half-step with the right foot. Lift the elbows to bring the fists up in front of the shoulders. Turn the fists so that the fist hearts face down, fist surfaces facing forward and wrists cocked. The elbows are raised to about shoulder height. Strike forward with both fists to chest height, keeping the arms slightly bent, and the fists about an inch apart. Press the head up and look forward. (image 10.112)

- The action of *double horse turn around* is the same whether on the right or left side, just transpose the right and left actions.

Pointers

- Be sure to hook the lead foot well around. Turn quickly and bring the other foot in quickly to the supporting ankle. The whole movement must be well coordinated.
- Step forward quickly after turning around. Punch with force, and with whole body integration.
- Do the whole move as one action without interruption.

4.2d Double Horse Closing Move   shuāngmǎ xíng shōushì   双马形收势

Using the *left* double horse as example.

ACTION 1: Step the right foot forward to stomp beside the left foot, lifting the left foot to the right ankle and keeping the knees together. First pull the right fist back to the right waist with the fist heart up. Tuck and press the left fist down and drill the right fist forward and up to nose height while pulling the left fist back to the belly. Look at the right fist. (image 10.113)

ACTION 2: Advance the left foot a half-step without moving the right foot, to take a *santi* stance. Hit out with a splitting palm with the left hand, the same as the *standard split*. (image 10.114)

10.113

10.114

- The closing of *double horse* is the same as that of *single horse*, that is: drill the right fist out, stomp the right foot, then split with the left hand and left foot forward. The only difference is that you are starting out with the right hand in a different place, which makes the movement different. You need to consider this carefully and get a feel for it.
- There are other versions of *double horse*. In them, the fists perform a double hit the same as described above, but the actions prior to the hit and the stepping differ. Both methods are traditional.

    One is to pound down with both fists, drawing back, then turn them over and hit forward. The fists follow a vertical circle down and back.

188 HORSE, *MA XING*

The other is to turn each fist over independently at either side, completing a horizontal circle, then hit forward.

4.3 METHOD THREE: DODGING HORSE

yáoshēn mǎ xíng 摇身马形

Start from left *santishi*.

4.3a   Dodge to Right (Single) Horse yáoshēn yòu mǎ xíng 摇身右马形

ACTION 1: Advance the left foot diagonally to the forward left a half-step and lift the right foot to beside the left ankle. Extend the right hand forward with the palm down and fingers forward. When it reaches the left hand, circle both hands forward to the right and pull to beside the right ribs. Press the head up and look in the direction to which you will punch. (images 10.115, 10.116)

ACTION 2: Take a long step forward with the right foot and follow in a half-step with the left foot. Clench fists and lift them in front of the right shoulder, fist hearts down and fist surfaces forward, wrists slightly cocked. Punch forcefully forward and down to chest height. Hit with the left fist behind the right elbow, and keep the right arm slightly bent. Look past the right fist. (image 10.117)

4.3b   Dodge to Left (Single) Horse yáoshēn zuǒ mǎ xíng 摇身左马形

ACTION 1: Advance the right foot a half-step diagonally to the forward right and follow in the left foot to beside the right ankle. Unclench the hands with the palms down. Extend the left hand forward of the right hand and circle both hands leftwards to beside the left ribs. Shift the body a bit to the right front. Look at both hands. (image 10.118)

ACTION 2: Take a long step forward with the left foot and follow in with the right foot a half-step. Clench the hands and lift them in front of the left shoulder, fist hearts down and fist surfaces forward, wrists slightly cocked. Punch the left fist forcefully forward to chest height. Punch with the right fist to behind the left elbow. Keep the left arm slightly bent. Press the head up and look forward. (image 10.119)

10.118

10.119

- Right and left are the same. Continue to repeat according to your fitness and the size of your training area.

Pointers

  o When the lead foot steps out diagonally the body should dodge at a bit of an angle to show a characteristic dodging right and left.

  o When the lead foot steps diagonally the hands hook and pull to the opposite side.

  o The fists punch with the final step, landing at exactly the same time.

4.3c Dodging Horse Turn Around yáoshēn mǎ xíng huíshēn 摇身马形回身

Describing with the <u>left</u> *dodging horse* as example.

ACTION 1: Advance the left foot a half-step with the foot hooked in. Turn the body around one-eighty degrees to the right to face back in the direction you just came. Lift the right foot to beside the left foot and shift onto the left leg. As the body turns around, circle the right fist around to the right, keeping it at chest height with the elbow at shoulder height. Bring the left fist around with it, both fist hearts down. Look at the left fist. (image 10.120)

10.120

ACTION 2: Take a long step forward with the right foot and follow in a half-step with the left foot. Continue to circle the right fist to bring it just in front of the right shoulder. As the right foot advances, strike out with the right fist to chest height. Hit with the left fist just inside the right elbow. Look past the right fist (image 10.121)

- The turn is similar whether turning from right or left position.

Pointers

  ○ Pointers for *dodging horse turn around* are the same as those for *single horse turn around*.

4.3d Dodging Horse Closing Move

yáoshēn mǎ xíng shōushì　　摇身马形收势

- The action of *dodging horse* closing is the same as that of *single horse* closing.

4.4 METHOD FOUR: REVERSE STANCE HORSE

àobù mǎ xíng　　拗步马形

Start from left *santishi*.

4.4a Reverse Stance Right (Single) Horse　àobù yòu mǎ xíng　拗步右马形

ACTION 1: Take a long step forward with the right foot and lift the left foot beside the right ankle, keeping the knees together. Thread the right hand over the left arm with the palm up, and, when it reaches the left hand, clench both fists. Lift the right hand up and bend the elbow to draw the fist back to in front of the right shoulder, turning the fist heart down. Turn and cock the left fist with the fist heart down in front of the right shoulder. Press the head up and look forward. (image 10.122)

ACTION 2: Take a long step forward with the left foot and follow in the right foot a half-step. Strike forward with the right fist to chest height, fist heart down and wrist slightly cocked, arm slightly bent. The left fist finishes behind the right elbow with the

arm rounded and fist heart down. Look past the right fist. (image 10.123)

4.4b Reverse Stance Left (Single) Horse àobù zuǒ mǎ xíng 拗步左马形

ACTION 1: Advance the left foot a half-step and lift the right foot beside the left ankle. Unclench the hands and lift them to nose height, drawing them forward and down in a brushing action. As they arrive in front of the left shoulder, clench into fists. Press the head up and look forward. (image 10.124)

ACTION 2: Take a long step forward with the right foot and follow in a half-step with the left. Punch the left fist forward to chest height, punching the right fist to behind the left elbow. Both fist hearts are down and the left wrist is slightly cocked with the arm bent. Press the head up and look forward. (image 10.125)

Pointers

- The pointers are the same as the standard *single horse*, described above. Only the stance is different.

4.4c Reverse Stance Horse Turn Around

àobù mǎ xíng huíshēn   拗步马形回身

Starting from *reverse stance <u>right</u> horse*.

ACTION 1: Hook-in the left foot in front of the right toes and turn the body around towards the right to face back in the direction from which you came. Lift the right foot, unclench the hands and brush forward and down toward the left

192 HORSE, *MA XING*

shoulder. Clench the hands, press the head up and look forward. (image 10.126)

ACTION 2: Take a long step forward with the right foot and follow in the left foot a half-step. Punch out into a *reverse stance left single horse* as described above. (image 10.127)

- Turning to the left or right is similar, just transpose right and left in the description.

4.4d   Reverse Stance Horse Closing Move

àobù mǎ xíng shōushì   拗步马形收势

- The action of *reverse stance horse closing move* is the same as that of *single horse model closing move*.

PROBLEMS OFTEN MET IN THE HORSE MODEL

PROBLEM 1: The student takes only a small step forward with the rear foot.

CORRECTIONS: Remind the student to charge forward as he brings the rear foot through, thinking of flying forward. When the lead foot takes its half-step forward, press the knee of the rear leg down to minimize the angle of the shank with the ground. This increases the power for the forward drive as it brings the shank as close to horizontal as possible. The student needs to work on leg strength to be able to use this type of power.

PROBLEM 2: The student moves the hands separately from the body when he does the hand circles.

CORRECTIONS: Remind the student that all hand actions work in concert with the body. The actions should be practised slowly at first to search for the feeling and find the coordination between the body and the hands. When the hands draw a vertical circle, the torso should lengthen and tuck slightly, When the hands draw a horizontal circle, the torso should move slightly forward and back. This is the specific way in which the body can assist power output, according to the principles of biomechanics.

PROBLEM 3: The student does not dodge the body when doing *dodging horse*, but simply moves the arms or feet.

CORRECTIONS: Remind the student that the stepping should be diagonal, and

CHAPTER TEN: THE TWELVE ANIMAL MODELS 193

that the body should shift immediately to the lead leg. The head should lead the action, and the body should lean slightly forward so that, when the hands do their action, the whole body shows a dodging action.

PROBLEM 4: The student steps to the side when doing the *reverse stance horse*.

CORRECTIONS: Remind the student to step straight forward, both with the lead foot and the rear foot as it strides through. Bring the rear foot in to lightly touch the ankle of the supporting leg, to ensure that the legs do not open up while stepping.

POWER GENERATION FOR THE HORSE MODEL

Single Horse

There are a variety of ways to perform *single horse* – some punch with the lead fist heart up, some punch with the fist tucked to ram straight, and some punch with an upright fist. These differences have come about as each teacher passed on what he learned. Looking at the action of a horse and thinking of imitating the horse's ability, I feel that the true way is to punch straight with the wrist cocked.

The footwork for the horse must cover distance and have good speed, using the rear foot to drive and the front foot to charge. This shows the galloping skill of the horse, its attitude of 'chasing the wind and the moon without relief'.

- When the rear fist threads under the lead arm you should stretch the upper back and close the chest, settling the elbow and tucking the lower back.
- When the fist rises and rolls back you should lengthen the lower back and pull the shoulder back slightly.
- When the fist turns over and punches forward, you should urge the shoulder forward, solidify the body core, and breathe out when you release power. This is done as the lead foot lands, using whole body power.

Double Horse: The double horse is a double pounding, shoving punch. Keep the body square to punch equally with both fists. When the fists turn over to punch down, urge the shoulders forward and drop the elbows, press the head up, and use the elbows to lead the fists down. At this time lengthen the lower back slightly and open the chest slightly, as if barging with the chest. When you lift the fists in front of the face, lift the elbows to shoulder height to store power, then when you turn, tuck, and charge the fists forward, close the chest, urge the shoulders forward, solidify the lower back, and extend the arms. Coordinate this with an expulsion of breath to assist releasing power. Fortifying the body core sets it back – using the kidney area to urge the shoulders, the shoulders to urge the elbows, and the elbows to drive the fists.

Dodging Horse

The footwork of *dodging horse* takes the body to the side by stepping the lead foot to an angle as the body dodges to the angle, then the rear foot comes through to stride straight forward. Be sure when dodging the body to the forward angle to first tuck it back a bit – this is Xingyiquan's characteristic 'dropping back to go forward, loading right to go left'. Use the waist as the fulcrum to lead the shoulders so that the shoulders move the arms. This keeps the whole body connected so that the whole body dodges.

The hand technique of the dodging action is: both hands hook and pull down and back, and then lift and hit forward and down, drawing a large circle. When pulling down and back, be sure to use the power of the waist by settling the shoulders and elbows, so that the shoulders are moved by the lower back, the elbows are moved by the shoulders, and the hands follow the elbows. This is a full, whole body power, and the hands and feet work together.

Reverse Stance Horse

The *reverse stance horse* draws a vertical circle with the hands in front of the body.

The *dodging horse* draws a horizontal circle.

The *single horse* draws a vertical circle up from below.

The *double horse* draws a vertical circle down from above. There is a different double horse that draws a horizontal circle at the sides.

- All variations of horse model have the same essential point: all pound forward. This is the key to horse model, the true meaning of horse model, and what shows the sense of the horse.

- The horse model is a complete action and must be done as one movement without a pause in the middle of the action. It should be completed in one breath. You may pause at the end of the strike.

BREATHING CYCLE FOR THE HORSE MODEL

All the variations of horse model use the same breathing pattern.

- Inhale as the lead foot advances a half-step and the hands circle.

- Exhale to launch your power as the rear foot comes through to stride forward and land, as the hands strike forward.

PRACTICAL APPLICATIONS FOR THE HORSE MODEL

The horse model, whichever one you use, is a charging shove or ram into the opponent, to strike the head, chest, ribs, or whatever opportunity presents. You can strike with one or both fists. The key lies in getting in close to the opponent, to get within his space.

- *Single horse* first hooks any oncoming attack up, then rolls over, tucking and hitting into the chest area. The key is to step through to the opponent's groin area. You may also hook and press the opponent's attack down, then hit.

Speed is essential in the horse model.

- *Double horse* knocks the opponent's arms down with both hands, then moves the body in to shove or strike the chest with both fists. It can also be a double hook to separate the opponent's arms to make a space to strike through to the centre.
- *Dodging horse* steps forward while dodging to the side, dropping the body out of the way, then stepping in to attack the face. You can use it as you like, as long as you drive in hard so that the opponent loses all ability to react.
- *Reverse stance horse* slaps the opponent's hands down and then moves quickly in to strike.

The horse model can also be used as a defensive counter-attack. The forearms can press down on the opponent's arms so that his punch cannot be realized and you can get the strike in. This is an effective technique, but you can't do it unless you have trained deep skills and can fiercely drive in, totally committed.

THE POEM ABOUT THE HORSE

马形歌诀

马形练疾击碏功，

单双摇拗扬威名。

横冲直撞栽拳打，

勇猛向前意在冲。

The horse model develops speed and the ability to gallop.

Whether single, double, dodging or reverse, all are famous for their prowess.

Charge across and pound straight in with the fists.

Drive forward bravely, focused only on the charge.

FIVE: ALLIGATOR MODEL

鼍形

INTRODUCTION TO THE ALLIGATOR MODEL, *TUO XING*

The alligator is amphibious but lives mostly in the water. It is very strong and fierce, and an excellent swimmer. Its skill is 'swimming in the water and conquering the waves' and its special ability is 'overturning rivers and seas.' For this reason, the masters chose to imitate its skills. When training alligator model the intent should be that of diving straight through ever-oncoming waves of a river or the sea. If you move quickly then it is like overturning the river or sea, separating the waters. If you move slowly then it like swimming in a slow winding current, following the natural flow of the stream; you go slowly and naturally like resting in your own home. The alligator model can change anytime from up or down, left or right, forward or backward, fast or slow. It always maintains the feeling of swimming in water.

When practising, use the waist as the fulcrum and sweep the arms left and right from it. The footwork goes forward in a zigzag. The hand technique twists, rolls, drills and turns over. The whole body works together and turns naturally. Attack and defense are hidden in the actions, and a short power is hidden in the slow action. Hard and soft intermingle, and the whole form is very natural.

METHODS OF PERFORMING ALLIGATOR MODEL

5.1 STANDARD ALLIGATOR: ADVANCING ALLIGATOR
jìnbù tuó xíng   进步鼍形

5.1a Advancing Left Alligator

jìnbù tuó xíng zuǒshì   进步鼍形左势

Start from left *santishi*.

ACTION 1: Shift back to the right leg and turn slightly right, pulling the left hand down to in front of the belly and withdrawing the left foot to in front of the right foot. Look at the left hand. (image 10.128)

10.128

CHAPTER TEN: THE TWELVE ANIMAL MODELS   197

ACTION 2: Step the left foot forty-five degrees to the forward left and bring the right foot in beside the left ankle without touching down (you may lightly touch the ball of the foot if you need to). Turn the left hand palm up and lift it in front of the chest. Then turn the palm down and brace out to the left at shoulder height. Bring the right hand to the

belly, palm up. Brace the left arm in a curve with the palm down and the elbow below the shoulder. Look at the left hand. (images 10.129 and 10.129 front)

5.1b Advancing Right Alligator   jìnbù tuó xíng yòushì   进步鼍形右势

ACTION: Take a step to the forward right with the right foot and follow in the left foot to beside the right ankle (you may touch down, but should not). Lift the right hand from the belly to the chest then turn it palm down to draw it across diagonally to the right to brace out at shoulder height with the elbow slightly below the shoulder. Lower the left hand and turn it palm up in front of the belly. Look at the right hand. (images 10.130 and 10.130 front)

Pointers

- Pay attention to the angle when stepping the lead foot forward. You should step in a zigzag pattern and land firmly, following in with the rear foot quickly.

- The left foot and hand should arrive together, as should the right foot and hand. Use the waist to draw the shoulders across, the shoulders to draw the elbows, and the elbows to draw the hands.

- The whole action should be coordinated and flow without a break. The arms should work together to draw circles. The bodywork should move forward and back, right and left with the zigzag footwork. The move should have both fast and slow actions within it.

- o You should move softly. You should not release any hard power.

5.1c Alligator Turn Around   tuó xíng huíshēn   鼍形回身势

The *turn around* is always the same movement, whether starting from left or right side, or from advancing or retreating.

ACTION 1: The stepping foot hooks out as it lands. The other foot steps again and hooks in, pointing to the toes of the lead foot. Turn the body around to face the direction from which you just came. The hands continue to move in relation to the feet – when the left foot lands the left hand braces out, when the right foot lands the right hand braces out. The whole action is the same as usual. (image 10.131)

ACTION 2: When turning from a *retreating alligator*, instead of retreating again, step forward with the foot hooked out. Then step the other foot hooked in outside the foot that just landed and turn the body around. Keep the arms moving with the feet the same as usual. Keep the whole body coordinated and follow the action of the hands with the eyes. (image 10.132)

- Right and left actions are similar.

Pointers

- o Be sure to first hook-out and then hook-in with the feet. Turn quickly and be sure to get turned completely around.
- o Maintain coordination between the body, feet and hands to continue the alligator action as you turn.

5.1d Alligator Closing Move   tuó xíng shōushì   鼍形收势

When you reach your starting point in left *alligator*.

ACTION 1: Step the right foot straight forward and follow in the left foot to beside the right ankle without touching down. Clench the right hand and drill it up to nose height, turning over the ulnar edge. Bring the left hand back to the belly and clench it. Look at the right hand.

ACTION 2: Step the left foot forward without moving the right foot to sit into a *santi* stance. Perform a splitting palm with the left hand to take a *santishi*, and then finish as usual.

5.2 RETREATING ALLIGATOR   tuìbù tuó xíng   退步鼉形

Starting from left *santishi* or <u>left</u> *alligator*.

5.2a   Retreating Right Alligator   tuìbù tuó xíng yòushì   退步鼉形右势

ACTION: Shift the weight forward then step the right foot diagonally back to the right, and then shift onto the right leg. Lift the left foot beside the right ankle, or touch down if you need to. Turn the right hand palm up and bring it from the belly past the chest to the face and turn it palm down, then brace out to the forward right at shoulder height. Keep the right arm rounded to brace with the elbow a bit below shoulder height. Lower the left hand to the belly and turn it palm up. Look at the right hand. (images 10.133, 10.134)

- If starting out from <u>left</u> *alligator*, just directly step the right foot back to the right without first doing a forward shift.

5.2b   Retreating Left Alligator   tuìbù tuó xíng zuǒshì   退步鼉形左势

ACTION: Retreat the left foot to the rear left and shift onto the left leg, lifting the right foot beside the left ankle (or setting it down beside the left foot). Bring the left hand, palm up, past the chest to in front of the face then turn it palm down and draw it horizontally across to the left to brace out at shoulder height. Keep the left arm rounded to brace and keep the elbow lower than the shoulder. Lower the right hand and roll it to turn palm up in front of the belly. Look at the left hand. (images

10.135, 10.136)

Pointers

- When retreating, step at bit of an angle. Shift quickly but steadily.
- The hands must move together with the feet in a continuous, unbroken manner.

PROBLEMS OFTEN MET IN THE ALLIGATOR MODEL

PROBLEM 1: The student is stiff, not gentle.

CORRECTIONS: Remind the student to use intent instead of brute force. This must not be overdone, however, to the point of slackness. Keep the spirit full and reaching to all parts, but do not use brute strength.

PROBLEM 2: The student does not coordinate the hands with the feet, so that the step arrives before the hands, or the hands push out before the step.

CORRECTIONS: Remind the student to pay attention to the coordination between the hands and feet, and to practise over and over, paying close attention to the exact timing.

PROBLEM 3: The student has a weak, floating power.

CORRECTIONS: The first thing is to practise more. The second is to pay attention to using the body. Remind the student to lead all action from the lower back and body core, so that the waist is the axis. Then the student may connect the power to the shoulders and elbows.

PROBLEM 4: The student only pays attention to the lead hand and leaves the rear hand stiff or powerless.

CORRECTIONS: Once the action of the lead hand is correct, more attention must be paid to the rear hand. The hands must work together for the action to be completed properly. The rear hand should have a closing in power as it comes back to the body, rolling back with power.

PROBLEM 5: The student rises and falls in the steps.

CORRECTIONS: There may be some rise and fall between movements, but not too much. Remind the student to pay attention to the knees and to coordinate the stepping with bending the knees to the correct angle.

PROBLEM 6: The student blocks across with the elbows above shoulder height.

CORRECTIONS: Remind the student that when the elbows are up the shoulders shrug up. When the shoulders shrug then the *qi* cannot settle. So, the elbows must not rise above the shoulders, they must settle slightly below the shoulders.

POWER GENERATION FOR THE ALLIGATOR MODEL

- The alligator model moves back and forth without hesitation. It is rounded without slackness, and turns with agility. The intent and spirit are full and the power is subtle.

- You may practise the *advancing alligator* and *retreating alligator* together, advancing for a while, then retreating.

- The power is subtle, held in the intent. Be sure not to use brute force in the arms. The mind is focused but the body is relaxed. When power is connected to the mind then there will be no gaps, but it will flow continuously like swimming in water. Imagine the alligator swimming to guide your practice.

- Be sure to step to forty-five degrees when doing the advancing or retreating alligator. First land the foot, then bend the knee for stability and grab the ground with the toes. When the rear foot does the follow-in step, bring the knees together and sit down, pressing the head up.

- The hands need to act together – one up, one down; one out, one returning. They alternately rotate inward and outward, knocking across horizontally and rolling back in. Be sure to lead the action of the hands from the elbows, the action of the elbows from the shoulders, and the action of the shoulders from the waist. Be sure also to coordinate the hands with the feet.

- The point of contact of the horizontally blocking arm is the ulnar surface of the forearm and the outer edge of the palm. The arm should form an arc with the chest. Keep the chest contained and keep the elbow below shoulder level. The rear hand should lower with a rolling-in power, keeping the shoulder settled to maintain a closing, relaxed power.

- The centre of gravity needs to move with the footwork, right and left, backwards and forwards. Keep the waist agile and lead its movement with the head. Load right to move left, load left to move right. Practise this carefully and thoughtfully to find the power, keeping the whole body together without any slackening. The action should be gentle and show internal power.

BREATHING CYCLE FOR THE ALLIGATOR MODEL

The alligator model uses natural and unrestricted breathing, light and smooth. The movements are gentle and go along with natural breathing. Breathe with the action, but do not hold your breath or use brute force.

PRACTICAL APPLICATIONS FOR THE ALLIGATOR MODEL

Examining the structure of alligator model, the footwork moves in a zigzag pattern either forward or backward, while the hands circle to either side of the body. The goal of these actions is to dissipate an opponent's attacking force. So, it is mainly an evasive move. The angled stepping, whether forward or backward, avoids the attack of the opponent. The hands are held ready to grab, with the forefinger and thumb open and the other fingers hooked. The main technique is to hook onto the opponent's arm and pull, lead, or knock it across, so that the oncoming punch loses its effectiveness. The power of a pull or lead comes from the shoulders and elbows being well connected. There is a hidden attack in the lower hand, which can come through if opportunity presents. It can strike at will. You may also step forward and use the outer edge of the upper palm to cut at the opponent's neck. You may also step in close to strike with the elbow – remember the classics say that the elbow is also a striking surface.

THE POEM ABOUT THE ALLIGATOR

鼍形歌诀

鼍形意境游水中，

两臂拨水在腰功。

裹带钻翻加肘打，

进退曲折意先行。

The mood in the alligator model is to swim in the water.

The arms push aside the water using the power from the waist.

Wrap and draw, drill and turnover, adding in an elbow to strike.

To advance and retreat, bend and flex, the mind steps first.

SIX: CHICKEN MODEL

鸡形

INTRODUCTION TO THE CHICKEN MODEL, *JI XING*

Chicken model imitates the actions of fighting roosters. It is not a simple imitation, however, but the result of years of development by the masters. Do not seek to copy a rooster, but seek its manner. The primary techniques of chicken model are: *golden rooster stands on one leg, pecks rice, shakes its feathers, heralds the dawn,* and *spreads its wings.* Each regional style of Xingyiquan practises a slightly different chicken model but there is great similarity in these basic techniques. When practising chicken model you should show this type of idea: the chicken is brave, it has the ability to stand on one leg, it can shake fiercely, it has a fighting spirit, and it pecks very accurately. The rooster is a natural fighter, it knows how to get in on an enemy, it is skillful at pecking and biting with its hard beak, it is skillful at grabbing, pouncing, kicking, and stomping with its sharp claws, and it can fly to the sky. It can advance and retreat instantaneously, getting in and out of any opening, alternating feet, and taking every opportunity. It will continue to fight even when its face is covered in blood. It conceals defensive moves in its attack and attacking moves in its defense, so that it attacks and defends at the same time, continuing always to attack with high and low techniques.

METHODS OF PERFORMING CHICKEN MODEL

The Four Techniques of the Rooster is the most common method of practicing chicken model. *Golden rooster stands on one leg* is practised separately. *Golden rooster spreads its wings* and *thrusts a foot* are also practised as a technique. These three methods all show the character of chicken model excellently.

6.1 METHOD ONE: GOLDEN ROOSTER STANDS ON ONE LEG (AS A SEPARATE PRACTICE)

    jīnjī dúlì   金鸡独立

6.1a   Right Golden Rooster Treads on Snow

    jīnjī tà xuě yòu shì   金鸡踏雪右势

Start from left *santishi*.

204 CHICKEN, *JI XING*

ACTION 1: Advance the left foot a half-step without moving the right foot, and shift forward so that most of your weight in on the left leg. Lift the right heel and bend the right knee. Lift the right hand to the sternum and thread it forward under the left arm with the palm down. Withdraw the left hand, pulling it back to the chest with the palm down. Urge the right shoulder forward slightly and drop the right wrist so that the fingers are at shoulder height. Press the head up and look at the right hand. (images 10.137, 10.138, and 10.138 front)

ACTION 2: Take a step forward with the right foot and quickly follow in the left foot to place it by the right ankle without touching down. Keep the knees together and stand firmly on the right leg with the knee bent. Thread the left hand forward under the right arm with the palm down and fingers forward. Bring the right hand back to in front of the chest and extend the left shoulder. The left hand is at shoulder height with the wrist slightly cocked. Press the head up and look at the left hand. (images 10.139, 10.140, and 10.140 front)

ACTION 3: Advance the left foot a half-step while threading the right hand forward. Advance the right foot a step while threading the left hand forward. This is the same as described in actions 1 and 2.

- Continue on in this manner according to the size of your practice area.

6.1b Left Golden Rooster Treads on Snow

jīnjī tà xuě zuǒ shì   金鸡踏雪左势

Start from right *santishi*.

ACTION 1: Advance the right foot a half-step without moving the left foot. Shift forward and lift the left heel. Thread the left hand forward under the right arm and withdraw the right hand. Both palms are angled downwards. (image 10.141)

ACTION 2: Take a step forward with the left foot and quickly follow in the right foot to by the right ankle without touching down. Stand firmly on the left leg with the knee bent. Thread the right hand forward under the left arm. The action is the same as that described above in *right golden rooster treads on snow*, just transposing right and left. (image 10.142)

10.141   10.142

Pointers

- Be sure to maintain the same height when moving forward. You must not bounce up and down. The key to this is to control the amount of flex in the knees.

- When the rear foot comes through to take a step you should strive for distance and land with stability. The follow-in step should be agile and quick. The knees should stay together. The stepping should be quick and continuous. The one legged stance should be stable, with a slight pause.

6.1c Golden Rooster Treads on Snow Turn Around

jīnjī tà xuě huíshēn shì   金鸡踏雪回身

- Using the <u>right</u> *stand on one leg* as example.

ACTION 1: Step the left foot a half-step, landing with the foot hooked in. Hook-in well so that the body can turn around a full one-eighty degrees. Shift to the left leg, lift the right foot to touch down by the left foot, and bend the left knee to stand steadily. Bring the right hand around flat with the body, so that it moves right and then back as the body turns to face in the way from which it came. Circle the left hand also flat across to the right. When the left hand arrives in front of the body, bring the right hand back to in front of the chest. Look at the right hand. (image 10.143)

ACTION 2: Without moving the feet, thread the right hand forward over the left hand and bring the left hand back to in front of the chest.

ACTION 3: Continue on the same as the advancing *golden rooster treads on snow*.

- *Golden rooster treads on snow* may be done as a one sided practice, doing the right form going one way, and turning and coming back with the left form. It may also be done alternating left and right.

Pointers

- When the lead foot hooks in to turn, be sure to hook-in as much as you can.
- Turn the body quickly around. Shift the weight quickly but with stability. Circle the hands with the body turn, so that the whole movement is well coordinated.

6.2 METHOD TWO: FOUR TECHNIQUES OF THE CHICKEN   jīxíng sìbǎ dòngzuò   鸡形四把动作

Start from left *santishi*.

6.2a   Golden Rooster Stands on One Leg   jīnjī dúlì   金鸡独立

ACTION: This is the same as the *golden rooster treads on snow* described above. Do two on the right side.

6.2b   Golden Rooster Pecks a Grain of Rice   jīnjī shí mǐ   金鸡食米

ACTION: Advance the left foot and follow-in the right foot to slide-stomp behind the left heel. Land with a thump. Clench the right hand and punch straight ahead at chest height, fist eye up. Tuck the left hand onto the right wrist. Look at the right fist. (images 10.144, and 10.144 other side)

CHAPTER TEN: THE TWELVE ANIMAL MODELS

10.144

10.144 FROM OTHER SIDE

6.2c   Golden Rooster Shakes its Feathers   jīnjī dǒu líng   金鸡抖翎

ACTION: Retreat the right foot then withdraw the left foot a bit, to form a half horse stance with the weight more on the right leg. Withdraw the right fist as the right foot steps, bending the elbow and drawing it back to bring the fist up and rightward to just in front of the right temple, turning the fist heart out. The elbow may be slightly raised. Turn the left hand to brace down to the left, palm out at hip height. Look at the left hand. (image 10.145)

10.145

6.2d   Golden Rooster Blocks Up
jīnjī shàng jià   金鸡上架

ACTION 1: Turn the torso ninety degrees by driving the left foot back and pivoting the right foot straight. Keep the same force in both arms. (image 10.146)

ACTION 2: Take a step forward with the left foot. Land firmly and follow in quickly with the right foot, placing it at the left ankle. Squat, keeping the knees together. Unclench the right hand and bring it forward and down to chop finishing at the left hip with the palm out. Thread the left hand past the chest to in front of the right shoulder with the fingers up and palm in. Press the head up and look to the forward right. (image 10.147)

10.146

10.147

6.2e Golden Rooster Heralds the Dawn   jīnjī bào xiǎo   金鸡报晓

ACTION: Take a step forward with the right foot and follow in a half-step with the left foot to take a *santi* stance. As the right foot lands, slice the right hand forward and up to eyebrow height with the wrist cocked. Turn the left hand in and pull down to beside the left hip. The right arm is slightly bent, the shoulders and elbows set down, and the buttocks settled. Press the head up and look past the right hand. (image 10.148)

6.2f Step Forward, Left Split   shàngbù zuǒ pīquán   上步左劈拳

ACTION 1: Withdraw the right foot, pause, then advance it a half-step. Bring the left foot to beside the right foot. When withdrawing, clench the right hand and pull it back to the belly. When advancing, drill the right fist forward and up. Clench the left hand in place at the belly. (image 10.149)

ACTION 2: Take a step forward with the left foot and follow in a half-step with the right foot, keeping most weight on the right leg. Slide the left hand along the right arm to split forward to chest height and pull the right hand back to the belly. Look past the left hand. (image 10.150)

6.2g Stamp, Right Split

zhènjiǎo yòu pīquán   震脚右劈拳

ACTION 1: Withdraw the left foot to beside the right ankle without touching down, by dorsi-flexing the ankle. Clench the left fist and pull it back to the belly, then drill up by the sternum and forward to nose height. The right fist remains at the belly. Look at the left fist. (image 10.151)

ACTION 2: Land the left foot with a thump and lift the right foot. At the same time, slide the right fist forward along the left arm to unclench and chop down at chest height. Pull the left hand back to the belly. Settle the buttocks down and press the head up. Look past the right hand. This position should be fairly low. (image 10.152)

6.2h   Golden Rooster Pecks a Grain of Rice   jīnjī shí mǐ   金鸡食米

ACTION: Step the right foot forward and follow in with the left foot. Do a driving punch with the left fist and cover the left wrist with the right hand. This is the same as movement 6.2c, just punching with the other fist. (images 10.153 and 10.153 other side)

6.2i   Golden Rooster Shakes its Feathers

6.2j   Golden Rooster Blocks Up

6.2k   Golden Rooster Heralds the Dawn

These three are the same as movements described above, transposing right and left sides. Traditionally, the four techniques of chicken model are done on one side, but I feel it is better to balance the body and be able to do the actions on either side.

Pointers:

- o   The punch in *golden rooster pecks rice* hits timed with the rear foot landing. Be sure to keep the whole body coordinated to punch with full power.

- o   *Golden rooster shakes its feathers* uses a full, coordinated power. Be careful to accurately place the hands.

o Take a step forward when doing *golden rooster blocks up*, and land with stability. Coordinate the footwork with the hand action.

o Take a step forward for *golden rooster heralds the dawn*, and follow in quickly. The lead hand slices up as the lead foot lands.

6.2l   Chicken Model Closing Move   jī xíng shōushì   鸡形收势

- Do as many repetitions as your training space and fitness allow. Do the closing move when you get back to the starting point.

If you are in a <u>right</u> split then hook in the right foot and pull the right fist back and turn around to the left, drill the right fist forward and advance the left foot to split with the left hand. Then close the same as usual from left *santishi*.

If you are in a <u>left</u> split, then clench the left hand and pull it back, hook-in the left foot, turn around to the left, advance the right foot and drill the right fist out. Then step the left foot forward and split forward with the left hand. Then close the same as usual from left *santishi*.

6.3   CHICKEN MODEL METHOD THREE

Start from left *santishi*.

6.3a   Golden Rooster Pecks a Grain of Rice

jīnjī shí mǐ   金鸡食米

ACTION: Step the left foot forward a half-step then bring the right foot up with a shovel step, landing with a thump. Clench the right fist and punch forward to chest height with an upright fist. Tuck the left hand on the right wrist. Look at the right fist. (image 10.154)

10.154

6.3b   Golden Rooster Spreads its Wings

jīnjī zhǎn chì   金鸡展翅

ACTION 1: First withdraw the right foot a half-step and sit back, crossing and drilling the fists up. Turn the fist hearts in, left arm inside the right, and drill up to head height. Then turn and unclench the hands, bracing out to the left and right. (images 10.155, 10.156)

10.155

CHAPTER TEN: THE TWELVE ANIMAL MODELS   211

ACTION 2: Withdraw the left foot further to beside the right foot, landing with a thump. While bringing the foot back, continue to circle the hands to the right and left, so that they finish by closing in together at the belly. Press the head up and look forward. (image 10.157)

10.156

10.157

6.3c   Golden Rooster Thrusts a Foot

jīnjī dēng jiǎo   金鸡蹬脚

ACTION: Advance the left foot a half-step and stand steadily with the knee slightly bent. Lift the right knee and then the foot, to kick with the ankle dorsi-flexed. Kick to chest height. Put the wrists together and open the palms and fingers to apply a carrying power forward and up to jaw height. Look forward. (image 10.158)

10.158

6.3d   Golden Rooster Shakes its Feathers   jīnjī dǒu líng   金鸡抖翎

ACTION: Land the right foot forward with the foot hooked in and follow in the left foot slightly. Turn the body ninety degrees to the left, keeping most weight on the left leg in a half horse stance. Clench the left fist and bring it forward and up. Roll the right hand in to the chest then brace down to the right with the palm facing out, the thumb web down, in front of the right knee. Unclench the left hand, bend the elbow, and pull back above the left temple with the palm out. Look at the right hand. (images 10.159 and 10.159 from the other side)

10.159

10.159 OTHER SIDE

212　CHICKEN, *JI XING*

6.3e　Step Forward, Left Split　　shàngbù zuǒ pīquán　　上步左劈拳

ACTION 1: Turn the body ninety degrees rightward to face forward. Withdraw the right foot a half-step, turn the right hand over and pull it back to the belly, clenching it. Keep the left hand at the head. (image 10.160 transitional)

ACTION 2: Advance the right foot a half-step and bring the left foot in without touching down. Cover with the left fist, bringing it forward and down to the belly. Drill the right fist forward and up to nose height. Look at the right fist. (image 10.161)

ACTION 3: Take another step forward with the left foot and follow in a half-step with the right foot. Bring the left hand through to do a split at nose height and pull the right hand back to the belly. Look at the left hand. (image 10.162)

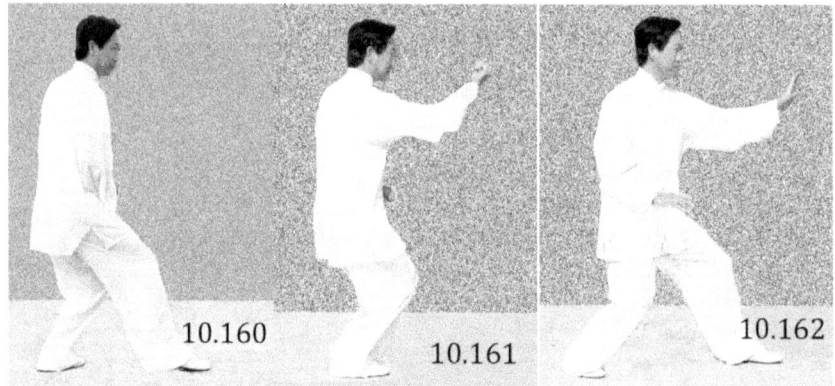

6.3f　Stamp, Right Split　　zhènjiǎo yòu pīquán　　震脚右劈拳

ACTION 1: Withdraw the left foot to beside the right ankle without touching down, by dorsi-flexing the ankle. Clench the left fist and pull it back to the belly, then drill up by the sternum and forward to nose height. The right fist remains at the belly. Look at the left fist.

ACTION 2: Land the left foot with a thump and lift the right foot. At the same time, slide the right fist forward along the left arm to unclench and chop down at chest height. Pull the left hand back to the belly. Settle the buttocks down and press the head up. Look past the right hand. This position should be fairly low.

- This movement is the same as that described in the four techniques of chicken model, movement 6.2g.

6.3g　Golden Rooster Pecks a Grain of Rice　　jīnjī shí mǐ　　金鸡食米

This movement is the same as 6.3a, just on the other side. Continue on to do all the moves on the other side.

- This chicken model is practised on both sides, continuing on as space and energy permit. Turn around from a split position, using the normal *split turn around*. The closing is also the same as that of split.

Pointers

- The action *golden rooster spreads its wings* must be circular – the hands must draw a circle and then come in to the belly timed exactly as the foot comes in.
- The hands must do the carrying move as the foot stamps.
- The action *golden rooster shakes its feathers* is not quite the same as that done earlier. That done in the four techniques of chicken model is a retreating move, while this is an advancing move. Land the foot hooked in and keep the body's power integrated.

PROBLEMS OFTEN MET IN THE CHICKEN MODEL

Chicken Stands on One Leg

PROBLEM 1: The student's stance height rises and falls while stepping forward.

CORRECTIONS: Remind the student to pay more attention to the flex in the knees when moving onto the leg to maintain an even height.

PROBLEM 2: The student steps too much to the side, swinging right and left instead of stepping forward.

CORRECTIONS: Remind the student to step straight forward, keeping the footwork within shoulder width at the most.

PROBLEM 3: Some students thread the hands straight forward with no settling power in the palms. Others thread straight through with no lifting power in the wrists.

CORRECTIONS: Remind the student to keep the arms slightly bent when threading forward, about 160 degrees. Remind them to drop into the palms by settling the wrists, using the heel of the palm to strike. Remind them also to lift the wrists first, and then to drop them.

PROBLEM 4: The student is unsteady in the one-legged stance.

CORRECTIONS: Remind the student to keep the knees together and to grab the ground with the toes of the supporting foot. They should also press the head up and tuck the buttocks down, settle the qi down and urge the shoulders into the move to aid stability.

Four Chicken Techniques

PROBLEM 1: The student lifts the foot to stamp hard when doing the punch.

CORRECTIONS: As the foot comes in it should strike the ground with a large surface, shoveling or raking in before the stamp. Some people just want to make a big noise, but this does not assist the power output to the fist. The punch is forward, so the foot needs a forward moving action into the thump.

PROBLEM 2: The student has no integrated body power when trying to shake the 'feathers' – the shoulder girdle.

CORRECTIONS: This action needs a lot of repetition. In addition, the final position may be done as a stake standing exercise so that the body knows what position it is seeking when using power and speed. While in the final position, and while gently doing the action, seek out the whole body power and the lines of force, to gradually develop the action and position.

PROBLEM 3: The student stands unsteadily or lifts the raised foot too high when doing the upper block.

CORRECTIONS: Remind the student to sit down slightly into this action, keeping the legs together and pressing the head up while settling the buttocks down. The student should also develop the habit in similar moves of always placing the lifted foot at the ankle of the supporting foot, dorsi-flexing to keep the foot parallel to the ground.

PROBLEM 4: The student just uses arm strength when doing *report the dawn*.

CORRECTIONS: This move should show the body's integrated power. Before releasing power, the body should first gather force, closing in before opening. Be sure that the student moves the shoulders, so that the action of the elbows is launched from the shoulders, that of the hands comes from the upper arms. The elbows should maintain a certain angle as the arm cuts up. The shoulders and hands must work together. This needs to be practised a lot to find the integrated power.

PROBLEM 5: The student does a small action for the stamping split.

CORRECTIONS: The stamp is on the spot, so the hand should drill up higher than usual, lengthening the torso. As the foot lands, the stance should be lower than usual, shrinking the body. This makes the move more difficult and more effective for performance.

Chicken Model Method Three

PROBLEM 1: The student lifts the foot to stamp when doing *golden rooster spreads its wings*.

CORRECTIONS: The student should wait after withdrawing the foot, shifting back after settling. The lead foot should be pulled in by closing the hip and dragging the thigh, to drag the foot in to thump with the heel on the ground.

PROBLEM 2: The student does a straight lifting kick for *golden rooster thrusts a foot*.

CORRECTIONS: This is a heel thrust kick; the knee should be lifted bent, and then thrust straight into the heel with the foot dorsi-flexed.

PROBLEM 3: The student does not coordinate the feet with the hands during *golden rooster spreads its wings*.

CORRECTIONS: The hands drill up as the rear foot withdraws. The hands turn and circle to the sides as the weight shifts back. The hands roll together to the belly as the lead foot withdraws and lands with a thump. The student should practise this repeatedly to develop the coordination.

POWER GENERATION FOR THE CHICKEN MODEL

Chicken Stands on One Leg

When you do the threading palms, first raise the wrists and then drop the wrists and sink into the palms, urging the shoulders forward and settling the elbows to release power. Be sure to sit down and settle into the buttocks, reach the shoulders and thread the palms through with a sinking drop. This is like a chicken reaching its head with each step it takes. Be sure to lift the wrists and then settle them.

This technique develops quick footwork and the ability to stop and go. It must be quick. The steps must cover distance, and the stops must be steady.

Four Chicken Techniques

The punch in *golden rooster pecks a grain of rice* is done by turning the waist and urging the shoulder forward, and is timed as the rear foot does a rubbing step in. After the lead foot has landed firmly, turn the waist and close the hips to bring the rear foot up to land the whole foot with a rubbing action forward and down, making a sound. Be sure not to lift the foot and stamp. Be sure to raise the head and straighten the neck, close the hips and tuck in the buttocks, settle the *qi* to the *dantian*, and release power with an exhalation of breath.

When you step back for *golden rooster shakes its feathers*, the torso should first lead the action. The lead foot pushes off to the rear and the whole body gathers power, then you can suddenly release the power. As the right fist lifts and turns as it pulls to the back, the power is directed through the elbow. As the left hand turns the elbow and rounds the arm, settle the shoulder and brace outward; the power is directed to the heel of the palm. The arm actions must be completed simultaneously with the backward step, and coordinated with an expulsion of breath, so that the power comes from the whole body.

Just before *golden rooster blocks up*, twist the torso. Then take a long step forward and land firmly. The rear foot must follow in quickly, closing the knees in tightly together. The lead hand chops down as the rear hand threads up, so that the hands have a wrapping power between them. Close the shoulders, open the upper back, press the head up, and settle the buttocks down.

Golden rooster reports the dawn is actually a scoop. The power of an upward scoop is in the shoulders. Land the lead foot, scoop one hand forward and up, and lower the other hand all as one action – there must be no mistiming. *Golden rooster reports the dawn* can be either a scooping shoulder strike or a scooping punch. The scooping shoulder strike is applied through the shoulder and upper arm. The scooping shoulder strike is an angled pressing power done once the footwork gets you in close enough. The scooping punch is applied to the heel of the lead hand. For the scooping punch, you need to sit into the hips and lengthen the spine, relax and extend the shoulder, and urge the upper arm forward to release power. The power differs, as does the application and use.

For *step forward, split,* to help take a long and stable step forward, withdraw the lead foot slightly and then advance a half-step. Pull the lead hand back as you withdraw the lead foot, so that foot and hand act together. Drill the lead hand forward as you advance the lead foot a half-step. Then step forward as the rear hand chops forward.

Golden rooster drinks water is a splitting palm combined with a stamp. The lead hand should clench and pull back as the lead foot withdraws. The fist drills up as the knee lifts. The knee should lift to hip height. Lengthen the spine slightly and rise to lend power to the drilling up fist. Settle the torso down, stomp the foot, pull back, chop the rear hand out, and lift the other foot all at once. All actions are done at once with total coordination and whole body power.

Chicken Model Method Three

Golden rooster spreads its wings uses a twisting, drilling power as the fists cross and drill upward. It uses a bracing power in both arms with the chest contained and the arms rounded as the fists turn over and draw a circle. When the hands gather in front of the abdomen, the arms should have an inward and downward wrapping, embracing power, with the elbows hugged tightly to the ribs. The hands should gather in as the foot withdraws, so that feet and hands are coordinated. When the elbows hug the ribs the fists can strike the belly to help sink the *qi* to the *dantian*.

Golden rooster thrusts a foot must be fast – the foot must lift to kick as soon as the other foot steps a half-step forward. The kicking leg must move quickly and the supporting leg should be slightly bent with the toes gripping the ground for stability. To kick, first lift the knee with the foot pulled back to present the heel, and then thrust forcefully forward, straightening the knee. Both palms lift up, keeping the elbows closed in, lengthening the spine and releasing the shoulders to extend the arms. The kick must come at the same time that the palms lift.

Golden rooster shakes its feathers comes immediately after the kick, starting to thrust forward strongly from the supporting leg to send the kicking leg forward to land. The landing foot stomps into the ground, so you need to twist the torso and hook in the foot. When the hands open out to brace upper and lower, left and right, they must complete the action as the foot lands. The hands must first gather power, and then open out, the left hand in front and the right hand behind. Contain the chest, close the shoulders, twist the hands, turn the elbows over, twist the waist, stomp the foot and brace up and down with the palms. The focus is in the lower hand. The power should be full and the technique use whole body

power.

BREATHING CYCLE FOR THE CHICKEN MODEL

- Take a small breath in during *golden rooster stands on one leg*. After each power move relax immediately to assist in breathing in. Inhale also during each action that opens up the chest (this principle applies to all such actions in Xingyiquan). For example, breathe in as you circle the arms out to the sides during *golden rooster spreads its wings*.

- Exhale on all the power moves to assist in launching power.

PRACTICAL APPLICATIONS FOR THE CHICKEN MODEL

- In Xingyiquan, all power release moves are effective strikes. The chicken model has many power release moves, and so has many applications.

Golden rooster stands on one leg uses fast footwork to enter quickly to take over the centre of the opponent, threading the hands into his face in order to throw him into confusion. The palms can then drop to strike his chest.

Golden rooster pecks a grain of rice uses the lead hand to hook and press the opponent's fist, entering in with the footwork to punch with the rear fist to his solar plexus.

Golden rooster shakes its feathers can strike with an entry step or a retreating step. One hand blocks up to pull back as the other hand tucks in to strike as the waist turns to enter the body sideways.

- The key lies in the footwork. The lead foot must get in tight to the opponent's body so that you can reach his hip or belly.

Golden rooster blocks up is an entry step with a chopping lean. One hand is down and one is above the shoulder, turn the body sideways and get the feet in with a T step, first gathering and then releasing power.

Golden rooster heralds the dawn is a scoop, that is, a strike that lifts forward and up from below.

Golden rooster spreads its wings is a retreating defensive move. The hands brace up out to the sides then drop and roll in. The upward brace deals with a high attack, and the low roll-in deals with a low attack.

Golden rooster thrusts a foot is a kick to the opponent's chest with a simultaneous lifting strike with both hands to his jaw. It strikes low and high, feinting high while striking low. The main technique is the kick.

The Poem About the Chicken

鸡形歌诀

金鸡踏雪独立能，

抖翎发威身劲整。

展翅蹬脚上下取，

食米报晓上架行。

Golden rooster treads on snow shows the ability to stand on one leg.

Shake the feathers emits all the body's enormous power.

Spread wings and *thrust a foot* deal with high and low.

Peck a grain of rice, *report the dawn*, and *block up* all move forward.

SEVEN: SWALLOW MODEL

燕形

Introduction To The Swallow Model, *Yan Xing*

Swallow model is the most agile of Xingyiquan's animal models, and develops nimbleness and quickness. Swallow model combines martial techniques with the agility that the swallow shows when it swoops over the water, flies straight up to the sky, or wheels over in flight.

One should understand these images when doing swallow model: to do *swallow pierces the sky,* the body lengthens, the hands turn as if they were wings, turning suddenly up to dive down. The image of *swallow skims the water* is dropping down to the water, scooping some up in flight, then rising. The drop stance needs to squat fully down and the lead hand protects you as the rear hand comes from below to rise into a groin strike. As the legs push off to rise, you strike the opponent's torso. Your movements must rise and fall, rising like flying high on wings, and dropping like hiding under the ground. You must leap forward, stand on one leg, slice the palm, punch quickly and with agility, and your strikes must be solid and firm. You should leap for distance and land lightly but firmly, seeking a combination of nimbleness with stability, a power in lightness, combining hard and soft and combining form and spirit as one.

Each branch of Xingyiquan does swallow model slightly differently, and each has its own characteristics. Almost all Xingyiquan books describe *swallow swoops over the water.* Some are done higher and some lower, according to how each teacher taught. Sometimes the name is the same for different movements, and sometimes the movements are the same for different names. Here I will introduce two versions of swallow model that contain some of the main methods.

Methods Of Performing The Swallow Model

7.1 SWALLOW MODEL METHOD ONE

Start from left *santishi*.

220 SWALLOW, YAN XING

7.1a   Swallow Pierces the Sky   yànzǐ zuāntiān   燕子钻天

ACTION 1: Rotate both palms to face up and thread the right hand forward under the left arm, shifting forward. As the right hand approaches the left hand, extend the right hand up. Bend the left elbow and turn the palm down to press down past the chest. Thread the right hand up past the head and shift back to the right leg, then bring the right hand back and down to shoulder height. Look at the right hand. Slice the left hand down and forward, and look at the left hand. (images 10.163, 10.164)

ACTION 2: Advance the left foot a half-step and push off to jump. Take a long step forward with the right foot and land firmly, keeping the left knee up in a right one legged stance. Lower the right hand by the waist then thread it forward and up under the left arm, turning the palm up when the hand passes head height. Bend the left elbow and turn the hand over to stab down in front of the groin with the little finger on the outside. Lift the left knee to waist height. Look forward. (images 10.165, 10.166)

7.1b   Swallow Skims the Water   yànzǐ chāo shuǐ   燕子抄水

ACTION 1: Turn ninety degrees to the right and bend the right knee to a full squat, extending the left foot to the left to form a left drop stance. Thread the left hand forward along the inside of the left leg, rolling the arm under to turn the palm up, until it is at the left foot. Brace back with the right hand, palm out and arm rounded. Look at the left hand. (images 10.167a, 10.167b and 10.167b front)

CHAPTER TEN: THE TWELVE ANIMAL MODELS

7.1c Step Forward, Slice to the Groin   shàngbù liāo yīn zhǎng   上步撩阴掌

ACTION 1: Thread the left hand forward and shift forward, bending the left knee to support with the left leg, rising slightly. (image 10.168)

ACTION 2: Take a step forward with the right foot, turning the foot out crossways. Do not move the left foot, and sit into a resting stance. Slice the right hand forward to strike with the palm forward at waist height. Tuck the left hand onto the right wrist and raise the body slightly, lifting the left heel. Look at the right hand. (image 10.169)

7.1d Left Low Punch

zuǒ xià bēngquán   左下崩拳

ACTION: Take a long step forward with the left foot and follow in with the right foot. Clench both fists and tuck in the left elbow. Slide the left fist along the right arm to punch forward and down with the fist heart down, at belly height. Pull the right fist back to the belly with the fist heart up. Look in the direction of the left punch and press the head up. (image 10.170)

7.1e Step Forward, Right Split shàngbù yòu pīquán 上步右劈拳

ACTION 1: Advance the left foot a half-step and follow in with the right foot to beside the left ankle without touching down. Pull the left fist back to the belly, then bring it up to the sternum and drill forward to nose height, twisting the ulnar edge upwards. (image 10.171)

ACTION 2: Take a long step forward with the right foot and follow in a half step with the left foot. Bring the right hand along the left arm to chop forward to shoulder height and pull the left hand back to the belly. Press the head up and look forward. (image 10.172)

7.1f Swallow Turn Around yàn xíng huíshēn 燕形回身

- The *swallow model turn around* is the same as that of split, adding another split to change sides. First do a split, and then continue on to the next move.

Pointers

  o During *pierce the sky* the hands must not stop. The right hand threads up as you jump, and the entire action is done all as one move.

  o During *skim the water* you must squat fully into the drop stance. The arms should form a straight line. Be sure to slide the left hand along the leg. Do not stop between *pierce the sky* and *skim the water*, but perform them as one move.

  o During *step forward, slice to the groin* bring the right hand through with the right foot. Tuck the legs tightly together. Reach the right hand forward as you strike.

  o Punch with the left fist as the left foot lands its forward step.

7.2 SWALLOW MODEL METHOD TWO

Start from left *santishi*.

7.2a Swallow Pierces the Sky yànzǐ zuāntiān 燕子钻天

- This is the same as described above in 7.1a

CHAPTER TEN: THE TWELVE ANIMAL MODELS   223

7.2b   Swallow Skims the Water   yànzǐ chāo shuǐ   燕子抄水

- This is the same as described above in 7.1b.

7.2c   Swallow Spreads its Wings   yànzǐ zhǎn chì   燕子展翅

ACTION 1: Thread the left hand towards the left foot and shift forward to the left foot, bending the left knee and rising slightly. Come through with the head, keeping the left hand extended at waist height and extending the right hand to the rear. Look at the left hand. (image 10.173)

ACTION 2: Bend the right elbow and bring the hand to the waist, then thread up and forward under the left arm with the palm up. Bend the left elbow and rotate the palm so that it faces in in front of the chest. The palms are crossed in front of the chest with the elbows down. (image 10.174)

ACTION 3: Take a long step forward with the right foot, landing firmly and bending the knee to a half squat. Follow up the left foot to beside the right ankle without touching down. Keep the knees together and dorsi-flex the left ankle. Separate the arms to left and right, the elbows slightly bent, the palms upright (left forward and right back), the palms both open and with the fingers up, at shoulder height. Look at the left hand. (image 10.175)

7.2d   Advance, Right Driving Punch   jìnbù yòu bēngquán   进步右崩拳

ACTION 1: Take a long step forward with the left foot and follow in a half-step with the right. As the right foot comes in to the left heel, half-squat on both legs. Clench the right fist and bring it in to the waist, then punch forward with the fist eye up. Tuck the left palm inward to touch the right wrist. Punch to chest height. Press the head up and look at the right fist. (image 10.176)

224 SWALLOW, *YAN XING*

10.176

7.2e Step Forward, Right Split shàngbù yòu pīquán 上步右劈拳

ACTION 1: Pull both hands back to the belly and advance the left foot a half-step. Drill the left fist up by the sternum and forward to nose height with the ulnar side twisted up. Follow in with the right foot without touching down. Look at the left fist. (image 10.177)

ACTION 2: Take a long step forward with the right foot and follow in a half-step with the left to take a *santi* stance with the right foot forward. Slide the right fist along the left arm, unclench the hands, and chop the right hand forward at shoulder height while pulling the left hand back to the belly, both palms down. Press the head up and look past the right hand. (image 10.178)

10.177

10.178

- Continue on to repeat moves 7.2a, b, c, d, and e on the other side.

7.2f Swallow Turn Around and Closing Move

- The *turn around* and *closing move* are the same as for the first method of swallow model.

Pointers

  o *Swallow spreads its wings* is made up of three actions, but they should be continuous. Take a long step forward with the right foot, landing solidly and at the same time as the hands complete their action.

CHAPTER TEN: THE TWELVE ANIMAL MODELS

- The hands and feet arrive together in *advance right driving punch*, the same as in *rooster pecks a grain of rice*.
- The feet and hands arrive together in *step forward right split*, using whole body power.

PROBLEMS OFTEN MET IN THE SWALLOW MODEL

PROBLEM 1: The student is uncoordinated when doing *swallow pierces the sky*.

CORRECTIONS: Tell the student to pay attention when the rear hand starts to thread forward, that the lead hand should start to draw back with a covering action. As the rear hand threads up, the lead hand should thread down. As the rear hand drops back, the lead hand should slice forward. Overall, the hands move at the same time and follow the rule: one forward and one back, one up and one down. Repeating these actions in this way many times will bring coordination

PROBLEM 2: The student's drop stance is too high and unstable when doing *swallow skims the water*.

CORRECTIONS: The higher the stance, the more difficult it is to keep stable, as the centre of gravity is high. The cause of a high stance is that the supporting leg is not squatting fully down – the body should be completely down and the other leg should extend out along the ground. This should be the same as Longfist style's *drop stance thread palm*. If the student is not flexible enough to do this, then he should do more hip and ankle flexibility training.

PROBLEM 3: As the student threads his hand forward in *swallow skims the water* he does not butt forward with the head, but simply comes straight up.

CORRECTIONS: Although this is not considered a huge error, it shows a low quality of movement. You should express the ability of the swallow to drop down, scoop water and then rise. This should be a unique action. The drop stance should go all the way down, then the hand should thread forward and the head should lead into the action before rising.

PROBLEM 4: The student does not smoothly connect *swallow pierces the sky* with *swallow skims the water*, leaving a big gap between the two actions.

CORRECTIONS: When first teaching, one must break down the movements, showing each one separately to make the requirements clear and explain all the details. But once the movements have been learned, you must remind the student to connect them. The action and power flow must be smooth and coordinated.

PROBLEM 5: The student does not connect the hand opening with the foot landing in *swallow spreads its wings*.

CORRECTIONS: Make sure the student prepares the hands by crossing them before stepping – the right hand outside the left. Then step forward and separate the hands to front and back as the foot lands. Have the student do the action slowly to gain the coordination, and only add speed once the movement is comfortable.

PROBLEM 6: The student keeps his torso too erect in *slice to the groin*, or places the hand too high.

CORRECTIONS: Remind the student to lean the torso forward slightly into the *slice to the groin*. The strike up should be done with a slightly bent arm, and the right shoulder should settle down, so that the hand reaches forward as the left foot steps out. The body should settle down and the palm should strike up to waist height. Remind the student to practise to coordinate the actions of the footwork, hand and shoulder.

PROBLEM 7: When doing the *low driving punch* the student cuts down instead of punching.

CORRECTIONS: Remind the student to pay attention to the action and placement of the elbows. When punching, the elbows should roll in so that when the body issues power it is applied through the shoulders, so that one hand goes forward as the other goes back, one up and one down.

POWER GENERATION FOR THE SWALLOW MODEL

The actions of *swallow pierces the sky* and *swallow skims the water* must be done continuously without a break in power. To keep the power smooth, do not stop in mid-movement.

Swallow pierces the sky emphasizes the forward-backward shifting of the body. As the rear hand threads forward so does the centre of gravity. When the hand threads up and then pulls back, the centre of gravity shifts back. Use the waist to draw the shoulder, and the shoulder to draw the elbows, turning while moving. The hands need to coordinate: the right hand goes up as the left hand goes down; the right hand goes back and the left hand goes forward; the right hand goes forward as the left hand goes back. Use the power of the body core, use the shoulders to draw the arms into coordinated movement, so that the whole body works as one.

The movement *swallow pierces the sky* must use the forward movement of the body, as the body moves forward past the lead foot, putting the rear hand forward and up; only then push off the lead foot and take a long step forward with the rear foot. Push off strongly with the rear foot to take everything forward, as long and high as possible. If you are practising *swallow pierces the sky* as a single technique, as the rear foot lands you should stand steady on one leg. Lift the other knee in front of the chest and slice up with the rear hand, stabbing the lead hand down with both arms slightly bent. This one-legged stance is the actual *swallow pierces the sky*. If you are combining *swallow pierces the sky* with *swallow skims the water*, then bring the rear foot up and forward to aid the drive forward, and when landing, turn the foot out and bend the knee to squat. First lift the other knee, then drop down and extend the leg along the ground with the foot hooked in.

Swallow scoops water is a drop stance as the hand threads forward, so you should drop as low as possible. You must squat fully on the supporting leg with the shank tight to the thigh, the belly on the thigh, and the buttocks sitting down as much as possible. Turn the foot out to forty-five degrees with the knee on line with it. Hook the other foot in and extend it out as close to the ground as possible, keeping the whole foot on the ground. When doing *swallow scoops water*, be sure to first tuck the shoulder under to be able to twist the arm and extend it along the leg. The rear hand slices up towards the rear. The key to the move lies in drilling the head forward to butt towards the extended foot, pushing into the rear leg to move the centre of gravity forward. Once the lead elbow has gone past the extended foot, then bend the knee and rise, twisting and threading the lead hand. Settle the shoulder and drop the elbow to put power into the arm twist.

Step forward slice to the groin is a relatively low posture. The rear hand comes through to slice as the rear foot steps through with the foot crossways. Get power into the slice by turning the waist, rolling the torso, and reaching with the arm. The legs cross with the thighs tucked tightly together, and the torso leans forward slightly.

- Do not hesitate between *swallow pierces the sky*, *skim the water*, and *slice to groin*. Complete the three actions as one move, with one continuous power flow.

The *low driving punch* can also be called *planting punch*. There are three actions involved – step and land the foot, punch forward and down, and pull the other hand back to the abdomen. These must be completed together, with one explosive move and breath. When launching power to the punch, be sure to drop one shoulder forward and down, and to pull the other up and back, to put power into the fists. Pay special attention to the lead elbow, keep it rolled in, so that the power is contained and complete.

Both types of swallow model share the moves *swallow pierces the sky* and *swallow skims the water*, but the rest of the actions are not the same. One strikes to the groin then punches down, the other spread the wings and then punches straight. Each has its own application and its own nature.

During *swallow spreads its wings*, as the rear foot steps through, it should take a long step and land firmly. The centre of gravity should move forward past the lead foot, and, as the rear foot thrusts forward, push strongly off the lead foot. In this way the step can cover a lot of distance. When stepping forward, be sure not to push the body upwards – the feet must drive straight forward. Land solidly on one leg with the knee bent and the toes grabbing the ground. Bring the rear foot up quickly to place the knees tightly together. Press the head up and tuck the buttocks in. As the arms open to the front and rear, they must finish the action as the rear foot comes through to land. Close the chest when the rear hand threads forward and slices up and the lead hand rotates and covers in. Open the chest, urge the shoulders into the action, and firm the abdomen when the arms 'spread the wings'.

Advance driving punch is also called *golden rooster pecks a grain of rice*. It is a rear foot timed punch. Combine the rear foot landing and the punch with an exhalation of breath. Be sure to bring the rear hand to the belly before punching.

BREATHING CYCLE FOR THE SWALLOW MODEL

The general rule for breathing is: Each power release action uses an exhalation to help with the power output. Each opening-up action uses an inhalation. Each closing-in action uses an exhalation.

- Inhale when moving forward and up in *swallow pierces the sky*. Use a lifting breath to help you to rise.
- Exhale when dropping down in *swallow skims the water*. Use a settling breath, not a sharp power launching exhalation.

Your ability to breathe smoothly in coordination with your actions directly affects your quality of movement. When first learning new actions and when practising slowly, you need to concentrate on the actions to get them perfect, so just breathe naturally. Once the actions are done correctly then they will influence how you breathe, and you will gradually come to breathe correctly in coordination with your actions. These principles and the progression should be applied to all Xingyiquan training.

PRACTICAL APPLICATIONS FOR THE SWALLOW MODEL

- Swallow model develops flexibility and agility, especially the ability to rise and drop quickly.

In *swallow pierces the sky*, the rear hand that threads forward and slices up to pull back can be an upward block turning to a grab. If you cannot grab, then just knock away and use the lead hand to strike the opponent's chest or face. Move your body back to dodge. Move your body forward to strike. The techniques themselves can be freely used as you see necessary.

In *swallow skims the water,* you must drop down into a full drop stance for training, but in using it you don't usually need to drop so far, just enough to bring the body down, to turn it sideways to facilitate entering. Use the power in the upper arms with a hidden threading cut up into the opponent's groin or belly.

In *swallow pierces the sky*, one leg pushes off as you drive the other leg up to assist the jump for height and distance. To use this technique in combat, kick forward with this leg as the hand threads forward.

In *step forward to strike the groin*, the lead hand takes care of the opponent's hands by scooping up, knocking aside, pressing down, or hooking, so that the rear hand can come through to strike the groin. When using the technique, get the body in tight and use the lead hand to shut down the opponent and protect your head. This technique needs to be fast, to get in before the opponent can react. You can step in the rear foot or the lead foot, but you must stay low.

Advance low punch strikes the opponent's belly. Aim through to behind his body, thinking of going right through him.

Swallow spreads its wings brings the rear hand through to slice up, stepping the foot in quickly and striking with the lead hand. Aim for the opponent's chest or face. Be sure to turn the body sideways as you enter. *Advance punch* is a strike to the solar plexus.

THE POEM ABOUT THE SWALLOW

燕形歌诀

钻天抄水一气成，

撩打招法不容情。

缩起长落身法意，

劲顺意领气子通。

Pierce the sky and *scoop water* in one breath,

The groin strike is then not easy to fathom.

The body technique is to tuck in as you rise, lengthen as you land;

The power is smooth and the intent leads, so the *qi* naturally connects.

EIGHT: SPARROW HAWK MODEL

鷂形

Introduction To The Sparrow Hawk Model, *Yao Xing*

The sparrow hawk is one of the fiercest and quickest of the birds of prey. All acccipiters are small but make up for their size with their agility and fierceness.[21] In Xingyiquan, we copy the sparrow hawk's skill at folding its body and wings to thread through the trees, its bravery at flying up to the heavens, its skill at wheeling over, its might at spreading its wings, and its ferocity at grasping prey.

Sparrow hawk model is practised advancing on a straight line, turning the body to attack, wheeling the body to use surprise to get in low while appearing to go high, and tucking the body to advance and strike. The body technique is to tuck and rise, to hide and drop – rising and falling, drilling and wheeling to left and right as if flying. The hand technique should be crisp and tight. The footwork should advance quickly and follow in immediately.

When practicing sparrow hawk model you should show this type of intent: flying up and down, wheeling left and right, tucking to enter straight in like an arrow. Turn the body sideways as if passing through the trees. Punch like a bullet, pierce the sky fiercely, wheel over lightly as if flying. The whole body must be fully coordinated with no slackness. When 'spreading the wings' you must first roll in and then spread, the roll in conceals the body, rolling the power and the intent inward so that you can launch wide open with whole body power. Upper and lower, inner and outer are all united as one. When grabbing prey you should be fierce and powerful. In sum, sparrow hawk model should show a connected spirit, an agile and full power, fierce and quick hand techniques, and a fully coordinated body technique.

Methods Of Performing The Sparrow Hawk Model

There are two main methods of performing sparrow hawk model. One combines *sparrow hawk tucks in its body, enters the woods, pierces the sky,* and *wheels over.* The second combines *sparrow hawk folds its wings, enters the woods, grabs a sparrow, spreads its wings,* and *wheels over.* There are many similar actions in each method, though each emphasizes a different aspect. You should practise each on both sides to develop complete skill.

---

[21] Translator's note: Accipiters, or bird hawks, include a number of small hawks that fly through woods after small birds such as sparrows. It is usual, though not perhaps totally accurate, in Xingyiquan to translate *yaozi* as sparrow hawk.

CHAPTER TEN: THE TWELVE ANIMAL MODELS

8.1 SPARROW HAWK MODEL METHOD ONE

Start from left *santishi*.

8.1a Sparrow Hawk Folds its Wings   yàozǐ shù shēn   鹞子束身

ACTION: Clench both fists and bring the right fist up from the belly to the sternum, taking a long step forward with the right foot. Lift the left foot by the right ankle without touching down, keeping the knees together. While doing this, punch the right fist forward and down to belly height, fist eye forward, stabbing out over the left arm. Pull the left fist back towards the belly with the fist heart in. Look forward and press the head up. (image 10.179)

8.1b Sparrow Hawk Enters the Woods   yàozǐ rù lín   鹞子入林

ACTION: Take a long step forward with the left foot and follow in a half-step with the right foot. Bend the right elbow to drill the fist up to eyebrow height and lift the left fist to the sternum. Punch the left fist forward at chest height, fist eye up, as the left foot lands. Rotate the right forearm and drop the elbow, pulling the right fist back to the temple with the fist heart forward about a fist width away from the right temple. Look past the left fist. (images 10.180 and 10.180 front)

8.1c Sparrow Hawk Pierces the Sky   yàozǐ zuān tiān   鹞子钻天

ACTION 1: Advance the left foot a half-step and follow in the right foot to beside the left without touching down. Drop the right fist to the right waist with the fist heart up. Rotate the left fist then cock it with the fist heart down, tucking the forearm across the body. Look forward. (image 10.181)

232 SPARROW HAWK, *YAO XING*

ACTION 2: Take a long step forward with the right foot and follow in the left foot a half-step. Drill the right fist forward and out from inside the left wrist, finishing at nose height with the fist heart in and ulnar edge up. Cock the left fist down to press and pull back to the belly, fist heart down. Press the head up and look at the right fist. (image 10.182)

8.1d Sparrow Hawk Wheels Over   yàozǐ fān shēn   鹞子翻身

ACTION 1: Hook the right foot in and turn around one-eighty degrees to the left to face back in the way from which you came. Lift the right elbow and bring the right arm past the right ear, crossing the forearm over the head as you turn around to the left. Press the right forearm past the head to cover forward and down with the fist hear down. Keep the left fist at the belly. (image 10.183)

ACTION 2: Complete the right fist cover down to the belly without moving the feet. Shift the weight forward onto the left foot as you drill the left fist up by the sternum then forward along inside the right wrist to drill up to nose height, fist heart in. Look at the left fist. (image 10.184)

ACTION 3: Bring the right forearm across the body, lifting it up to the head outside the left fist. Bend the left elbow to bring the fist back to the chest. Turn the body rightward and shift back to the right leg. Pull the right fist back as the body turns, and circle it down to the right waist with the fist heart up. Bend the right knee to squat fully down, and extend the left leg out into a drop stance. Slide the left fist along the left leg, turning it so the fist eye faces down as it extends – the left fist should go past the left foot. Watch the left fist as it drills up, watch the right fist as it lifts crossways and back, then turn the head quickly to watch the left fist again as it extends forward with the drop stance. (images 10.185, 10.186)

CHAPTER TEN: THE TWELVE ANIMAL MODELS 233

 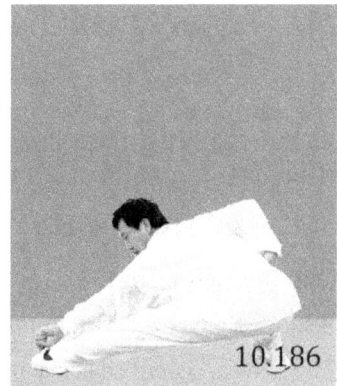

8.1e Sparrow Hawk Folds its Wings   yàozî shù shēn   鹞子束身

ACTION 1: Extend the left fist along the left leg and shift forward onto the left leg, bending the knee and rising slightly. Take a long step forward with the right foot and quickly bring the left foot up to the right ankle without touching down. Bring the right fist past the chest to punch forward and down, fist eye forward at belly height, crossing over outside the left fist. Bring the left fist back towards the belly. Look in front of the right punch and press the head up. Keep the arms tight to the ribs. (image 10.187)

- Repeat the moves again, continuing on as described above.

Pointers

- o Be sure to take a long step forward with the right foot when doing *sparrow hawk folds its wings*. Land firmly, and close the hands together.

- o *Sparrow hawk pierces the sky* is a right drilling punch, so the main points are the same as described in the chapter on drill.

- o The actions in the sparrow hawk model are an integrated unit, so you must practise them as a continuous whole. The entire body must be coordinated. Pay attention to the shifts in weight.

- To practise the other side of the sparrow hawk model, after *sparrow hawk pierces the sky*, take another step forward and do a *left aligned step drill*. Then carry on with *sparrow hawk wheels over*, *folds its wings*, *enters the woods*, and *pierces the sky* on the other side.

8.1f Sparrow Hawk Closing Move   yào xíng shōushì 鹞形收势

Once you get back to your starting place, complete *sparrow hawk folds its wings* and *sparrow hawk enters the woods*. Then cock the left fist to press and pull back to the belly. From there you can complete the form the same as from *santishi*.

8.2 SPARROW HAWK MODEL METHOD TWO

Start from left *santishi*.

8.2a Sparrow Hawk Folds its Wings   yàozǐ shù shēn   鹞子束身

The same as described above in 8.1a.

8.2b Sparrow Hawk Enters the Woods   yàozǐ rù lín   鹞子入林

The same as described above in 8.1b.

8.2c Sparrow Hawk Grasps a Sparrow   yàozǐ zhuō què   鹞子捉雀

ACTION 1: Advance the left foot a half-step and unclench the hands. Turn the left palm up and turn the right palm outward. Circle the left hand up, right, and back to beside the right waist, palm down. Circle the right hand back and down, also beside the right waist, palm up. Look at the left hand. (image 10.188)

ACTION 2: Step the right foot forward, hooked out in a cross step. Block with the left arm forward and up to shoulder height, forearm across the body. Thread the right hand forward to chest height as the right foot steps forward, turning the palm up. Look at the right hand. (image 10.189)

ACTION 3: Step the left foot forward and follow in a half-step with the right foot to take a *santi* stance. Lift the right hand to eyebrow height, turning the palm down. Slide the left hand along the right forearm to chop forward and down at waist height. Pull the right hand back to beside the right waist. Look at the left hand and press the head up. (image 10.190)

CHAPTER TEN: THE TWELVE ANIMAL MODELS   235

8.2d   Sparrow Hawk Spreads its Wings yàozǐ zhǎnchì   鹞子展翅

ACTION 1: Step the left foot forward a half-step with the foot hooked out. Lift the right foot to the left ankle without touching down. Clench the hands and pull the left fist back to the belly, then drill the left fist up by the sternum to eyebrow height, rotating the fist. Flex and lift the right elbow, keeping it dropped, to lift the right fist up to eyebrow height, circling forward and to the left. The fists end up crossed in front of the chest with the fist hearts in, the left fist inside the right fist. The body is turned ninety degrees to the left. Look at the right fist. (images 10.191 and 10.191 other side)

ACTION 2: Take a long step to the forward right with the right foot, landing it across the line of the form, and bringing the left foot in slightly, to sit into a horse stance. Unclench the hands and turn the palms down to brace out strongly at waist height to the left and right. The arms are curved and the power goes to the heel of the palms. Press the head up and focus forward. Look at the right hand. (images 10.192 and 10.192 other side)

8.2e   Sparrow Hawk Pierces the Sky yàozǐ zuān tiān   鹞子钻天

ACTION 1: Withdraw the right foot a little then take a step forward, bringing the left foot up to the right ankle without touching down. Clench the fists and bring the left fist back to the belly. Bring the right fist back the belly then drill it up by the sternum and forward to nose height. Look at the right fist. (image 10.193)

ACTION 2: Take a step forward with the left foot and follow in a half-step with the right foot. Turn the right fist heart down and across the body to tuck and press down with the forearm, pulling it back to the belly with the fist heart in. Drill the left fist by the sternum and forward to nose height

with the ulnar side turned up. Look at the left fist. (image 10.194)

8.2f   Sparrow Hawk Wheels Over   yàozǐ fān shēn   鹞子翻身

- This is the same as described in 8.1d, the only difference is that this time it turns around to the right. This way you get to practise in both directions.

8.2g   Sparrow Hawk Turn Around and Closing Move

zhuàn shēn, shòu shì   转身和收势

- The *turn around* and *closing move* of the second method of the sparrow hawk model are the same as that of the first method.

Pointers

- *Sparrow hawk folds its wings* and *sparrow hawk enters the woods* should be done as one action with no hesitation.

- *Sparrow hawk grasps its prey* is described as three actions, but must be done as one.

- During *sparrow hawk spreads its wings*, the right elbow cover must arrive as the left foot lands, applying one whole body power.

PROBLEMS OFTEN MET IN THE SPARROW HAWK MODEL

PROBLEM 1: In *sparrow hawk enters the woods*, during the action of lifting the right elbow and bringing in the right foot, the student turns the foot out too much, causing the knee to be turned out.

CORRECTIONS: Tell the student to keep the elbow in, so that the right fist first drills up, rotating fully, so that the body turns sideways for the punch. When the student brings in the right foot, remind him to use the knee to bring the foot in, keeping the knee tucked inward. This will prevent the problem of leaving the hip back, which allows the knee to arrive turned out, and the foot to turn across the stance.

CHAPTER TEN: THE TWELVE ANIMAL MODELS

PROBLEM 2: The student does not have whole body power during *sparrow hawk wheels over*, moving the hands and body independently, and showing a clear lack of internal power

CORRECTIONS: This problem can only be solved by practice. During repetitions, the student must pay attention to the power flow, looking for it in the line of the movements, and trying to get a feel for it. Practice of any movement must be done with this principle: first learn the movements correctly; train hard once they are well known. When thought is added to hard training then skill will evolve.[22]

PROBLEM 3: The student has power in the lead hand but not in the rear hand during *sparrow hawk spreads its wings*. Also, the hands and feet do not work together.

CORRECTIONS: Hand and foot coordination will come naturally with much thoughtful practice. The student must also pay attention to finding equal power in the hands. As the classics say, "when the lead hand strikes, the power launches from the rear hand". This is the only way to use whole body power, which is an even, heavy power.

PROBLEM 4: The student is unstable during *sparrow hawk wheels over*.

CORRECTIONS: Usually the cause of instability is shifting the weight back and forth too much and too forcefully. The student should pay attention to the hook-in step, making the foot placement slightly ahead. In this way, the body technique can move smoothly into the turn.

POWER GENERATION FOR THE SPARROW HAWK MODEL

First Sparrow Hawk Method

Sparrow Hawk Folds its wings, Sparrow Hawk Enters the Woods

- These moves should be done as one action, with no hesitation between them.

During *sparrow hawk folds its wings* the right stabbing punch must hit simultaneously with the right foot landing. To have power, the head presses up, the right shoulder urges forward slightly, the shoulders and elbows settle, the shoulders close in, the chest closes, the abdomen settles firmly, the buttocks drop, and the upper arms adhere tightly to the ribs.

Sparrow hawk enters the woods is an *aligned stance cannon fist*. The lead punch should arrive with the landing of the lead foot, so that the power is complete. To have an effective block, the blocking arm must drill up with the elbow tucked down, and then the body moves in sideways so that the block is a deflection – you must not turn the forearm sideways by lifting the elbow, which turns the

---

[22] Translator's note (verbal instruction from author): In this action, pretend you are holding a spear and twisting it from the hand holding the grip to send power to the hand holding the middle of the spear in front. This helps you find the power transfer through the body core.

action into a straight upper block. To get the correct power, rotate the right forearm, keeping the elbow down.

Sparrow Hawk Pierces the Sky

The fist must drill up as the foot lands. To have correct drilling power and protect the midline, the ulnar edge must twist upward.

To move from the *sparrow hawk enters the woods* into *sparrow hawk pierces the sky*, first bring the right fist down from beside the temple, pulling the right arm slightly back. This creates an inward and downward rolling power in the right forearm, rolling as it pulls back. Once it arrives at the waist, then it is ready to drill forward. As the fist drills forward, urge the fist from the elbow, the elbow from the shoulder, and the shoulder from the lower back, lengthening the lower back in order to send the shoulder forward. To use whole body power, you must be sure to first turn the left fist up and turn back, then bring the forearm across and hook and cover while pulling back. This ensures that both fists are moving from the power of the shoulders and elbows, and working together.

Sparrow Hawk Wheels Over

Moving the weight back and forth must come by using the waist as a fulcrum, so that the whole body remains coordinated. When the torso turns left and the weight shifts leftward to send the left drill out, the torso needs to reach forward slightly. When the weight shifts back and the torso turns right, transfer power from the waist to the shoulders, from the shoulders to the elbows, and from the elbows to the hands, so that the right forearm first slices upward, then the elbow pulls back. Bend the left arm to lift the elbow, stabbing the fist down to slide along the leg as it twists, being sure to keep the shoulders closed. Use a twisting power to circle the right fist down to the waist. The shoulder needs to open, close, and settle.

During the drop stance the weight should be completely on the right leg, which is fully bent to a full squat. The left fist slides down and forward along the top of the left leg, and must go past the left foot. Press the head forward into the movement, moving the centre of gravity forward. The left shoulder should open out and settle down so that the left fist can rotate fully with the fist eye up. Settle the elbow and bend it slightly, so that the left arm has a forward and upward scooping power as it moves forward with a twisting, drilling power.

- Older players do not need to sit right down into the drop stance, but the same power should be maintained in the hands. As the body turns the power should lengthen. The waist and shoulder action is key, so that the arms move together with the waist and the power is complete without slackness, soft but not loose, with a hidden power and no stiffness.

Moving from *sparrow hawk wheels over* to *sparrow hawk folds its wings,* the power should be smooth so that the movement is coordinated.

CHAPTER TEN: THE TWELVE ANIMAL MODELS 239

Second Sparrow Hawk method

Sparrow Hawk Grabs a Sparrow, Sparrow Hawk Spreads its Wings

- Although the two sparrow hawk forms differ in techniques, they should both show the spirit of the sparrow hawk.

The hands must circle into *sparrow hawk grabs a sparrow,* transfering power from the waist to the shoulders, from the shoulders to the elbows, and from the elbows to the hands. The rear foot should step through as the lead hand braces and the rear hand threads forward. The lead hand should have a bracing power forward and up with an upward and outward blocking power. Keep the arm bent so that the forearm and outer edge of the palm have power. As the rear hand stabs forward it needs a twisting, rolling, drilling power, and as it chops forward and down it first circles up a half circle so that it turns, drops, tucks, and pulls back with the forward step.

The action of *sparrow hawk spreads its wings* first closes down then opens out, which means that the power first gathers then launches. To roll in, close the chest and open the upper back, releasing tension in the shoulders and settling the elbows, closing in without telegraphing your intent. When bracing out, be sure to first turn the elbows up, then spread the chest and firm the abdomen, release the shoulders and brace outward with equal power in the right and left hands. The power is completed as you settle into the stance, with equal placement and power right and left, up and down.

BREATHING CYCLE FOR THE SPARROW HAWK MODEL

In general, inhale during transitional actions and exhale for the final power launch of each movement.

- Inhale during *sparrow hawk tucks its wings* and exhale during *sparrow hawk enters the woods.*

- Inhale in the initial action of *sparrow hawk pierces the sky* and exhale for the final action.

- Inhale in the dropping action of *sparrow hawk wheels over* and exhale for the rising action. Settle the breath into the belly to launch power.

- Inhale during the initial actions of *sparrow hawk grasps its prey* and exhale for the final grab.

- Inhale during the initial action of *sparrow hawk spreads its wings* and exhale for the final action.

PRACTICAL APPLICATIONS FOR THE SPARROW HAWK MODEL

- Practice and power application in forms differ considerably as to how you might apply the techniques. You can't expect to apply a move without changing it, and must be ready to react to anything that the opponent does. Forms are a means of practising techniques but do not expect to use the techniques in the theoretical 'model method' that you have practised.

Sparrow hawk tucks its wings and *sparrow hawk enters the woods* are one technique – an *aligned stance cannon punch* that uses a turned body to enter. The lead hand deflects so that the rear hand can get in to punch. The footwork should drive directly into the opponent's groin, hitting as you enter.

Sparrow hawk pierces the sky is a drilling punch to the nose. You need to get inside the opponent's defenses to strike upwards, so must step in to get the body close. The drill hides an elbow strike.

Sparrow hawk wheels over is either a way to hit as you turn around, or a feint up and strike down. You don't need to drop all the way down, because a large movement is slow and you must move quickly to be effective. "The only thing that cannot be beaten is speed." The cover and drill is a feint, and the lower strike is the real strike. You can step forward or back, depending on what is needed.

Sparrow hawk grasps its prey is a double handed aligned stance pull that changes into an entry with a push and stab. This softens the opponent and then you charge in for a strike to the chest.

Sparrow hawk spreads its wings uses one forearm to knock aside and the other arm to cover and roll down to make the opponent lose effectiveness. As your hands drop down and forward they can get in to strike the opponent's belly. You can also use the rear forearm to cover the opponent's arm and slide along it to strike crossways to his neck or throat. One is a low strike, and one is a crosscut to the throat; use what would work as the opportunity presents.

THE POEM ABOUT THE SPARROW HAWK

鹞子歌诀

鹞子入林侧身攻，

翻身顾后逞其能。

展翅捉雀形贯意，

劲力浑厚体均衡。

Sparrow hawk enters the woods attacks with the body turned sideways.

Wheel the body deals with things behind it, flaunting its great ability.

Spread the wings and *grasp the sparrow* have full intent throughout,

The power is dense and the body is balanced.

NINE: SNAKE MODEL

蛇形

INTRODUCTION TO THE SNAKE MODEL, *SHE XING*

The snake is a reptile that, although it has no legs, is known for its speed, agility, instantaneous reaction time, and whole body liveliness. Xingyiquan masters of old examined the movements and spirit of the snake to create the snake form. They created the rich, expansive, and beautiful techniques of the snake form by imitating its imposing look of a snake when it holds itself erect, its ferocity when it spits its tongue, its litheness at slithering through the grass, and its ability to coil around. We should show the skills and attitude of the snake when we practise: the litheness of a snake's body, its ability to bend and lengthen, its ability to encircle and coil, its softness and hardness, its overall ease of movement. If you hit its head then its tail will react, if you hit its tail then its head will react, if you hit its body then its tail and head will react together.

METHODS OF PERFORMING THE SNAKE MODEL

There are two traditional ways of performing the snake model. One is comprised of three movements: *white snake spits its tongue, white snake coils its body,* and *white snake slithers through the grass.* The other emphasizes the scooping lift. Both use Xingyiquan's zigzag stepping pattern, as if following the line of a slithering snake.

9.1   METHOD ONE OF THE SNAKE MODEL

Start from left *santishi*.

9.1a   White Snake Spits its Tongue[23]   báishé tù xìn   白蛇吐信

ACTION: Withdraw the left foot a half-step and lower the left hand to the belly. (no photo) Advance the left foot a half-step to the right with the foot turned out, shifting forward. Thread the left hand up to the sternum and forward to eye height, palm up. Do not move the right hand yet. Look at the left hand. (image 10.195)

---

[23] Translator's note: in movement names, a snake's forked tongue is sometimes written 芯, but it is usually written 信. The two are pronounced the same, and neither really mean a forked tongue. The character 信 is more common.

9.1b White Snake Coils its Body   báishé chán shēn 白蛇缠身

ACTION 1: Turn the left hand over, palm down, and circle it down and back to behind the left hip. Circle the right hand right and up to above the head. Keep both elbows bent. Rise, turning slightly leftward. Look at the left hand. (image 10.196)

ACTION 2: Stab the right hand directly down to outside the left hip, palm out. Thread the left hand in front of the right shoulder, palm up, tucking the left elbow into the chest. Twist the waist leftward and squat down into a resting stance, lifting the right heel. Look at the right hand at first, and as you sit down, look to the forward right. Press the head up. Sit onto the right heel. (image 10.197)

9.1c White Snake Slithers through the Grass   báishé bō cǎo 白蛇拨草

ACTION 1: Advance the left foot a half-step and take a long step to the forward right with the right foot, following in with the left foot a half-step. Slice the right hand rightwards and upwards to waist height with the thumb web up and the fingers forward. Pull the left hand back to the left hip, palm down. Sit the torso down, settling the weight between the feet. Look at the right hand. (images 10.198 and 10.198 front)

CHAPTER TEN: THE TWELVE ANIMAL MODELS   243

10.198   10.198
              FRONT

9.1d   White Snake Spits its Tongue   báishé tù xìn   白蛇吐信

ACTION: Sit back onto the left leg and withdraw the right foot a half-step. Bring the right hand back to the belly without pausing. Advance the right foot a half-step to the forward left with the foot turned out, shifting forward. Thread the right hand up by the sternum and forward to eye height. Do not move the left hand yet. Look at the right hand. (image 10.199)

10.199

- Continue on to left and right with the same action, alternating sides.

Pointers

- As the left foot advances it should circle and turn out. The left hand should pull back and then thread up to coordinate with the footwork.
- Twist the body and sit in coordination with the right palm stab down.
- Step the right foot forward to coordinate with the right scooping slice.

9.1e   Snake Turn Around   shé xíng huíshēn   蛇形回身

ACTION 1: If you finish on the <u>right</u> side *white snake slithers through the grass*, then stand up, swinging the left hand forward and up (fingers forward, little finger side up) until the hands form a line on either side of the body. Pivot around a full one-eighty degrees on the feet. Look forward. (image 10.200)

ACTION 2: The arms have swung so that they form a straight line with the right up and the left down. Twist the body and sit down into a resting stance, stabbing the right hand down outside the left hip, palm out, and circling the left hand up to the right shoulder, palm up. First watch the right hand as the hands move, then look to the forward left as soon as you sit down. (images 10.201, 10.202)

- The *snake form turn around* is simply *white snake coils its body*, done while pivoting. Left and right sides are similar, just transposing right and left.

9.1f Snake Closing Move shé xíng shōushì 蛇形收势

Continue on until you arrive where you started.

- From a <u>left</u> side *white snake slithers through the grass* stance:

Bring the left foot back beside the right foot. Cover and press down the left hand to the belly. Then lift both hands up, bring them together and turn them down, pressing down. Stand up and close.

- From a <u>right</u> side *white snake slithers through the grass* stance:

Bring the right foot back. Cover and press down the right hand to the belly. Then lift both hands up, bring them together and turn them down, pressing down. Stand up and close.

9.2 SECOND METHOD OF THE SNAKE MODEL

Start from left *santishi*.

9.2a Snake on Right Side shé xíng yòu shì 蛇形右势

ACTION 1: Advance the left foot a half-step, shift to the left leg, and bring the right foot in to touch the toes down, with the knee bent and the heel off the ground. Stab the right hand down from the belly to the left, palm out, fingers down, back of the hand adhering to the left hip. Bend the left elbow and bring the left hand to in front of the right shoulder, palm in, fingers forward. Look past the right shoulder. (image 10.203)

ACTION 2: Take a long step to the forward right with the right foot and follow in a half-step with the left foot, putting most weight on the left leg. Clench both fists and slice the right fist to the right and up to waist height, fist eye up. Pull the left fist back to beside the left hip. Drop the torso and lean forward slightly. Look at the right fist. (image 10.204)

9.2b **Snake on Left Side**   shé xíng zuǒ shì   蛇形左势

ACTION 1: Advance the right foot a half-step and shift onto the right leg, bringing the left foot in to touch the ball on the ground, heel up and knee bent so that the left heel is behind the right foot. Unclench the hands and stab the left hand down by the right hip, palm out and fingers down. Bend the right elbow and close the arm so that the hand is in front of the left shoulder, palm in, fingers up. Look in front of the left shoulder. (image 10.205)

ACTION 2: Take a long diagonal step to the forward left with the left foot and follow in a half-step with the right foot, putting most weight on the right leg. Clench the hands and slice the left fist left and up to waist height, fist eye up. Pull the right fist back to outside the right hip. Drop the body and lean forward. Look at the left fist. (image 10.206)

Pointers

- Advance the left foot and stab the right hand down simultaneously. Pay attention to twisting the waist and closing the shoulders.
- Step the right foot forward and slice the right hand up with fully connected power. The same goes for the other side.

9.2c   Snake Turn Around   shé xíng huí shēn   蛇形回身

- If you arrive at the end of the space on the <u>left</u> side *white snake slithers through the grass*,

ACTION 1: Hook-in step the left foot to outside the right foot so that the body turns around to the right two-seventy degrees. Lift the right foot, touching the toes down and shifting onto the left leg. Unclench the hands and stab the right hand down by the left hip. As the body turns around, bend the left elbow to hold the hand in front of the right shoulder.

ACTION 2: Advance the right foot diagonally and slice the right fist up.

- Turning from the <u>right</u> side is the same, just transposing left and right.

PROBLEMS OFTEN MET IN THE SNAKE MODEL

Method One of Snake Model

PROBLEM 1: The student does not thread the hand up during *white snake spits its tongue*, but simply takes the hand across then carries on.

> CORRECTIONS: Reinforce the correct movement pattern from the beginning. The hand must first thread through with the ulnar side turned over as much as possible. Then, to continue on, the hand will rotate palm down, and only then continue on to *coil around*.

PROBLEM 2: The student is unstable in the squatting position of *white snake coils its body*.

> CORRECTIONS: There are three main causes of loss of balance. A: The centre of gravity is not under control. B: the lead foot is not turned out enough in the resting stance. C: the torso leans forward too far. Watch for these tendencies in the student. Remind the student to lift the head up to maintain a centered torso.
>
>> The head is the 'leader of the six *yangs*', that is to say, if the head is upright then the torso will be straight. Pressing the head up will place the torso on the correct line and keep it centered, thus keeping the weight under control.
>
> For the resting stance, remind the student to turn the lead foot out and keep it flat on the ground to gain stability. In this stance the buttocks should sit all the way down, the waist should be bent, the chest contained, and the upper back tight, but the head should always press upwards.

PROBLEM 3: The student slices the arm up too high during *white snake slithers through the grass*.

> CORRECTIONS: The arm must come through no higher than the waist and no lower than the knee. The scooping slice is a strike to the groin.

CHAPTER TEN: THE TWELVE ANIMAL MODELS 247

PROBLEM 4: The student straightens his arm during *slither through the grass*.

CORRECTIONS: Have the student maintain a settled shoulder and elbow, which will help to maintain a bent elbow.

Method Two of Snake Model

PROBLEM 1: The student remains too straight during the step forward, stab down and thread up action.

CORRECTIONS: The student must experiment with what are the characteristics of the snake form. He must use the body, setting the shoulder into the direction that the scooping slice will be done, closing the shoulders and twisting the waist.

PROBLEM 2: The student straightens the arm during the scooping slice.

CORRECTIONS: The classics say, "too straight gives less force, too bent gives less reach". A certain angle is needed in the elbow to put force into the slice, so the shoulder should be extended and the elbow settled.

PROBLEM 3: The student drags the hip when doing the follow-in step.

CORRECTIONS: Leaving the hip behind during the step is a common error in Xingyiquan footwork. Usually it is caused by the rear foot turning out, which in turn turns out the knee. This prevents you from closing the groin, and makes the next driving step difficult to do, so it must be corrected. When practising footwork, have the student first bring the knee forward and only then complete the follow-in step with the foot. Pay attention that the foot is turned at less than a forty-five degree angle, so that the knee tracks straight. Only in this position can the leg push off strongly into the ground, and can the groin remain closed.

POWER GENERATION FOR THE SNAKE MODEL

Method One of Snake Model

- Although there are three actions, there is only one technique. There should be no obvious break between the actions, especially between *spitting the tongue* and *coiling the body*.

White snake spits its tongue: The left hand should thread up as the left foot lands, turned out. The left hand should pull back as the left foot withdraws. Hands and feet always work together. Pay attention to keep the fingers together as the left hand threads up, turning into the ulnar edge to roll the elbow in.

White snake coils its body: As the arms open and swing up, press the head up and rise in the torso. Then as the hands thread and stab, gathering in, squat down fully into the legs. The body technique is to first rise and open, and then drop and fold in. When you open you must open fully, and when you fold in you should shut down completely. When moving, pay attention that the right hand has a rolling in power as it drops into the stab – the palm should have a twisting power, twisting into the stab. The left hand should have a twisting, rolling, drilling power as it threads up. The shoulders and abdomen should close in and the torso bend, closing the chest, so that the whole body tucks and twists as you squat and stab with the hands.

White snake slithers through the grass: The right hand must complete the scooping slice as the right foot lands. Sit the torso down slightly to launch power, dropping into the buttocks, by tucking in the rear knee and stabbing it down. The shoulders move up and down, so coordinate the power launch through the shoulders, combining this with an exhalation to help gain more power. You must practise to find how to coordinate the shoulder and buttocks actions.

White snake coils its body is the preparatory action and *white snake slithers through the grass* is the launching action. You should try to find this power of shooting a spring in your practice. When coiling, you want to coil the spring tightly, pressing it down to store power. When going through the grass you want to suddenly shoot the spring out. You shoot out using all directions – forward and backward, left and right, inside and outside. This is a high quality power launch, using whole body power.

During the *snake turn around,* be sure to first rise, pivot on both feet, and then drop and stab. Raise the body high and drop tightly.

Method Two of Snake Model

- This method of doing snake is appropriate for older players, as it uses a fairly high, less difficult stance.

The hands and feet must be coordinated – as the lead foot advances one hand stabs down and the other threads up. The stabbing down hand gets its power from the turning of the waist, closing of the shoulders, rotating of the arm, and rolling in of the hip. The hand that threads up gets its power from a rolling in of the arm with a drill. The arms should be tightly held in front of the chest, so you need to contain the chest, tighten the upper back, press the head up, relax tension in the hips, and sit into the buttocks.

The slice must come as the foot lands. The rear foot must come through nearby the lead foot as it advances. The power is the same as *white snake slithers through the grass* explained above, the only difference is the use of the fist instead of the palm.

The *turn around* for this snake method is different from the first, so be sure to take a good hook-in step, hooking well in. When turning, press the head up. The rotation should be around the spine, and must be quick, so be sure not to move around too much. Keep the whole body coordinated.

- Keep the elbows appropriately bent during the stabbing and slicing actions. Never over-straighten the arms.

- The vital element of the snake model is the advancing scooping slice. You must find how to use the power from the body by sitting down into the action in order to have a strong shoveling, lifting, slicing action into the arm.

BREATHING CYCLE FOR THE SNAKE MODEL

First, work on the correct line of action of the hands and feet. Get every part of the technique correct and coordinate the hands and feet, without worrying about the breathing. Concentrate on the biomechanical action. Once the action is smooth, then you can concentrate on the power flow and the whole body power. Exhalation can then help you get more power into the strike.

- Inhale in rising actions and opening actions.
- Exhale in dropping actions and closing-in actions. Exhale sharply in power launching actions. Work carefully to coordinate the breathing closely with the actions of the snake form.

PRACTICAL APPLICATIONS FOR THE SNAKE MODEL

White snake spits its tongue is a threading strike to the face, and hides a hooking grab. If the opponent blocks with his hands, then you can turn over to hook onto his hand. If he doesn't block, then you thread directly to his eyes. This is not a heavy hit, but a quick stab to the eyes can throw him off and give your following attack a better chance at getting in.

White snake coils its body is a small, compact movement when used, although it is practised as a large movement. Draw a large circle with the hands in practice, but tighten this down to really use it. Dodge the head out of the way and hook onto the opponent's hand with your lead hand. You may also get in a shoulder strike during this action.

White snake slithers through the grass is a scooping throw, or a slice to the groin. One hand can block up and then pull down. When you step in you can shove with the shoulder or you can strike into the groin with your arm or hand. The key is to drive the footwork to enter through the opponent's main door.

- Although there are a variety of ways to perform snake form, almost all finish with the scooping strike. Each variation gives you a different application. You must learn to react and change techniques according to the situation, so the main thing you are practising is the way to use power throughout your body, so that you can use your power when and as you need.

> Do not practice as if the technique is set in stone. If you train empty movements then your training is dead; if you train the power within the forms then your training is lively.

SNAKE, *SHE XING*

THE POEM ABOUT THE SNAKE

蛇形歌诀

蛇形身法贵屈伸，

头闪肩撞藏在心。

进步攉挑腰膀力，

周身内外劲衡均。

The body technique of the snake is to flex and extend.

Dodge the head and hide the technique of a shoulder shove.

Enter with the footwork to shovel and scoop, using the strength of the back into the arm,

Using an even balance of inner and outer power throughout the whole body.

TEN: WEDGE-TAILED HAWK MODEL

鸟台形

Introduction To The Wedge-Tailed Hawk Model, *Tai Xing*

The classics say, "tai bird[24] has a direct nature, it has the ability to raise its tail straight up, it flies straight up then drops straight down onto its prey. Its innate skill is to lift its tail and fly up past the clouds, and then it can drop straight to grab its prey with its talons. So we copy its form to rise and fall like lightening, to use the tail, to change like the wind. Outwardly it is fierce, inwardly it is soft. It has an indescribable skill."

The action of the wedge-tailed hawk model[25] is to cross the hands in front of the body, open them to the sides, and then strike forward simultaneously. It emphasizes bringing the power from the tailbone, getting the power of the whole body into the arms. It uses Xingyiquan's zigzag stepping pattern, and the strike is forward and down.

Method Of Performing The Wedge-Tailed Hawk Model

10   Standard Wedge-Tailed Hawk Model

tāi xíng 鸟台形

Start from left *santishi*.

---

[24] Author's note: The character for 'tai' is sometimes written with a bird radical and sometimes with a fish radical. Both are pronounced 'tai'. Although they are pronounced the same, the meaning of the character is changed considerably with the different radicals, as one flies and the other swims. Within Xingyiquan, though, however the character is written, the form is performed much the same way. [Translator's. note: many typesets lack the bird radical character, so this is why it is often typed wrong. I had to put together two characters to make the bird radical character as it is not in the computer program.]

[25] Translator's note: This is also translated as 'Chinese ostrich,' 'phoenix,' and 'mythical tai bird' but I prefer wedge-tailed hawk, as this hawk does exactly this action with its talons, wings, and tail to catch rabbits, which are about the same size as it.

252 WEDGE-TAILED HAWK, *TAI XING*

10a **Wedge-tailed Hawk, Left** tāi xíng zuǒ shì 鸟台 形左势

ACTION 1: Advance the left foot a half-step and clench the fists, pulling the left fist back to the belly. Turn both fist hearts inward and keep them tight to the belly. Press the head up and look forward. (image 10.207)

ACTION 2: Take a long step forward with the right foot and follow in with the left foot to inside the right ankle without touching down. Drill the fists up to eyebrow height, fist hearts in, crossing the forearms in front of the chest, left inside the right. Turn the fists, open out to right and left, and circle back down to the sides of the body, fist hearts up. Press the head up and look straight ahead to the forward left. (images 10.208, 10.209, 10.210)

  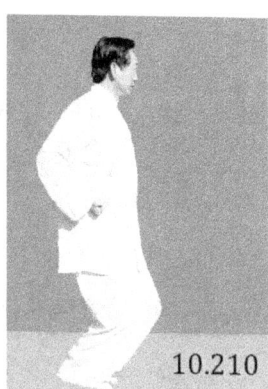

ACTION 3: Take a long step with the left foot to the forward left and follow in a half-step with the right foot, keeping most weight on the right leg. Punch both fists to the lower front at belly height, fist hearts up. Keep the arms slightly bent, and the fists about a fist-width apart. Press the head up and look past the fists. (images 10.211 and 10.211 front)

CHAPTER TEN: THE TWELVE ANIMAL MODELS 253

10b   Wedge-tailed Hawk, Right   tāi xíng yòu shì   鸟台 形右势

ACTION 1: Advance the left foot a half-step and bring the right foot up to the left ankle without touching down, keeping the toes up. Cross the fists and drill up with fist hearts in, right fist outside the left fist. Drill up to eyebrow height and then open to either side. Circle around and down to the sides, turning the fist hearts up. Press the head up and look to the forward right. (images 10.212, 10.213)

ACTION 2: Take a long step with the right foot to the forward right and follow in a half-step with the left foot, keeping the weight on the left leg. Punch to the forward right with the fist hearts up. Keep the arms slightly bent and the fists about a fist-width apart. Press the head up, settle the shoulders, and look past the fists. (image 10.214)

10c   Wedge-tailed Hawk, Left   tāi xíng zuǒ shì   鸟台 形左势

- This is the same as the *wedge-tailed hawk, right* described above in 10b, just transposing left and right.

Pointers:

- o Complete the circle of the fists down to the sides as the lead foot advances.
- o Complete the punch as the rear foot steps through and lands, so that the punch arrives with the foot.

10d   Wedge-tailed Hawk Turn Around   tāi xíng huí shēn   鸟台 形回身

If starting from *wedge-tailed hawk, left*:

ACTION 1: Step the left foot around to the outside of the right foot, hooking in, turning the body around two-seventy degrees to the right and sitting onto the left leg, lifting the right foot to the left ankle without touching down. Cross the fists and drill up, fist hearts in. On drilling up to eyebrow height, open them and circle down to the sides, fists hearts up. Press the head up and look to the forward right. (image 10.215)

ACTION 2: Step the right foot to the forward right and follow in a half-step with the left, keeping the weight on the left leg. Punch forward and down to belly height with both fists, fist hearts up. The fists are fist-width apart. Press the head up and look past the fists. (image 10.216)

10e Wedge-tailed Hawk Closing Move   tāi xíng shōushì   鸟台 形收势

Continue until you reach your starting point and turn around.

ACTION 1: If you are in a *left* side wedge-tailed hawk, turn the body forty-five degrees to the right and bring the right fist back to the belly. As the body turns, circle the left fist up and rightward, to cover and press down with the forearm across, fist heart down. Bring the left foot in beside the right foot, drill the right fist up and forward and press and pull the left fist back to the belly. Press the head up and look forward.

ACTION 2: Step the left foot straight forward without moving the right foot. Do a split with the left hand to settle into left *santishi*. Then close the same as usual from *santishi*.

- If you are in a *right* side wedge-tailed hawk, bring the right foot in and cover with the left forearm, drilling up with the right fist. Then step the left foot forward and split with the left hand to settle into left *santishi*, closing as usual.

PROBLEMS OFTEN MET IN THE WEDGE-TAILED HAWK MODEL

PROBLEM 1: The student shrugs his shoulders when drilling up and circling.

CORRECTIONS: Always be careful to keep the shoulders and elbows settled. Shrugging the shoulders not only breaks the basic positional requirements of most martial arts, it also causes problems of *qi* flow. The *qi* floats in the chest, causing the body to be light and the legs to be unsteady. The way to solve this problem is to concentrate on releasing tension in the shoulder muscles and settling them down, tautening the upper back muscles, while always maintaining a straight and upright head. The student must learn to feel the release in the shoulder joints and the settling down.

PROBLEM 2: The student circles the hands in front of the body instead of bringing them back to the waist before punching forward. This gives a short distance for the punch, and can cause the punch to turn into a poke.

CORRECTIONS: The student must correct the line drawn by the fists, to take them out and down to either side of the waist. He should pay attention to opening the elbows and drawing them back slightly. Then, for the punch, forcefully squeeze the elbows into the ribs and shove them forward, sending the fists forward in a strong punch.

PROBLEM 3: The student leaves too much distance between the fists in the punch.

CORRECTIONS: If the fists are too far apart then they could miss the target, and the power will not be compact. The student must practice getting a fist width – about ten centimetres – between the fists.

POWER GENERATION FOR THE WEDGE-TAILED HAWK MODEL

As the fists rise and cross they need to have drilling power. As the fists reach head height they turn out. At this point the torso should settle, the chest close, and the upper back stretch. When the fists circle to the sides the arms should have a bracing out power. The arms are rounded with slightly bent elbows. When the fists are lowered to the sides, the torso should lengthen slightly and the arms should have a rolling-in power. The fists must draw vertical circles at the sides, and at each instant during the circle there must be a full power; there must be no slackening off at any time.

The footwork to practise the form is a zigzag pattern. There should be no pause halfway through the stepping action.

The fists circle to the sides as the lead foot takes a half-step forward. The fists punch as the rear foot comes through to land.

As the fists circle and drop and the arms roll in, the head should press forward and up and the waist should straighten slightly. The shoulders should open, the chest should expand, and the abdomen should become firm. At this point the torso may rise slightly.

The punch comes as the foot lands. The fists should be tightly clenched with the fist hearts aligned flat. Press the head up, settle the shoulders down, and sit into the buttocks. The fists must continue to twist, as the punch depends on the arms squeezing the elbows into the ribs to send the fists forward. Exhale to launch power to send the fists out; the elbows follow, and the shoulders urge forward. Grab the ground with the foot as it lands.

To turn around the hook-in step needs to hook well in, the body needs to get around quickly and remain stable.

Breathing Cycle For The Wedge-Tailed Hawk Model

- Inhale as the arms circle around. Take a long breath in.
- Exhale to punch. Use a short and powerful breath out.

Practical Applications For The Wedge-Tailed Hawk Model

The drill up and circle is a defensive move. You can stick to the opponent's arm and roll through to enter. You should draw a large circle in practice, but when really using it, a small circle is more effective.

The double punch is to between the waist and belly. This is a short punch, thrown when the body is in close, so you need to step in through the 'main door'. If you can get the body in close then you can get the punch in, landing the punch as the foot lands.

- The main technique of the wedge-tailed hawk form is to get in close with the body. The main attacking action is the double punch just below the waist with the fist hearts up. You can hit with one or both fists, and you can hit to the floating ribs.

The Poem About The Wedge-Tailed Hawk

鸟台 形歌诀

展翅升空上下飞，

双拳直捣纵步追。

拳势贯在均衡劲，

四梢相齐显其威。

Spread the wings and soar in the sky, flying up and down.

Double fists strike straight, chasing with a direct step.

The value of the technique is in its even balanced power.

Its might lies in the four tips working together.

ELEVEN: EAGLE MODEL

鷹形

Introduction To The Eagle Model, *Ying Xing*

The eagle, a bird of prey with a hooked beak, a short neck, and feathery feet with long talons, has a fierce nature. Xingyiquan's eagle form borrows its skill at grasping prey, so the hand shape is called an eagle claw. When practising you should feel the eagle soaring in the wilderness, circling slowly with open wings, then suddenly spotting its prey, tucking the wings and dropping, grabbing it in its talons and then taking it to its beak. There is nothing the prey can do to escape this ferocity. The eagle form is traditionally also called 'eagle clutching'. The most important aspect is to drop into the grab with the head up and the eyes spirited like an eagle.

Methods Of Performing The Eagle Model

The eagle grab is done either in a reverse stance [opposite hand and foot forward] or an aligned stance [same hand and foot forward]. The hand technique and power application is the same, only the footwork differs.

11.1 METHOD ONE: REVERSE STANCE EAGLE

àobù yīng xíng   拗步鷹形

Start from left *santishi*.

11.1a   Eagle in Left Reverse Stance   zuǒ àobù yīng xíng   左拗步鷹形

ACTION 1: Clench the left fist and pull it back to the belly. Clench the right hand at the belly. Withdraw the left foot to in front of the right foot and shift onto the right leg. Drill the left fist up by the sternum and forward to nose height, twisting the ulnar edge over. Press the head up and look past the left fist. (image 10.217)

ACTION 2: Take a long diagonal step to the forward left with the left foot and follow in a half-step with the right foot, shifting forward to place the weight between the legs. Drill the right fist up by the sternum then along inside of the left forearm. Once the fists cross then unclench them, turning the palms down. Pull the left hand back to the belly and chop the right hand forward to waist height. The direction of the strike is aligned along a line drawn midway between the feet. Press the head up, settle the shoulders and elbows, and look at the right hand. (images 10.218 and 10.218 front)

11.1b Eagle in Right Reverse Stance yòu àobù yīng xíng 右拗步鹰形

ACTION 1: Advance the left foot a half-step and lift the right foot inside the left ankle. Clench the right hand and pull it back to the belly, then drill it up by the sternum and forward to nose height, twisting the ulnar edge up. Look past the right fist. (image 10.219)

ACTION 2: Take a long diagonal step with the right foot to the forward right and follow in the left foot a half-step, shifting the weight forward to between the legs. Bend the left knee and press it down. Drill the left fist up by the sternum then along inside the right forearm until the fists cross. Then unclench the hands and turn the palms down. Pull the right hand back to the belly and split forward and down with the left hand to waist height. Release tension in the shoulders and settle the elbows. Keep the left arm slightly bent. Press the head up and look at the left hand. (image 10.220)

11.1c Eagle in Left Reverse Stance   zuǒ àobù yīng xíng   左拗步鹰形

ACTION 1: Advance the right foot a half-step and lift the left foot inside the right foot. Clench the left hand and pull it back to the belly, then drill it up by the sternum and up to nose height, turning the ulnar edge up. Look at the left fist.

ACTION 2: Take a long step to the forward left with the left foot and follow in a half-step with the right foot, shifting the weight forward between the legs. Drill the right fist up by the sternum then along the left forearm, and when the fists cross, unclench them both and turn the palms down. Pull the left hand back to the belly and split forward and down to waist height with the right hand. Settle the shoulders and elbows, keep the right arm slightly bent, press the head up, and look at the right hand.

Pointers

- Pull the left fist back and drill forward timed exactly with the withdrawal of the left foot.
- Land the left foot and the right hand split at exactly the same time. Be sure to press the head up as you look down, turning only the eyes down.
- Right and left sides are the same action, just transposing right and left.

11.1d Eagle Turn Around   yīng xíng huíshēn   鹰形回身

Starting with the _right_ reverse stance eagle grab (right foot and left hand forward).

ACTION 1: Hook-in the right foot in front of the left foot, shifting onto the right leg. Lift the left foot and turn around to the left to face back in the way from which you came. Clench the left hand and pull it back to the belly, then drill it up by the sternum and forward to nose height, twisting the ulnar edge up. Do not move the right fist. (image 10.221)

ACTION 2: Step the left foot diagonally to the forward left and follow in a half-step with the right foot. Open the right hand and slide it along the left forearm to split forward and down to waist height. Look at the right hand. (image 10.222)

10.221

10.222

- Turning in the other direction is the same, just transposing right and left.

EAGLE, *YING XING*

Pointers

- You must hook-step in and turn around quickly. Be sure to maintain stability as you lift the other foot to ankle height.
- The split in the turn around is the same as the normal eagle grabbing.

11.1e Eagle Closing Move yīng xíng shōushì 鹰形收势

Once you get back to the starting point, turn around to face in the same direction as the opening position.

- From *left* reverse stance eagle grab

ACTION 1: Withdraw the left foot to beside the right foot. Clench the right fist and pull it back to the belly then drill it up to nose height, ulnar edge twisted up. Look at the right fist.

ACTION 2: Advance the left foot a half-step directly forward and split forward with the left hand to settle into a left *santishi*. Close as usual from *santishi*.

- From *right* reverse stance eagle grab

ACTION 1: Withdraw the right foot to beside the left foot and shift to the right leg. Clench the left fist and pull it back to the belly. Clench the right fist and drill it up by the sternum, then forward to nose height, twisting the ulnar edge up. Look at the right fist.

ACTION 2: Advance the left foot a half-step directly forward without moving the right foot, to settle into a left *santishi*. Split the left hand forward and pull the right hand back to the belly. Press the head up and look straight ahead. Close as usual from *santishi*.

11.2 SECOND METHOD: ALIGNED STANCE EAGLE

shùnbù yīng xíng 顺步鹰形

Start from left *santishi*.

11.2a Eagle in Right Aligned Stance yòu shùnbù yīng xíng 右顺步鹰形

ACTION 1: First withdraw the left foot a bit, then advance it a half-step, following in with the right foot to inside the left ankle. Clench the left fist and pull it back to the belly, then drill it up by the sternum and forward to nose height, ulnar edge twisted up. Look at the left hand. (image 10.223)

ACTION 2: Take a long step forward with the right foot and follow in a half-step with the left foot. Drill the right fist up by the sternum then forward along the left forearm. When the fists cross, unclench the hand and turn the palms down, splitting forcefully out with the right hand at waist height and pulling the left hand back to the belly. Press the head up, release through the shoulders and settle the elbows. Look at the right hand. (image 10.224)

11.2b   Eagle in Left Aligned Stance   zuǒ shùnbù yīng xíng   左顺步鹰形

ACTION 1: First withdraw the right foot a bit then advance a half-step, following in with the left foot just inside the right ankle. Clench the right hand and pull it back to the belly, then drill it up by the sternum and forward to nose height, ulnar edge twisted up. Look at the right fist. (image 10.225)

ACTION 2: Take a long step forward with the left foot and follow in a half-step with the right foot. Drill the left fist up by the sternum then forward along the right forearm. When the fists cross, unclench the hands and turn the palms down. Split forcefully out with the left hand at waist height and pull the right hand back to the belly. Press the head up, release through the shoulders and settle the elbows. Look at the left hand. (image 10.226)

Pointers

- o   All the pointers are the same as the *reverse stance eagle*. Only the footwork differs.

11.2c Aligned Stance Eagle Turn Around and Closing

shùnbù yīng xíng zhuànshēn hé shōushì   顺步鹰形转身和收势

- The turn around is the same as the turn of split, only the splitting action is lower than in split, and the hands are held in an eagle claw shape.

- Closing is the same as that of split.

PROBLEMS OFTEN MET IN THE EAGLE MODEL

PROBLEM 1: The student does not use the eagle claw.

CORRECTIONS: Some people do not use the eagle claw, and there is nothing wrong with this. The eagle claw does, however, better bring out the spirit of the eagle.

PROBLEM 2: The student does not have a strong scissoring action in the legs in *reverse stance eagle*.

CORRECTIONS: The student must bring in the foot from the hip. First land the lead foot, then bring in the rear foot a half step by rolling the hip, closing the knee, and bringing in the foot. The head must be pressed up and the buttocks must sit down, so that there is a raking power between the feet. The rear foot pushes through the heel. With these actions there will be a good scissoring strength between the legs.

PROBLEM 3: The student does not have a whole body power in the landing of the split.

CORRECTIONS: The first thing is to have the student understand what whole body power is. When using power, each segment throughout the whole body must be integrated to a high degree, using the mind. The student must practise each movement such that once one segment moves there is nothing in the body that does not move in total integrated coordination. Use this method: first collect the *qi* and settle down, then move from the root to the tips, sequentially connecting and transferring power. In this way the student can gradually collect his dispersed power to make it whole, and eventually reach the goal of emitting power into the tips.

PROBLEM 4: The student drops his head and bends at the waist to look at the lead hand that is at waist height.

CORRECTIONS: Dropping the head and bending over at the waist is a major error in most martial art styles. The student must press up into the head in the final position and keep the spine of the upper back straight, sitting into the buttocks. As the hand chops down the head presses up to counterbalance. Never let the student bend the back or stick out the buttocks.

POWER GENERATION FOR THE EAGLE MODEL

The hand shape differs from the usual hand shapes in that it is held in an eagle claw. The thumb web is stretched open, the thumb opening strongly, and the other fingers are separated slightly. The last and middle joints of the fingers are bent. The palm is concave, and the wrist sits slightly.

The lead hand grabs and pulls back as the lead foot withdraws slightly. Then the lead foot advances a half-step as the lead hand drills forward. Both hands must split downward as the foot lands.

- The footwork of the *reverse stance eagle* advances in a zigzag pattern, and that of the *aligned stance eagle* advances in a straight line.

Once the hand has clenched and pulled back it should not hesitate, but drill directly up. The foot should also not hesitate once it withdraws, but should immediately advance. The lower back should straighten and the torso should lengthen as the fist drills up. Then when the hands drop down to the chest, the abdomen should close and the torso should press forward slightly, dropping the lead shoulder and lifting the rear shoulder slightly. The elbows should settle down and stay bent so that the palms can press down. The wrist should be slightly cocked, the fingers bent, and the palm held concave.

The head must maintain a vertical line by pressing up while the eyes look down. The legs must have a scissoring power with the knees closing in, the rear knee driving down, the rear heel slightly off the ground. Twist the waist, roll in the hips, close the knees, and coordinate this with the splitting action of the hands to launch power.

- Although *reverse stance eagle* advances in a zigzag pattern, the hands draw a straight line with an imaginary line down the midline of the feet.

- To get the turn of *aligned stance eagle* the foot must hook in considerably. The body must turn around quickly, and the foot must hook in as the fist drills forward. Help maintain body stability by pressing up into the head.

BREATHING CYCLE FOR THE EAGLE MODEL

Always practise with a clear rhythm, distinguishing between action and stillness, and do not rush the movements. Follow your breathing pattern to do each move one at a time, keeping the body balanced and keeping your power full, so that breathing is smooth.

- Inhale as the fist drills up.

- Exhale as the hands split down.

PRACTICAL APPLICATIONS FOR THE EAGLE MODEL

The eagle model has two alternate foot placements for the same technique – either reverse stance or aligned stance. The aligned stance can move in from outside or inside. The key in either case is to get the body in close, as that is the only way to take the opponent out.

- The drill up can take care of an attack, so can be thought of as the defensive move, but it can also be used as an attack.

- Always protect your midline; take charge of the midline; rush the midline.

Xingyiquan classics say, "never send out a fist without results, never bring it back without taking an opportunity." After you've drilled up then you can open the hand for a grab, pull, hook, or controlling technique. If you can grab clothes then grab clothes, otherwise grab the 'meat'. Once you've controlled the opponent's arm then enter and press him down, striking his chest or belly with the other hand.

> Drilling both fists up as the lead foot enters both defends the centre and shoves into the opponent. Get the body in tight to shove, hitting with the entire torso, taking over the main door, always attacking the midline. The main door is the space between the opponent's feet, the midline is the opponent's centre, and is the part of the opponent's body that you want to hurt.

THE POEM ABOUT THE EAGLE

鹰形歌诀

鹰形练时爪似钩，

起钻落翻拗顺走。

拧腰裹胯坐臀力，

精神气力功为首。

When training eagle model the hands should be like hooks.

Drill as they rise and turn as they land; stepping either into reverse stance or aligned stance.

Twist the waist and roll in the hips, sitting the buttocks down to get strength.

Deep skill lies in the spirit, *qi*, and strength.

TWELVE: BEAR MODEL

熊形

Introduction To The Bear Model, *Xiong Xing*

The bear is a ferocious animal. It appears slow in nature but is unyielding. It has the strength of shaking the body and shoulders, the ability to stand erect right up into the neck, and a natural stance with a lively lower back and relaxed shoulders. So Xingyiquan uses this shape and intent in the techniques. The intent behind your moves is to react like a bear. The bear lives in the wilds, it ambles along slowly with relaxed and soft shoulder girdle and back. It gathers its food in a leisurely way, calmly and peaceably. But, should it meet an attack, it is quick to anger, and shakes its whole body, spreads its forelegs and stands straight up, raises its head and slaps with its paws. It charges forward and doesn't relent until its enemy is dead.

The Xingyiquan classics talk of 'chicken legs, dragon body, bear arms, and tiger head'. This describes the key to the position and function of each body segment. Chicken legs describes the how to stand on one leg and move quickly. Dragon body describes how to use the waist effectively by flexing and extending. Bear arms describes how to relax and settle the shoulder girdle. Tiger head describes how to have a fierce spirit, putting fear into the opponent.

You must pay attention in bear model to charge in with the footwork to get the body in, pressing up the head with a straight neck. The hands guard and shield the centre, completely controlling the centre.

Method Of Performing The Bear Model

Start from left *santishi*.

12a Black Bear Leaves its Den   hēixióng chūdòng   黑熊出洞

ACTION: Advance the left foot a half-step with the toes hooked in slightly, and follow in the right foot a half-step with ball of the foot on the ground, the heel slightly raised. Bend the right knee, shift the weight forward mostly onto the left leg, and lean forward slightly. Clench both fists and press the left forearm across the body to cover and take the fist down to the belly, fist heart down. Drill the right fist up by the sternum and out inside the left fist, ulnar edge turned out, fist at nose height. Press the head up, tuck the jaw in, and look at the right fist. (images 10.227 and 10.227 front)

10.227
10.227 FRONT

12b   Old Bear Shoves from its Shoulder   lǎoxióng zhuàng bǎng   老熊撞膀

ACTION: Advance the left foot a half-step and step the right foot forward a long step, following in with the left foot. Shift forward so most weight is on the right leg. Bend the right elbow to bring the right fist to the left chest, fist heart down. Slice forward and up to block with the left forearm outside the right arm, unclenching and taking the hand to the left shoulder, the left palm supporting the right fist surface. As the right foot lands, lift the right elbow and strike forward with the tip. Press the hands together and use the right elbow and Shoulder to butt forward. Look past the right elbow. (image 10.228)

10.228

12c   Black Bear Leaves its Den   hēixióng chūdòng   黑熊出洞

ACTION: Advance the right foot a half-step with the foot hooked in slightly. Follow in a half-step with left foot, touching the ball of the foot down with the heel raised. Bend the left knee downward, shift forward onto the right leg and lean slightly forward. Bring the right forearm across the body, fist heart down, to cover and press down, pulling the fist back to the belly. Drill the left fist out from in front of the chest, forward and up inside the right forearm to nose height, fist heart in, ulnar edge turned up. Press the head up, tuck the chin in, and look at the left fist. (image 10.229)

10.229

CHAPTER TEN: THE TWELVE ANIMAL MODELS 267

12d   Old Bear Shoves from its Shoulder   lǎoxióng zhuàng bǎng   老熊撞膀

ACTION: Advance the right foot a half-step and step the left foot forward a long step, following in a half-step with the right foot. Shift the weight forward to the left leg. Drill the right fist up outside the left forearm to slice up to nose height, then pull it back in front of the right chest, unclenching. Bend the left elbow and bring the fist back in front of the chest. Lift the left elbow and bring it on line. Press the right palm into the left fist surface, and press the hands together to strike with the left elbow as the left foot steps forward. Shift forward to butt with the left arm. Look past the left elbow. (image 10.230)

- Continue on alternating right and left sides as many times as you have space and energy to do.

Pointers

- Be sure to shift forward as you advance the left foot, and to drill the right fist through as you step.
- The forward step of the right foot should be long and quick, and land as the right elbow butts forward.
- The entire sequence must link together smoothly.

12e   Bear Turn Around   xióng xíng huíshēn shì   熊形回身势

From the <u>left</u> side *old bear shoves from its shoulder*.

ACTION 1: Step the right foot forward, hooking in outside the left foot and shifting onto the right leg. Turn the body around to the left to face the way in which you came. Lift the left foot to inside the right ankle without touching down. As you turn around, turn the right palm up and thread up, stab the left fist down to the left; press the head up, and look at the right hand. After you have turned, look at the left fist. (image 10.231)

ACTION 2: Take a long step straight forward with the left foot, hooking the toes in. Follow in a half-step with the right foot, landing on the ball with the heel lifted and the knee bent. Shift the

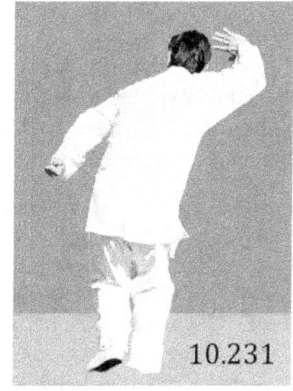

weight forward towards the left leg and lean forward slightly. Lift the left fist as the body turns, to cross the forearm and press down, fist heart down, pulling it back to the belly, fist heart on the belly. After the right hand drills up, as the body turns, clench the fist and bring it down to the right waist, then, as the left foot steps forward, drill the right fist forward and up inside the left arm, to nose height, fist heart in, ulnar edge turned up. Press the head up and look at the right fist. (image 10.232)

- The *turn around* from the right side is similar, just transposing right and left.

Pointers

- You must take a good hook-in step and get around quickly. It is the rear foot that comes forward to do the hook-in step.
- As you do the hook-in step thread both hands – one threading the forearm and one stabbing back, keeping the whole body coordinated.

12f   Bear Closing Move   xióng xíng shōushì   熊形收势

- On arriving at the starting place and turning around into the <u>left</u> side *old bear shoves from its shoulder*.

ACTION 1: Step the right foot forward and stamp it just beside the left foot. Quickly lift the left foot, no higher than the right ankle. Backfist forward and up with the left fist to nose height, then, without stopping, turn the fist over, hook and pull back to the belly, fist heart down. Lower the right hand, clinching it and drill up by the sternum then forward to nose height, ulnar edge twisted up. Press the head up and look at the right fist.

ACTION 2: Step the left foot forward without moving the right foot, slide the left hand along the right forearm and split to shoulder height with the palm down, pulling the right hand back to the belly, to settle into a *santishi*. Press the head up and look at the left hand.

- On arriving at the starting place and turning into the <u>right</u> side *old bear shoves from its shoulder*.

ACTION: Step the left foot forward without moving the right foot, to sit into a *santi* stance. Circle the right fist up and forward, with the peak of the fist forward and fist heart in. Slide the left hand along the right forearm to split forward at shoulder height, and unclench the right hand, turning it in and pulling it back to the belly. Press the head up and look at the left hand.

- Complete the *closing move* the same as usual from left *santishi*.

PROBLEMS OFTEN MET IN THE BEAR MODEL

PROBLEM 1: The student does not straighten the neck properly, tilting the head up to look forward instead.

CORRECTIONS: Remind the student to tuck the chin in and think of butting forward and up with the head. The proper body position will also help – the chest contained and the upper back stretched, the torso leaning forward slightly. The eyes must look up at the fist without tilting the head up. The head should be slightly dropped while the eyes are raised to look forward.

PROBLEM 2: The student bends the elbow too much or straightens it too much during *black bear leaves its den*.

CORRECTIONS: The student should bend the elbow to about ninety to one hundred degrees as he drills up. The angle should be more acute than that of a normal *drilling punch*.

PROBLEM 3: The student does too small a movement into the elbow strike of *old bear shoves from its shoulder*, resulting in a stiff shove.

CORRECTIONS: This results from not giving enough consideration to the body technique of gathering and releasing, which is dependant on an easy moving shoulder girdle. After the rear fist drill up it pulls back to butt the elbow forward. At this time the waist must be supple and the shoulder must turn back slightly. After that, you can step forward and butt with the elbow. In this way the elbow strike can be strong because it uses the full power of a shoulder strike.

POWER GENERATION FOR THE BEAR MODEL

- The key to power in all the actions of the bear model is to press the head forward and up while pressing the torso slightly forward. The classics say, "The bear has the strength of holding its neck straight, the power of cutting across its shoulder girdle, and the ferocity of charging out of its den." The body technique should show the strength of straightening the neck and the ferocity of a wild animal protecting its den.

During *black bear leaves its den*, three actions must be done simultaneously to have full power: the lead foot advances, the lead fist covers and presses, and the rear fist drills out. The head must press forward and up and the body must charge forward, pushing strongly off the rear foot. As the fist drills up the shoulder must first pull back slightly and then close in forward. This small shoulder movement must be coordinated with a turning of the waist and closing of the chest. The upper arm must adhere tightly to the ribs so that as the fist drills out the shoulder moves forward with a butting, shoving power. Butt simultaneously with four parts: the shoulder, elbow, fist, and head.

During *black bear leaves its den*, the lead foot should be turned in slightly as it advances. This rolls the knee in slightly. The rear foot should lift the heel, stabbing the rear knee down. The buttocks should be tucked in and the hips rolled in as well, so there is a closing power between the knees.

Old bear shoves from its shoulder is not a shoulder or an upper arm shove, but is an elbow strike. The elbow should strike as the rear foot lands forward. Since an elbow strike is a short range technique the weight must shift forward. This shift must not be overdone, however, but should be held within the forward third of the stance. To butt with the elbow, the shoulder should first close then open, showing an intention to shove with the shoulder. First lift the elbow and then – as the rear hand assists the front fist, giving a combined force from the hands – lengthen the spine, extend the shoulder, and step into the hit so that the elbow can strike strongly forward.

BREATHING CYCLE FOR THE BEAR MODEL

- Inhale during all gathering movement.

- Exhale during all advancing power launching movements – while drilling up and while butting with the elbow.

In general, use the technique of a long inhale and a short exhale to help store and release power and develop whole body power.

PRACTICAL APPLICATIONS FOR THE BEAR MODEL

- The bear model uses a strong charging attitude and power. It charges in to strike with the shoulder or elbow, so the body should lean a bit into the action to help. Since the head then is slightly forward, be sure to protect the head with both hands.

Black bear leaves its den uses the lead hand to press down and knock aside an opponent's punch. You can then advance and get in a drilling punch to the opponent's chest, jaw, or nose. Be sure to charge into the opponent's groin or past his feet, getting the body in as closely as possible. This technique will not work if you do not get the body in.

The butt uses the rear hand to block up or pull away the opponent's arm, then you can advance and strike with the elbow to the chest or ribs. The key is quick footwork, getting the body in close very quickly.

Once you have got in close for the elbow strike, there is a hidden backfist. You can quickly snap out a backfist to the opponent's face. The backfist isn't a strong hit but it can throw him off and allow you another opportunity to continue your attack.

THE POEM ABOUT THE BEAR

熊形歌诀

熊形出洞守护能,

竖项钻打欺身用。

排手冲步顶肘去,

得机得势定输赢。

The bear charges out of its den with the ability to protect.

It straightens its neck, drills a hit, and intimidates.

It slaps and charges in to strike with its elbows.

It takes advantage of every opportunity so will certainly win.

THIRTEEN: EAGLE AND BEAR COMBINED

鹰熊合演

INTRODUCTION TO THE EAGLE AND BEAR COMBINED, *YING XIONG HE YAN*

The eagle and bear models each traditionally have their own individual practice, and, although there are differences between methods, they are basically very similar. The *eagle and bear combined* is another widespread traditional method of practice. The animals are combined this way because the pair rhymes with *yingxiong* – hero – which expresses the spirit of the practice. The essence of eagle is the grasping, and that of bear is the uprightness, so combining them combines their strengths.

METHOD OF PERFORMING THE EAGLE AND BEAR COMBINED

Start from left *santishi*.

13a Left Reverse Stance Eagle   zuǒ àobù yīng xíng   左拗步鹰形

ACTION: This is the same as the *left reverse stance eagle* described above in the eagle model.

13b Black Bear Leaves its Den   hēixióng chūdòng   黑熊出洞

ACTION: Clench the right hand and pull it back to the belly. Advance the left foot a half-step straight forward, the foot hooked in slightly, and follow in a bit with the right foot, raising the heel and bending the knee. Drill the right fist up by the sternum and forward to nose height, fist heart in, ulnar edge up. Lean forward slightly, press the head up, and look at the right fist.

13c Right Reverse Stance Eagle   yòu àobù yīng xíng   右拗步鹰形

ACTION: This is the same as the *right reverse stance eagle* described above.

13d Black Bear Leaves its Den   hēixióng chūdòng   黑熊出洞

ACTION: This is the same as movement 13b described above, just transposing right and left.

CHAPTER TEN: THE TWELVE ANIMAL MODELS

Pointers

- All the movement requirements and the use of power are the same as eagle model and bear model when practised separately. It is just the transitions that differ, so you need to concentrate on understanding the transitional actions.

- The lead foot should advance as the rear fist comes through to drill forward.

13e   Eagle and Bear Turn Around

yīng xióng hélián huíshēn   鹰熊合练回身

Turn around when you arrive at eagle grabs. The description is given starting from the _left_ _reverse stance eagle_

ACTION 1: Lift the left foot and hook-out step directly forward. Step the right foot forward, hooking in just in front of the left toes, shifting onto the right leg. Lift the left foot to by the right ankle. Bring the right hand around with the body turn, circling left, up, right, and down, to finish at the waist. While the right hand draws its circle, circle the left hand down, left and up to nose height, then cover across the body with the left forearm at shoulder height. Look at the right hand as it circles, then when it pulls back to the waist, turn the head to look at the left hand. (image 10.233)

ACTION 2: Take a step forward with the left foot and follow in a bit with the right foot, lifting the heel and bending the knee. Finish the left forearm cover and pull the fist back to the belly. Drill the right fist up by the sternum and forward to nose height, ulnar edge turned up. Press the head forward and up, tuck in the chin, and look past the right fist. (image 10.234)

- Turning the other way is similar, just transposing left and right.

13f   Eagle and Bear Closing Move   yīng xióng hélián shōushì   收势

- This is the same as _eagle closing move_.

Power Generation For The Eagle And Bear Combined

The key to connecting *eagle grasp* to *black bear leaves its den* is the driving forward foot. The foot charges straight forward with the foot turned in slightly and the weight shifts forward. As the hand pulls back to the belly the head should press up, the shoulders settle down, and the waist lengthen. When the fist drills forward the waist should turn, the chest close in, so that the fist leads, the elbow follows, and the shoulder urges forward. Keep focused on the shoulder girdle/upper arm and elbow, so that the drilling fist is backed up by a butting power from the shoulder.

- The *turn around* changes from *eagle grabs* to *black bear leaves its den*, so be sure to first do a hook-out and then a hook-in step. The hands need to draw their own circles in a coordinated way, balancing the up/down and left/right, so that the power is evenly expressed.

Practical Applications For The Eagle And Bear Combined

See the explanations in the sections on the eagle model and the bear model.

The Poem About The Eagle And Bear

鹰熊合练歌诀

鹰熊斗智，

取法为拳。

阴阳暗合，

形意之源。

The eagle and bear fight wisely.

Their techniques were taken to make a fighting style

In which *Yin* and *Yang* secretly combine.

This is the source of Xingyi.

PRONUNCIATION OF PINYIN, THE CHINESE NATIONAL PHONETIC ALPHABET (WITH INTERNATIONAL PHONETIC ALPHABET EQUIVALENTS)

INITIALS (words can start with these consonants, or have a zero initial)

PINYIN	IPA	ROUGH PRONUNCIATION GUIDE
p	p^h	Like English pet with a considerable puff of air.
b	p	Similar to the *pinyin* "p" but without the puff of air (unvoiced, neither English pet nor bet).
t	t^h	Like English tag with a considerable puff of air.
d	t	Similar to the *pinyin* "t" but with no puff of air (unvoiced, not dog).
k	k^h	Like English kill with a considerable puff of air.
g	k	Similar to the *pinyin* "k" but with no puff of air (unvoiced, not English get).
c	ts^h	Like exaggerating English cats.
z	ts	Like the *pinyin* "c" but without the puff of air (unvoiced).
ch	$tʂ^h$	Somewhat similar to English chat with a puff of air, but with the tip of the tongue rolled back.
zh	tʂ	Like the *pinyin* "ch" but with no puff of air (unvoiced).
q	$tɕ^h$	Somewhat similar to English chat with a puff of air, but with the front of the tongue raised and the tip on the lower teeth.
j	tɕ	Like the *pinyin* "q" but without the puff of air (unvoiced).
m	m	Like English met.
n	n	Like English net.
f	f	Similar to English fat, but with the teeth just touching lightly behind the lower lip.
s	s	Similar to English set.

sh	ʂ	Somewhat similar to English s<u>h</u>ow, but with the same tongue placement as the *pinyin* "ch" and "zh."
x	þ	Somewhat similar to English s<u>h</u>ine but with the same tongue placement as the *pinyin* "q" and "j."
h	χ	Raise the back of the tongue and let the breath come through the obstructed passage without vibrating the vocal cords.
l	l	Like English <u>l</u>et.
r	ɹ	Like the *pinyin* "sh" but with voicing.

FINALS

n	n	Like English pi<u>n</u>.
ng	ŋ	Like English si<u>ng</u>.

VOWELS

a	A a ɛ	Usually close to English f<u>a</u>ther (not p<u>a</u>t). Like y<u>e</u>t when written "-ian" or "yan."
e	ɣ e ɛ ə	Usually similar to English p<u>e</u>t, can tend towards a mid vowel.
i	i ɭ ɪ	Usually similar to English b<u>ee</u>. Similar to w<u>e</u>t when written "ui." After c, z, s, ch, zh, sh, and r it is similar to s<u>ir</u>.
o	o u	Usually close to English r<u>o</u>ll. Similar to c<u>ow</u> when written "ao," and <u>owe</u> when in "ou."
u	u y	Usually similar t English o b<u>oo</u>t. After the *pinyin* "x", "q", and "j" and in the vowel groups starting with these consonants, it is pronounced "ü".
ü	y	Similar to French <u>ü</u>. It is written after "n" or "l," because these are the only positions where both "u" and "ü" are possible
y	i	Partially like an English 'y', tending towards i.
w	u	Partially like an English 'w', tending towards u.

INITIAL CONSONANTS

place of articulation	Unaspirated Stops	Aspirated Stops	Unaspirated Affricates	Aspirated Affricates	Nasals	Fricatives	Voiced Continuants
	manner of articulation						
bilabials	b	p			m		
labio-dentals						f	
dental-alveolars	d	t	z	c	n	s	l
retroflexes			zh	ch		sh	r
palatals			j	q		x	
velars	g	k				h	

TONES IN PINYIN

NUMBER	PINYIN	NAME	RANGE
1	¯	high level	55
2	´	high rising	35
3	ˇ	dipping	214
4	`	high falling	51
none	° or blank	neutral	in context

With tone sandhi, tones may change according to the preceding or following tone. The tone marking is put over the main vowel when there are two vowels written together (usually involving the pronunciation of y or w).

ABOUT THE TRANSLATOR

Andrea Falk has practised external and internal Chinese martial arts since 1972, and has concentrated on internal styles since 1981. She started Xingyiquan with Xia Bohua in 1981. In 2001 she met Di Guoyong, and has trained with him ever since.

Andrea honed her skills in Vancouver, Beijing, and Shanghai – with a Bachelor of Arts majoring in Chinese, a Bachelor of Physical Education and later a Master of Physical Education with an emphasis on biomechanics and coaching science from the University of British Columbia. She trained in wushu full time from 1980 to 1983 at the Beijing Physical Culture Institute, earning an advanced studies diploma in Wushu under the tutelage of professor Xia Bohua. There she gained the basics of Yang and Chen style Taijiquan, Baguazhang, Xingyiquan, Chaquan, and modern Wushu (Changquan and weapons). She also spent the summers of 1984 and 1986 at the Beijing Physical Culture Institute. She started learning purely traditionally after 1986, visiting China on extended trips as often as possible. She trains Chen style Taijiquan and Baguazhang as an inside apprentice of Huan Dahai (and with elder martial brothers) in Shanghai, and Xingyiquan and Baguazhang as a close student and friend of Di Guoyong in Beijing. When not in China or traveling to teach, she is usually in Québec city or at a cottage in the Laurentian hills, Canada.

Andrea has worked teaching and translating since 1983. She founded the wushu centre in Montreal in 1984, in Victoria in 1992, and in Quebec city in 2007. She has taught Chen Taijiquan, Baguazhang, and Xingyiquan around the world, but mostly in Canada and England. For years Andrea translated books for her own students, and in 2000 established tgl books and the website www.thewushucentre.ca to bring the best Chinese martial arts books to a wider audience.

trois gros lapins traversent le chemin

ISBN 978-1-989468-07-4

www.ingramcontent.com/pod-product-compliance
Lightning Source LLC
Chambersburg PA
CBHW071814230426
43670CB00013B/2450